P9-BTN-769

KEEPING GOD'S EARTH

The Global Environment
in Biblical Perspective

EDITED BY Noah J. Toly and Daniel I. Block

IVP Academic

An imprint of InterVarsity Press
Downers Grove, Illinois

Apollos
Nottingham, England

InterVarsity Press, USA
P.O. Box 1400
Downers Grove, IL 60515-1426, USA
World Wide Web: www.ivpress.com
Email: email@ivpress.com

APOLLOS (an imprint of Inter-Varsity Press, England)
Norton Street
Nottingham NG7 3HR, England
Website: www.ivpbooks.com
Email: ivp@ivpbooks.com

©2010 by Noah J. Toly and Daniel I. Block

InterVarsity Press®, USA, is the book-publishing division of InterVarsity Christian Fellowship/USA® <www.intervarsity.org> and a member movement of the International Fellowship of Evangelical Students.

Inter-Varsity Press, England, is closely linked with the Universities and Colleges Christian Fellowship, a student movement connecting Christian Unions throughout Great Britain, and a member movement of the International Fellowship of Evangelical Students. Website: www.uccf.org.uk

Scripture quotations, unless otherwise noted, are from the New Revised Standard Version of the Bible, copyright 1989 by the Division of Christian Education of the National Council of the Churches of Christ in the USA. Used by permission. All rights reserved.

Design: Cindy Kiple
Cover images: Foodcollection RF/Getty Images
Interior images: Megan Tamaccio

USA ISBN 978-0-8308-3883-7
UK ISBN 978-1-84474-450-3

Printed in the United States of America ∞

Library of Congress Cataloging-in-Publication Data

Keeping God's earth: the global environment in biblical perspective /
edited by Noah J. Toly and Daniel I. Block.
    p. cm.
  Includes bibliographical references and index.
  ISBN 978-0-8308-3883-7 (pbk.: alk. paper)
  1. Human ecology—Religious aspects—Christianity. 2. Human
ecology—Biblical teaching. 3. Evangelicalism. I. Toly, Noah. II.
Block, Daniel Isaac, 1943-
  BT695.5.K44 2010
  261.8'8—dc22

                                                                    2010008328

British Library Cataloguing in Publication Data

A catalogue record for this book is available from the British Library.

P 20 19 18 17 16 15 14 13 12 11 10 9 8 7 6 5 4 3 2 1
Y 27 26 25 24 23 22 21 20 19 18 17 16 15 14 13 12 11 10

CONTENTS

122277

ABBREVIATIONS

AB	Anchor Bible
ABD	Anchor Bible Dictionary
BDAG	W. Bauer, F. W. Danker, W. F. Arndt, F. W. Gingrich, *Greek-English Lexicon of the New Testament*
BECNT	Baker Exegetical Commentary on the New Testament
BETL	Bibliotheca ephemeridum theologicarum lovaniensium
Bib	*Biblica*
BJRL	*Bulletin of the John Rylands University Library of Manchester*
BSac	*Bibliotheca sacra*
BZ	Biblische Zeitschrift
BZAW	Beihefte zur Zeitschrift für die alttestamentliche Wissenschaft
CBET	Contributions to Biblical Exegesis and Theology
CHANE	Culture and History of the Ancient Near East
COS	*The Context of Scripture,* ed. W. W. Hallo, 3 vols. (Leiden: E. J. Brill, 1997-2002)
DCH	*Dictionary of Classical Hebrew,* ed. D. J. A. Clines (Sheffield, U.K.: Sheffield Academic Press, 1993-)
FAT	Forschungen zum Alten Testament
HALOT	*The Hebrew and Aramaic Lexicon of the Old Testament,* L. Koehler, W. Baumgartner and J. J. Stamm, 4 vols. (Leiden: E. J. Brill, 1994-1999)
HTS	Harvard Theological Studies
IEJ	*Israel Exploration Journal*
JBL	*Journal of Biblical Literature*
JSNTSup	Journal for the Study of the New Testament: Supplement Series
JSOT	*Journal for the Study of Old Testament*
JSOTSup	Journal for the Study of Old Testament: Supplement Series
KTU	*Die Keilalphabetischen Texte aus Ugarit,* ed. M. Dietrich, O. Loretz and J. Sanmartin, Alter Orient und Altes Testament (Neukirchen-Vluyn: Neukirchener Verlag, 1976)
LHB/OTS	Library of Hebrew Bible/Old Testament Studies

NAC	New American Commentary
NICNT	New International Commentary on the New Testament
NICOT	New International Commentary on the Old Testament
NIDNTT	*New International Dictionary of New Testament Theology*
NIDOTTE	*New International Dictionary of Old Testament Theology and Exegesis*, ed. W. A. VanGemeren, 5 vols. (Grand Rapids: Zondervan, 1997)
NIGTC	New International Greek Testament Commentary
NIVAC	NIV Application Commentary
NSBT	New Studies in Biblical Theology
NTS	*New Testament Studies*
OBO	Orbis biblicus et orientalis
OBT	Overtures to Biblical Theology
OTL	Old Testament Library
OTS	Old Testament Studies
PEQ	*Palestine Exploration Quarterly*
Presb	*Presbyterion*
PRSt	*Perspectives in Religious Studies*
SBLDS	SBL Dissertation Series
SBLSS	SBL Supplement Series
Sem	*Semitica*
SHANE	Studies in the History of the Ancient Near East
TDOT	*Theological Dictionary of the Old Testament*, ed. G. J. Botterweck and H. Ringgren (Grand Rapids: Eerdmans, 1974-)
TDNT	*Theological Dictionary of the New Testament*, ed. G. Kittel and G. Friedrich, 10 vols. (Grand Rapids: Eerdmans, 1964-1976)
TrinJ	*Trinity Journal*
UBL	Ugaritisch-biblische Literatur
UT	C. H. Godon, *Ugaritic Textbook*, Analecta Orientalia 38 (Rome: Pontifical Biblical Institute, 1965).
VT	*Vetus Testamentum*
VTSup	Vetas Testamentum Supplements
WBC	Word Biblical Commentary
WTJ	*Westminster Theological Journal*
ZAW	*Zeitschrift für die alttestamentliche Wissenschaft*
ZNW	*Zeitschrift für die neutestamentliche Wissenschaft*

PART ONE

INTRODUCTION

KEEPING GOD'S EARTH

Toward an Evangelical Response to
Environmental Challenges

Noah J. Toly and Daniel I. Block

BURGEONING CITIES, DECREASING BIOLOGICAL DIVERSITY, inequitable access to clean water, and increasing atmospheric concentrations of energy-trapping gases are among the most significant challenges the world faces at the beginning of the twenty-first century. For a long time, such issues have been perceived as fundamentally technical issues. If we apply advances in science and technology we can solve the problems we face. However, as Garrett Hardin has famously noted, many environmental challenges belong to the set of problems for which there are no technical solutions or, as Kai Lee has suggested, for which there are no uncontroversial optimal solutions.[1] This implies the necessity but insufficiency of normal empirical—whether experimental or historical—science.

Normal science seeks an accurate understanding and representation of the world through systematic observation and experimentation. The scientific enterprise, across both natural and social sciences, is devoted

---

[1]Garrett Hardin, "The Tragedy of the Commons," *Science* 162, no. 3859 (1968): 1243-48. Kai N. Lee, "Appraising Adaptive Management," *Conservation Ecology* 3, no. 2 (1999): 1-9. See also Mark Sagoff, *The Economy of the Earth* (Cambridge: Cambridge University Press, 1988) and William P. Ophuls with A. Stephen Boyan Jr., "The American Political Economy II: The Non-Politics of Laissez Faire," in *Ecology and the Politics of Scarcity Revisited: The Unraveling of the American Dream* (New York: W. H. Freeman, 1992), pp. 237-53.

to formulating and testing explanations for phenomena, and to explaining and predicting relationships and outcomes. This includes the observation of environmental change and the discernment of the origins and implications—the causes and consequences—of such change. It is according to scientific investigation that we detect the immediate causes of environmental challenges, understand the effects of environmental conditions, and know the relationships between one issue (for example, biodiversity loss) and another (say, climate change).

The discernment of causes and effects is of inestimable importance for mitigating environmental degradation, adapting to environmental change, and maintaining environmental integrity. When it comes to managing human relationships with non-human creation, we must know which actions lead to what consequences. Conventionally scientific approaches to knowledge can tell us whether or not soil contamination at brownfield sites might cause cancer. Conventionally scientific approaches might tell us if we are likely to jeopardize biodiversity by destroying a certain portion of habitat. Conventionally scientific inquiry can tell us what pollutes our water and what harm that pollution might bring to human and non-human life, alike. Such approaches can even guide our interventions and suggest whether or not a particular action is likely to mitigate a specific problem and help us anticipate the likelihood of the success of a particular adaptation solution.

But no conventionally scientific approach can tell us what ends we should pursue or what kinds of consequences we should value. That is, scientific inquiry does not tell us whether or not we should welcome cancer, and why. It does not tell us if—and if so, for whom—cancer is an acceptable tradeoff for the benefits of investing in something other than brownfield remediation. It cannot tell us how we should regard biodiversity. It cannot tell us how to assess the risks of water pollution. Environmental explorations bring us quickly to the intersection of science and ethics. Environmental issues beg questions of what we take to be the good life.

For example, discussions of climate change move quickly and easily between atmospheric physics, risk management, economics and politics. Atmospheric physicists have proven the opacity of certain gases—

CO_2, for example—to energy radiating from the earth's surface. These disciplines can reveal to us the origins of such gases, the capacity of the earth to recycle these gases, the length of time for which these gases persist in the atmosphere, the likely effects of high atmospheric concentrations upon the climate, and even physically plausible mechanisms by which to reduce concentrations of these gases. Economics can help us predict likely tradeoffs, the value of goods and services we will need to forego in favor of reducing concentrations. But as soon as we ask the questions "Should we reduce greenhouse gases?" and "If so, by how much?" we have ventured beyond the strictly scientific.[2]

These are not scientific questions for which we *discover* answers. These are ethical and risk management questions about which we *negotiate* answers. Indeed, under the auspices of the United Nations Framework Convention on Climate Change and with the input of nongovernmental organizations, governments now bargain over an acceptable atmospheric chemistry. Their delegates *need scientific research* to do their work, but they *are not doing science*.

For this reason, Leigh Glover has described climate science as "post-normal science," citing Ravetz and Healy, or "civic science," citing Cortner.[3] Post-normal science is concerned with "the resolution of uncertainty in the context of conflicting values and agendas" and exhibits explicit, rather than implicit, management of social influence, interpretation and application. Post-normal science is not primarily applied science, but practical science. That is, it is not primarily basic science applied to emergent situations, but it is a science that responds to specific problems.

A similar school of thought has emerged across the social sciences.

---

[2]Some might presume to answer these questions with strictly economic reasoning, suggesting that this approach provides a neutral, objective and universally accessible vantage point from which to discriminate between options. However, even the presumption that all trade-offs are commensurable is a controvertible (while sometimes helpful) and politically charged notion.

[3]Leigh Glover, *Postmodern Climate Change* (New York: Routledge, 2006). See also J. R. Ravetz, "What Is Post-Normal Science?" *Futures* 31, no. 7 (1999): 647-53; S. A. Healy, "Extended Peer Communities and the Ascendance of Post-Normal Politics," *Futures* 31, no. 7 (1999): 655-69; H. J. Cortner, "Making Science Relevant to Environmental Policy," *Environmental Science and Policy* 3, no. 1 (2000): 21-30. Of course, any reference to "normal" or "post-normal" science evokes Thomas Kuhn's *The Structure of Scientific Revolutions* (Chicago: University of Chicago Press, 1962).

In his 2005 book, *The Flight from Reality in the Human Sciences*, Ian Shapiro argues for a "problem-driven inquiry" in which social inquiry responds to problems "identified in ways that are both theoretically illuminating and intelligible to outsiders."[4] And in 2001, Bent Flyvbjerg shook up much of social inquiry with his book *Making Social Science Matter: Why Social Inquiry Fails and How It Can Succeed Again*. In it, he argues that social inquiry is at its best when modeled after the Aristotelian concept of *phronēsis*: "Variously translated as 'prudence' or 'practical wisdom . . .' *phronēsis* goes beyond both analytical scientific knowledge (*epistēmē*) and technical knowledge or know-how (*technē*) and involves judgments and decisions made in the manner of a virtuoso social and political actor."[5] Flyvbjerg suggests that phronetic inquiry must ask the following four questions:

1. Where are we going?
2. Who gains and who loses?
3. Is this desirable?
4. What should be done?[6]

While hotly contested in the epistemic community to which they are addressed, the approaches identified by Shapiro, Flyvbjerg and others[7] may be precisely the sort of post-normal inquiry that is necessary in the face of mounting ecological crises.

Adapted to environmental issues, *phronēsis* would involve decisions made in the manner of virtuoso communities in response to environ-

---

[4]Ian Shapiro, *The Flight from Reality in the Social Sciences* (Princeton: Princeton University Press, 2005).

[5]Bent Flyvbjerg, *Making Social Science Matter: Why Social Inquiry Fails and How It Can Succeed Again* (Cambridge: Cambridge University Press, 2000), p. 2.

[6]Ibid.

[7]Flyvbjerg has sparked substantial controversy in several disciplines, resulting in a debate in the journal *Politics and Society* (see 31, no. 1 [2003] and 32, no. 3 [2004]). See also Sanford F. Schram and Brian Caterino, eds., *Making Political Science Matter: Debating Knowledge, Research, and Method* (New York: New York University Press, 2006); Kristen Renwick Monroe, ed., *Perestroika: The Raucous Rebellion in Political Science* (New Haven, Conn.: Yale University Press, 2005). The extent to which this debate has penetrated the discipline of economics is less, but may be reflected, somewhat, in the "post-autistic economics" movement (www.paecon. net), in the electronic journal, *Real-World Economics Review*, the *Heterodox Economics Newsletter* and the book *Real-World Economics: A Post-Autistic Economics Reader* (New York: Anthem Press, 2007).

mental challenges. And this is a necessarily synthetic task. Scientific inquiry enjoys a place among these issues, answering the question, "Where are we going?"[8] And it can begin to answer the question, "Who gains and who loses?" describing likely absolute and relative changes in states of affairs. But even the identification of variables important to this second question is value-inflected. And perspectives on what it means to gain or to lose are certainly value-inflected. Even human survival is a contested value—though it is a widely accepted, plausibly mutual and intersubjectively useful value for advancing decisions among for the most part like-minded people. One need only consult the work of some misanthropic deep ecologists to discover that some are ambivalent at best about human survival. Dave Foreman, for example, has suggested that humans are a cancer on the earth, that the optimum human population is zero, and that he would not shed a tear at the prospect of human extinction. As the name of the organization he founded suggests, *EarthFirst!*, such eco-centric movements subordinate all other values to ecological integrity.

Christians are called to subordinate all other values to God and his good news. We might call such a movement "KingdomFirst!" As expressed in Martin Luther's hymn "A Mighty Fortress," "Let goods and kindred go / This mortal life also / The body they may kill / God's truth abideth still / His kingdom is forever." Expressing no disdain for human life or survival, still the hymn subordinates survival to a theocentric position. Dave Foreman and Martin Luther both relativize human survival. No science can serve as arbiter between them.

Discernment of this sort demands faith-inflected and submissive engagement with revelation, both general and special. For the Christian engaged with creation care, biblical and theological concerns must be epistemologically and ethically promiscuous. That is, they must couple indiscriminately with everything else we know.

As evangelicals we affirm that all truth is God's truth. This aphorism yields two corollaries. First, since nature (God's works) does indeed reveal truth about God (Ps 19:1-6; Rom 1:18-23) and about it-

---

[8]Even then, we must admit to the situationally inflected and value-laden task of naming the place to which we're headed.

self, the Christian search for truth through scientific investigation is transformed into a sacred exercise deserving of utmost rigor and discipline. The essayists in this volume who have wrestled with issues of urbanization, biodiversity, water resources and climate change describe the issues facing us in graphic terms. Evangelicals need to hear what science is telling us about these crises—not because science is the ultimate arbiter of truth, trumping all other sources, but because when faith discovers understanding, what is known to all through common grace gains new and profound significance. It is not that science is deified as Science, but that science becomes a medium by which God's truth is recognized. Evangelicals need not fear the work of scientists, as if this will diminish one's perception of the role and the hand of God in the universe. On the contrary, as Sir John Houghton reminded the community of Wheaton College in a chapel address on January 24, 2007,[9] the greater the discoveries of our scientists, the greater the God behind those remarkable realities. And when our scientists remind us of the degradation of God's good earth, we need to hear their call for action.

Second, since all truth is God's truth, for a distinctly Christian disposition toward the findings of science, evangelicals will appeal to special revelation (God's Word). Having declared this, we recognize that this may not be as simple as it sounds. Nowhere do the Scriptures envision the crises that are the subjects of this volume. They recognize that the weather is the link between the resources of heaven and the needs of earth, but biblical authors had no comprehension of how high and low pressure systems work, nor could they envision the effects of global warming on the polar ice caps and the implications of the release of all this water on our coastal cities. If anything, they declare that this will not be a catastrophic development—at least not on a global scale: so long as the earth remains, the seasons with their distinctive meteorological features will succeed each other with perfect consistency (Gen 8:22). While the Scriptures speak of post-diluvian local floods, God promises by covenant never again to let the waters threaten creaturely

---

[9]Sir John Houghton, "Big Science Big God: Science and Faith in a Strong Embrace" (chapel address, Wheaton College, Wheaton, Ill., January 24, 2007).

or human life en masse (Gen 9:11). The Old Testament knows about conflicts over water resources on a small scale,[10] but it could not have envisioned the degradation of water resources we witness today through pollution and irresponsible exploitation.[11] The same is true of the pressures modern developments have placed on non-human life and the complications created by massive urbanization. This has led some to argue that since the question of safeguarding the environment did not enter the thinking of characters in the narratives of Scripture or the authors of the texts of Scripture, we should abandon all efforts to establish biblical responses to the crises that we face. Cyril Rodd asserts as forcefully as possible that *"the question of safeguarding the environment did not enter into their* [Old Testament writers'] *thinking."* He claims, "there is no *explicit* demand to *care for* the environment, because it did not occur to anyone in ancient Israel to make such a plea."[12]

Admittedly, biblical authors could scarcely have imagined the ecological effects that our industrialized and technological culture has produced, but to say they were disinterested in creation care seems extreme on several counts.[13] First, the creation accounts of Genesis 1 and 2 place humans squarely in the center of God's maintenance of the earth. As his images we are charged with the duty and privilege of governing the world as he would were he physically present (Gen 1; cf. Ps 8) and to serve and guard the earth in the earth's interest (Gen 2:15). Second, even if the Scriptures could not conceive of modern ecological problems, they create a worldview in which humans are cast as keepers, not only of their brothers and sisters but also of their environment. If God cares for the sparrows (Mt 10:29-31; Lk 12:6-7) and the lilies of the field (Mt 6:28-30; Lk 12:27-28), surely we should also.

But Rodd's caution raises an important hermeneutical issue: If the

---

[10]See Abraham's struggle over wells with Abimelech (Gen 21:22-32) and Isaac's with the Philistines and the herdsmen of Gerar (Gen 26:12-33).

[11]Unless of course Yahweh's turning the Nile to blood in Ex 7:14-25 is considered this kind of pollution, but here the issues are quite different.

[12]Cyril S. Rodd, *Glimpses of a Strange Land: Studies in Old Testament Ethics*, OTS (Edinburgh: T & T Clark, 2001), p. 249, italics in original. For response to Rodd, see further, Daniel Block's essay in chapter 5 of this volume.

[13]So also Christopher J. H. Wright, *Old Testament Ethics for the People of God* (Downers Grove, Ill.: InterVarsity Press, 2004), p. 105.

Scriptures do not address current environmental crises directly, how do
we use them responsibly for developing a response that is fundamentally biblical and distinctly Christian? Douglas Moo's opening essay
below wrestles with these issues from a biblical theological perspective,
paying particular attention to the implications of the eschatological vision of the New Testament for a Christian ecotheology. But what authority does the Old Testament have for evangelicals? The issue is complex and calls for careful consideration of several factors.

First, we recognize that while all the writings of the Old Testament
are products of a specific ethnic and theological community, they address both cosmic and ethnocentric realities. Although the opening
chapters of Genesis set the stage for God's special relationship and history with Israel, that stage is indeed cosmic. And the perspectives reflected in Genesis 1–11 are intended as the property of all humanity.
The original Adam and then Noah, the second Adam, are the ancestors of all. Indeed, in a move unparalleled elsewhere in ancient Near
Eastern literature, Genesis 10 presents the human population of the
earth as one large extended family. Therefore, the mission assigned to
our first ancestors is the mission of all. As images of God, we have inherited both the status and the responsibilities of Adam and Eve.[14]

Second, in reading the Old Testament texts we distinguish among
descriptive, reflective and prescriptive texts. Although the narratives are
written from a particular theological perspective, these accounts give us
a picture of the reality that was Israel. For the most part, historians do
not prescribe how Israelites should have dealt with what we now refer to
as ecological issues. Rather, they describe how they handled them, and
given their pervasively rebellious condition, more often than not, the
picture they paint is negative. Given the nature of narrative—even theologically driven narrative—the normative values reflected must often be
derived by inference, that is, by asking, "What view of God, the world,
humanity and the relationships among these three does this account
reflect?" And how does it relate to the normative view? While the perspectives, voices and actions of characters in the narratives are often

---

[14]The New Testament is clear on the determinative and normative nature of the opening chapters of Genesis for all humanity. See Rom 1:18-23; 5:14; 1 Cor 15:22, 45; 1 Tim 2:13-14.

flawed, the perspective of the narrator is deemed normative.

Psalmists and prophets address issues of faith and ethics from a reflective perspective. While evangelicals affirm that they are equally inspired, they also recognize that they represent human and divine responses to reality respectively. In the Psalms and wisdom writings we hear poets celebrating both the creative and providential power of God,[15] and his grace in ascribing to humans a vital role in the administration of the world he has created (Ps 8). We often hear these same voices in the prophets,[16] but to these are added voices of lament, especially over the cosmic effects of human failure (for example, Hos 4:1-3). Evangelicals hear the voice of God in the compositions of poets and prophets who respond to Israel's actual experiences.

Biblical scholars typically refer to the specific documents that make up Israel's constitutional literature and that are cast as prescriptive texts as the "Law of Moses" or the "Law of the Lord." While we doubt the validity of the "law," as the appropriate generic category,[17] the narratives of Genesis-Deuteronomy incorporate a series of more or less self-contained prescriptive documents: the Decalogue (Ex 20:2-17; Deut 5:6-21), the Book of the Covenant (Ex 20:22–23:19), the Manual of Worship (Ex 25–31; Lev 1–16), the Holiness Conventions (Lev 17–26), and the Deuteronomic Torah (Deut 12–26; 28).[18] These regulations provide the Israelites with a detailed picture of how they are to respond to God's grace toward them—liturgically, ethically, economically—but they also function paradigmatically for Christians. Israel had a distinctive mission in God's program of salvation for a fallen world. She was set high above the nations for the praise, honor and glory of Yahweh, her Redeemer and the Creator of the world (Deut 26:19; 28:1, 9-10),

---

[15]For example, Ps 19; 29; 33; 95; 105; 135; 136; 148; Prov 8:22-31; Job 38-39.

[16]Is 37:16; 40:12-31; 45:5-13, 18; 48:1-19; Jer 10:12-16; 51:15-19; Amos 5:8-9.

[17]Although the Hebrew word *tôrāh* is generally rendered *nomos*, "law," in the Septuagint, and this is the word carried over into the New Testament, technically this word means "teaching, instruction," and has the same semantic range as Greek *didaskalia* and *didachē*. Deuteronomy is not cast as "second law," but as Moses farewell pastoral addresses to his congregation.

[18]To these we must add a series of instructions revealed to Israel in the course of their journey from Egypt to the Promised Land: regulations concerning Passover and the Festival of Unleavened Bread (Ex 12–13), Religious Conventions (Ex 34:10-27); Miscellaneous Regulations (Num 5–6; 15; 18–19; 28–30; 35–36).

and as Yahweh's special treasure, Israel was assigned a priestly function (Ex 19:5-6), so that through her Yahweh might bless all the peoples of the earth (Gen 12:3). All the documents that make up Israel's constitutional literature serve this mission. In Israel, the nations observe what the gracious hand of God can accomplish and how God's people respond to that grace. The constitutional texts were not written primarily to provide judges with prescribed answers for legal and ethical cases presented to them, but to create a worldview. Israel's relationship to her land and to Yahweh serve as microcosms of the relationship between humanity, the world (including living and non-living things) and the Creator. When we read these texts we need always to be asking: What underlying perspective/ethic is reflected here that we should apply to our modern situation? For this reason, the laws and teachings of the Torah provide a wealth of wisdom for people of every age on how to respond to human poverty and deprivation, how to handle domestic animals, and how to wrestle with fundamental issues related to food production and survival. Particularly, the Torah calls individuals to abandon self-interest and to demonstrate covenant commitment to others by always acting in their interests. This discovery alone should rein in the individualism, greed and acquisitiveness that characterize the modern Western minority world.

Even if we de-emphasize or reject the line of reasoning that would require special concern for non-human life, and the conviction that human beings were created to take care of the world, rather than that the world was created for us, the appeal for creation care may be justified on purely humanitarian grounds. People's lives are at stake. If the process of global warming continues, many millions living in coastal regions will be driven from their homes by rising ocean waters caused by melting ice and thermal expansion of the seas. Unless we address the problems of overcrowding and lack of sanitation in many of the world's cities, premature death will rob their citizens of life; disease, poverty and unemployment will continue to dehumanize them and rob them of their dignity. Unless we manage the earth's rich agricultural resources well, and unless we find ways of distributing the fruit of the ground to empty stomachs around the globe, millions who have been created in

God's image will die prematurely. And unless we learn to share our water resources more equitably and make this vital treasure available in sufficient quantity and quality, many in the Two-Thirds World will perish. Surely Jesus' commendation of those who have given a cup of cold water to the thirsty in Matthew 10:42 extends to all who drill wells and devise means of delivering that water that the thirsty may drink.

The time has come for evangelicals to care for—and not just talk about—the earth. The signatories to "An Evangelical Manifesto" were correct in recognizing that evangelicals must be concerned not only with the church but also the wider world, especially to the plight of millions who are poor, vulnerable, marginalized and without a voice in their communities.[19] Let us extend this concern to all of creation. May the Lord wake us all up to our privileged status as his deputies and representatives and to our responsibilities in caring for all of God's good earth.

---

[19]See "An Evangelical Manifesto: A Declaration of Evangelical Identity and Public Commitment," signed May 7, 2008, Washington, D.C., available at <www.anevangelicalmanifesto .com/>.

1

ESCHATOLOGY AND ENVIRONMENTAL ETHICS

On the Importance of Biblical Theology to Creation Care

Douglas J. Moo

In 1843, Ludwig Feuerbach claimed that "Nature, the world, has no value, no interest for Christians. The Christian thinks only of himself and the salvation of his soul."[1] Feuerbach was not the first to accuse Christianity of an excessive anthropocentrism, and he was certainly not the last. Such charges have, indeed, become especially common during the last forty years, as many environmentalists trace to Christianity one of the ideological roots of the current "ecological crisis." Perhaps the best-known of these accusations came in a paper read in 1967 by Lynn White Jr., titled "The Historic Roots of our Ecological Crisis."[2] White argued that environmental degradation was the indirect product of Christianity, which he labeled (in its Western form), "the most anthropocentric religion the world has ever seen."[3] The biblical claim that humans have dominion over creation has shaped the typically Western "instrumentalist" view of nature: that the natural world exists solely to

---

[1]John Reumann, *Creation and New Creation: The Past, Present, and Future of God's Creative Activity* (Minneapolis: Augsburg, 1973), p. 8, citing Ludwig Feuerbach, *The Essence of Christianity* (New York: Harper & Row, 1957), p. 287.

[2]Lynn White Jr., "The Historical Roots of Our Ecologic Crisis," *Science* 155 (1967): 1203-7. White's paper has been reprinted in many places; references in this article are to idem, in *The Care of Creation: Focusing Concern and Action*, ed. R. J. Berry (Downers Grove, Ill: InterVarsity Press, 2000), pp. 31-42.

[3]White, "Historical Roots," p. 38.

meet human needs. Wedded to unprecedented scientific and technological advancements, Christian anthropocentrism has brought us pollution, global warming and widespread species extinction.[4]

As might be expected, orthodox Christians have been especially
keen to register their reservations about White's thesis. As bookends to
these responses, we may mention Francis Schaeffer's ground-breaking
1973 book *Pollution and the Death of Man*,[5] which was motivated to a
considerable extent by White's essay; and Alister McGrath's *The Reenchantment of Nature*, published in 2002.[6] But more important for my
purpose than this continuing dispute about the ideological roots of the
environmental crisis is the proliferation over the past half-century of
books and articles seeking to discover in the Bible and in Christian
theology resources to positively address this crisis. They are far too varied even to categorize here. It should be noted, however, that evangelicals have made significant contributions to this discussion,[7] and a number of significant evangelical organizations dedicated to environmental
causes have arisen.[8] To be sure, evangelical reaction to environmentalism has been quite diverse. Some evangelicals have joined with social
and political conservatives to voice concern about what they perceive to
be evangelical environmentalists' overly negative attitude toward human ingenuity as manifested in technology and their tendency to ig-

---

[4]This chapter is a condensed version of my article "Nature in the New Creation: New Testament Eschatology and the Environment," published in the *Journal of the Evangelical Theological
Society* 49 (2006): 449-88.

[5]Francis Schaeffer, *Pollution and the Death of Man* (Wheaton, Ill.: Crossway, 1973).

[6]Alister E. McGrath, *The Reenchantment of Nature: The Denial of Religion and the Ecological
Crisis* (New York: Doubleday, 2002).

[7]For a survey of responses from evangelicals, along with an analysis of some of the religious
and social circumstances in which they developed, see David Kenneth Larsen, "God's Gar-
deners: American Protestant Evangelicals Confront Environmentalism, 1967-2000" (Ph.D.
diss., University of Chicago, 2001). A survey of early evangelical responses can be found in
Henlee H. Barnette, *The Church and the Ecological Crisis* (Grand Rapids: Eerdmans, 1972).
A survey broader in its scope, though dated, is Joseph K. Sheldon, *Rediscovery of Creation: A
Bibliographical Study of the Church's Response to the Environmental Crisis*, ATLA Bibliography
Series 29 (Metuchen, N.J.: The American Theological Library Association and the Scarecrow
Press, 1992). See also the helpful taxonomy of approaches set forth in Raymond Grizzle, Paul
E. Rothrock and Christopher B. Barrett, "Evangelicals and Environmentalism: Past, Present,
and Future," *TrinJ* 19 (1998): 3-27.

[8]The most significant organizations at the theoretical level are the Evangelical Environmental
Network (www.creationcare.org) and the AuSable Institute (www.AuSable.org). A Rocha is
an evangelical organization devoted to the practice of creation care (http://en.arocha.org).

nore the role of individual human rights in social policy.[9] And it is fair to say that most lay evangelicals, responding to the anti-Christian attitudes displayed by many environmentalists and following the lead of some influential Christian media figures, have a generally negative attitude toward environmentalism.

The negative view of environmentalism among many Christians can find some basis in the NT. The NT is heavily anthropocentric; the "world" is often viewed negatively; little is said about the natural world; and what little is said sometimes suggests that it is doomed to an imminent fiery end. Many evangelicals are therefore seriously convinced that concern for the environment is either a waste of time (God will ensure that the world will be preserved until its destined destruction) or a luxury we can't afford (we should deflect none of our time or resources from our core mission of evangelism). Let me say at the outset that I have no intention of suggesting that the redemption of human beings is not at the heart of God's plan or that the church should not make evangelism its primary goal. But I do want to suggest that the attitude of an "either-or" when it comes to evangelism and environmental concern is a false alternative, echoing the false alternative of evangelism versus social concern that was debated in the 1960s and 70s; both distinctions are profoundly out of keeping with the witness of Scripture.

In this paper, specifically, I want to buttress this claim by suggesting, in a necessarily preliminary manner, that the NT stands in continuity with the OT in affirming the continuing importance of the natural world in the plan of God. To be sure, this point has been made, and made well, by others. But I hope to contribute to the discussion by the way I argue the point.

My biblical-theological approach to the issue under discussion will set texts in the context of certain specific broader themes that bind the Scriptures together. Two are especially important for the present essay.

---

[9]See especially the writings of E. Calvin Beisner, *Prosperity and Poverty: The Compassionate Use of Resources in a World of Scarcity* (Wheaton, Ill.: Crossway, 1988); idem, *Prospects for Growth: A Biblical View of Population, Resources and the Future* (Westchester, Ill.: Crossway, 1990); idem, *Man, Economy, and the Environment in Biblical Perspective* (Moscow, Idaho: Canon Press, 1994) and idem, *Where Garden Meets Wilderness: Evangelical Entry into the Environmental Debate* (Grand Rapids: Acton Institute, 1997).

First, we will utilize the common perspective of inaugurated eschatology, with its critical distinction between the "already" of fulfillment and the "not yet" of consummation. Greg Beale and others have put forth the notion of "new creation" as at least one central unifying theme within this structure of eschatological realization.[10] Quite appropriately, granted the NT focus, most studies of "new creation" have focused on its anthropological aspects. I want to explore the place of creation itself in this eschatological program of new creation. Second, the theological and eschatological significance of the texts we are looking at can only be appreciated after they are set within the larger biblical story line. A brief and admittedly simplistic rehearsal of this story, with a focus on those stages of particular significance to our study, runs as follows. The first humans, created in God's image, fail to obey the Lord their God and bring ruin on themselves and the entire world. After the judgment of expulsion from the Garden and the Flood, God begins his work of reclaiming his fallen creation through Abraham and his descendants. From that line comes Israel, the nation God chooses to carry forward his grand plan of redemption. The nation is given the responsibility not only to worship God through their praise and obedience but also to be a "light to the nations": to be the means of God's blessing of the entire world. As both a blessing and a test, Israel is given a land. Israel's enjoyment of that land, indeed, her continuance in it, depends on her obedience to the covenant stipulations. Yet Israel fails on this score; and so the nation is sent into exile, removed from its land. But the prophets proclaim that the exile will one day be reversed. Central to many of the prophetic texts is this theme of return from exile, when God would bless his people anew, the land would once again be fruitful, and the ultimate purpose of God to bless the nations through Israel would be accomplished. Israel does, of course, return from exile, but it quickly becomes clear that this return falls far short of what the prophets had promised. And so a new deliverance is anticipated still. The NT claims that this deliver-

---

[10]For example, Greg Beale, "The Eschatological Concept of New Testament Theology," in *"The Reader Must Understand": Eschatology in Bible and Theology*, ed. K. E. Brower and M. W. Elliott (Leicester, U.K.: Inter-Varsity Press, 1997), pp. 11-52.

ance takes place in and through the coming of Jesus the Messiah. He, the second Adam, the true and ultimate image of God, obeys where Adam had disobeyed; through his death and resurrection he inaugurates the last days that the prophets had longed for. The true "return from exile" has finally taken place. Yet, as we have already noted, the ultimate benefits of that fulfillment are not yet seen. Through Christ's second coming God will consummate his redemptive work for the entire cosmos.

This very rough sketch of the shape of eschatological fulfillment as it unfolds in the biblical story brings nothing new to the table. But insufficient attention has been paid to the place of the cosmos in this scheme of fulfillment. Return to the land and the blessing of the land were very important in the prophetic witness. What happens to that theme in the NT? Any adequate answer to this question involves us in some very knotty and controversial hermeneutical issues. Some interpreters insist that the OT promises about a return to the land have not been fulfilled in the return from exile and must be fulfilled when Christ returns in glory. While this position deserves respect for the seriousness with which it takes the OT promises, I am not convinced finally that it does justice to what we might call the "universalizing" hermeneutic of the NT. Other scholars insist that the NT pattern of fulfillment points to Christ and his people as the "place" where the OT land promises now find their fulfillment. The Christological focus in the NT presentation of fulfillment of the promise is certainly justified. But I think there are suggestions within the NT that the land promise has not simply been spiritualized or "Christified," but universalized. In a necessarily tentative fashion, therefore, I will suggest that the land promise in the NT is expanded, in a manner typical of the shape of NT fulfillment, to include the whole world. Furthermore, I want to suggest that this restoration of "the world" is not to be spiritualized, nor can it be reduced to human beings only. It includes a material element. God is at work bringing blessing not only to his people but also to the physical cosmos itself.

The essay falls into three parts. I first look at several passages on the future of the created world. I will then turn to passages and concepts about the present state of the created world. I will conclude with some reflections on the ethical implications of the NT eschatological perspective.

The Final State of Nature: The "Not Yet" of Eschatological Fulfillment

Romans 8:19-22. Romans 8:19-22, along with Colossians 1:20, is the NT text most often cited in literature on biblical environmentalism. And justly so—it is the clearest expression of future hope for the physical world in the NT.

> The creation waits in eager expectation for the children of God to be revealed. For the creation was subjected to frustration, not by its own choice, but by the will of the one who subjected it, in hope that the creation itself will be liberated from its bondage to decay and brought into the freedom and glory of the children of God. We know that the whole creation has been groaning as in the pains of childbirth right up to the present time.[11]

The text comes toward the beginning of a section in which Paul celebrates the future glory that God's work in Christ assures to believers. The verses provide grounds for Paul's assertion in Romans 8:18: "I consider that our present sufferings are not worth comparing with the glory that will be revealed in us." How Romans 8:19-22 relates to Romans 8:18 depends on the most important exegetical issue raised by this text: what does the word *creation* (*ktisis*; occurring once in each verse) refer to? The majority of modern interpreters agree that *creation* in these verses refers to the "subhuman" creation. Following the lead of psalmists and prophets (for example, Ps 65:12-13; Is 24:4; Jer 4:28; 12:4), Paul personifies the world of nature in order to portray its "fall" and anticipated glory.

Three of the things Paul says about creation in these verses are especially important for our argument.

First, creation has been "frustrated" and is in "bondage to decay." In the background is the curse of the ground in Genesis 3:17-19:

---

[11]Quotations of the Bible in this chapter, unless otherwise noted, are from the TNIV.

To Adam he said, "Because you listened to your wife and ate from the tree about which I commanded you, 'You must not eat of it,'

"Cursed is the ground because of you;
through painful toil you will eat of it
all the days of your life.
It will produce thorns and thistles for you,
and you will eat the plants of the field.
By the sweat of your brow
you will eat your food
until you return to the ground,
since from it you were taken;
for dust you are
and to dust you will return."

In Romans 8:20, the "one who subjected it" is God, who pronounces the Genesis curse. Just what this curse is and how it has come about is not clear. But Paul suggests that human sin has led to some kind of change in the nature of the cosmos itself. It has been subject, he says, to "frustration," or "vanity"; the Greek word suggests that creation has not been able to attain the purpose for which it was created. And the word "decay" suggests the inevitable disintegration to which all things since the Fall are subject.

Our conclusions about the nature of the created world as a result of the Fall are therefore necessarily modest. What can be affirmed on the basis of Romans 8 is that the natural world itself has been affected in some way by the human fall into sin and is therefore no longer in its pristine created state. This element in the teaching of Romans 8 has important consequences for a properly Christian view of the natural world. Human sin has affected the state of nature itself and will continue to do so until the end of this age. As Moltmann notes, "To understand 'nature' as creation therefore means discerning 'nature' as the enslaved creation that hopes for liberty. So by 'nature' we can only mean a single act in the great drama of the creation of the world on the way to the kingdom of glory—the act that is being played out at the present time."[12]

---

[12]Jürgen Moltmann, *God in Creation: A New Theology of Creation and the Spirit of God* (Min-

And this brings us to our second and third points, which we can make more quickly. If creation has suffered the consequences of human sin, it will also enjoy the fruits of human deliverance. When believers are glorified, creation's "bondage to decay" will be ended, and it will participate in the "freedom that belongs to the glory" for which Christians are destined. Nature, Paul affirms, has a future within the plan of God. It is destined not simply for destruction but for transformation. The reversal of the conditions of the Fall includes the created world along with the world of human beings. Indeed, the glory that humans will experience, involving as it does the resurrection of the body (Rom 8:9-11, 23), necessarily requires an appropriate environment for that embodiment.

Finally, we should note that, in addition to Genesis 3, these verses in Romans almost certainly allude to various prophetic expectations. The single most important prophetic text echoed in these verses is Isaiah 24–27. Isaiah 24:1-13 describes the effects of sin in cosmic terms: "the heavens languish with the earth" (v. 4), "a curse consumes the earth" (v. 6). And why is the earth in this condition? Because "the earth is defiled by its people; they have disobeyed the laws, violated the statutes and broken the everlasting covenant" (v. 5). Isaiah goes on in these chapters to describe how that situation will be reversed. As Jonathan Moo has summarized the matter, the prophet looks

> to a time when the Lord will reign as king on Mount Zion (24:23) and the glory of the Lord [δοξα κυρίου] will be praised (24:14, 15) and manifested (25:1). On that day, the Lord will destroy "the covering that is cast on all peoples, the veil that is spread over all nations. He will swallow up death for ever, and the Lord God will wipe tears from all faces, and the reproach of his people he will take away from all the earth" (25:7-8). This is the day that God's people have waited and yearned for as they have sought him in their distress (25:9; 26:8, 9, 16). Indeed, they have been suffering as in birth pains [ὠδίνω] but they have not been able to bring about deliverance in the earth (26:17-18). But despite their seemingly fruitless labor, "the dead shall live, their bodies shall rise" and the "dwellers in the dust awake" (26:19) and, in the days to come, "Israel

neapolis: Fortress, 1993), p. 39.

shall blossom and put forth shoots, and fill the whole world with fruit" (27:6).[13]

Paul quotes from this section of Isaiah later in Romans (Is 27:9 in Rom 11:26-27), and other NT authors make extensive use of the imagery of these chapters. Paul's dependence on this section of Isaiah's prophecy in Romans 8 suggests that his conviction about the physical restoration of the entire world is to some extent derived from the prophetic hope for the restoration of Israel to her land—a restoration that in these chapters, and in a manner typical of Isaiah's prophecy, ultimately encompasses the whole world (see especially Isaiah 24:21-23; 27:6, 13). Moreover, this same idea may surface elsewhere in Romans. In Rom 4:13, Paul speaks of the promise to Abraham that he would be the "heir of the world." Genesis, of course, while emphasizing the worldwide extent of the blessing associated with Abraham, teaches that he would be heir of one particular land, Palestine. Paul clearly universalizes: but in what direction? Does the "world" here refer to human beings only? One might conclude so, since Paul's concern in this context is with the inclusion of Gentiles along with Jews as recipients of the promise to Abraham. However, while human beings are undoubtedly the focus, the concern Paul shows for the physical earth in Romans 8 suggests that "world" in Romans 4:13 may well include the earth also.[14]

New heavens and new earth. The hope for the liberation of creation that Paul expresses in Romans 8 clearly implies that the destiny of the natural world is not destruction but transformation. But this hope for a transformed world stands in some tension with passages in the NT which appear to announce that the last days will usher in an entirely new world. The most important of these passages are those in 2 Peter 3 and Revelation 21 that predict the "destruction" (2 Pet 3:10-12) or "passing away" (Rev 21:1) of the present heavens and earth as the pre-

---

[13]Jonathan Moo, "Romans 8.19-22 and Isaiah's Cosmic Covenant," *New Testament Studies* 54 (2008): 74-89.

[14]See esp. Is 11:10-14; 42:1, 6; 49:6; 54:3; Jer 4:2; Ps 72:8-11; Sir 44:21; *Jub.* 19:21; *2 Bar.* 14:13; 51:3. See on this N. T. Wright, "The Letter to the Romans," in *The New Interpreter's Bible*, ed. L. E. Keck (Nashville: Abingdon, 2002), 10:495.

lude to the appearance of a "new heaven and a new earth." The continuity between this world and the next one is difficult to determine. But this much can at least be said: the new world is a place of material substance. The phrase *heaven and earth* is a merism that refers to the entire universe. As G. K. Beale points out, therefore, Revelation 21:1 predicts "not merely ethical renovation but transformation of the fundamental cosmic structure (including physical elements)."[15] This language warns us against the persistent tendency in Christian tradition to picture the saints' eternal home as an ethereal and immaterial place up above somewhere. In fact, the NT, contrary to popular Christian parlance, does not usually claim that we will spend eternity in heaven, but in a new heaven and a new earth: a material place suited for life in a material, though of course transformed, body. Jesus' resurrection signals God's commitment to the material world. But the immediate question we need to answer is this: How are we to resolve the tension between the expectation that this world will be transformed and the expectation that this world will be destroyed and exchanged for a new one?

The interpretation of both 2 Peter 3 and Revelation 21 is complicated by their apocalyptic style, a style that features metaphoric language notoriously difficult to interpret. What are we to make of John's vision of the existing heaven and earth "passing away" or of his assertion that, at the time of the great white throne judgment, the "earth and the heavens fled from his [God's] presence, and there was no place for them" (Rev 20:11)? What does Peter mean when he predicts the "destruction of the heavens by fire" (2 Pet 3:12) or that "the heavens will disappear with a roar; the elements will be destroyed by fire, and the earth and everything done in it will be laid bare" (2 Pet 3:10) or that "the elements will melt in the heat" (1 Pet 3:12)? Are we to take this language as straightforward descriptions of a future physical reality, to be fulfilled perhaps in a nuclear holocaust or in the ultimate fiery explosion of the sun? Or are John and Peter using metaphors to depict an irruption of God's power to remake the world as we know it? A close look at the passages suggests that what is envisaged is not annihilation

---

[15]G. K. Beale, *The Book of Revelation*, NIGTC (Grand Rapids: Eerdmans, 1999), p. 1040.

and new creation but radical transformation.

We should begin with the ultimate source of the new heaven and new earth language: Isaiah 65:17 and Isaiah 66:22-24. John's vision of the New Jerusalem, which he uses to elaborate the nature of the new heaven and new earth, depends considerably on the language of these last chapters in Isaiah (as well as, of course, others in Isaiah and the prophets). Isaiah seems to picture a re-created universe. Exactly what this re-creation will look like is not clear. And Jewish literature does not resolve the matter, referring both to the renovation of this world and the replacement of this world with a different one. The language of Revelation 20:11 and Revelation 21:1 could certainly suggest that a new heaven and new earth replace the old ones.[16] But neither text is completely clear about the matter. Moreover, there are pointers in this context to the idea of renovation. In Revelation 21:5, God proclaims, "I am making everything new!" He does not proclaim "I am making new things." The language here suggests renewal, not destruction and re-creation. The language of Revelation 21–22 is full of references to the original creation, suggesting that John intends to portray the reverse of the curse, a return to the conditions of Eden (though the end advances beyond the conditions of Eden in significant ways as well).

Similar points can be made when we turn to 2 Peter 3. Several interpreters therefore conclude that Peter is using standard metaphors to refer to God's final judgment on human beings. There is some truth in this observation, since Peter parallels the destruction of this present world with the destruction of the former world through the Flood of Noah's day. Clearly the Flood brought judgment upon humankind; equally clearly, the Flood did not annihilate the earth. Yet we cannot finally eliminate some notion of a far-reaching change in the very universe itself. As we have already noted, "heaven and earth" quite regularly in Scripture refers to the created universe, not simply to the human world; and Peter's reference to the "elements" (2 Pet 3:10, 12), while

---

[16]David Mathewson provides a useful survey of interpretation on this matter in *A New Heaven and a New Earth: The Meaning and Function of the Old Testament in Revelation 21.1-22.5*, JSNTSup 238 (Sheffield, U.K.: Sheffield Academic Press, 2003), pp. 135-39. He comes down hesitantly on the side of annihilation/new creation.

much debated, probably also refers to the components of the physical world. Moreover, the whole argument in this part of 2 Peter 3 is cosmological in focus. Mockers deny that Christ will ever return in judgment because, they claim, "everything" goes on as it has since creation (2 Pet 3:4). Peter responds by reminding the mockers of three outstanding interventions of God in the cosmos: creation itself, the flood in the day of Noah, and the end of history as we know it. But it is not clear that Peter is predicting the destruction of the present universe.

First, we should note that the translation of 2 Peter 3:10 in some versions (for example, KJV, ASV, NASB), which has the earth and everything in it being "burned up," is almost certainly incorrect. The text is notoriously difficult, but almost all modern versions and commentators assume that the reading "will be found" is original. What this means is more difficult to determine, but perhaps the idea of being "laid bare" before God for judgment is the best option. Second, the language of burning and melting that is found in 2 Peter 3:7, 10, 12 must be read against the background of the OT, where such language is often a metaphorical way of speaking of judgment.[17] And even if some reference to physical fire is present, the fire need not bring total destruction. And that brings us to our third, and most important point: the Greek word for "destroy" in 2 Peter 3:10-12 is a verb that denotes, as the lexicon of Louw-Nida puts it, "to destroy or reduce something to ruin by tearing down or breaking to pieces."[18] This "destruction" does not necessarily mean total physical annihilation, but a dissolution or radical change in nature. The widespread metaphorical sense of the venerable English verb "undo" might accurately convey something of the sense. When a character in a C. S. Lewis novel exclaims that he is "undone," he does not mean that he has ceased to exist but that the very nature of his being

---

[17]See, e.g., Is 30:30; 66:15-16; Nahum 1:6; Zeph 1:18; 3:8; Mic 1:3-4; Is 63:19–64:1 LXX. Al Wolters suggests the language may refer to a refining process by which the present world is purged of evil. Idem, "Worldview and Textual Criticism in 2 Peter 3:10," *WTJ* 49 (1987): 405-13.

[18]Johannes P. Louw and Eugene A. Nida, *Greek-English Lexicon of the New Testament Based on Semantic Domains*, 2 vols. (New York: United Bible Societies, 1989), 20.53. The verb means basically "loose," "release," from which meaning the ideas of "break" (for example, Jn 10:35) and "destroy" or "break down" are derived. The closest parallels to the use of λυω in 2 Peter 3 are John 2:19 ("destroy this temple"); Ephesians 2:14 ("breaking down the dividing wall of hostility"); 1 John 3:8 ("to destroy the devil's works").

has been destroyed. We should also note that language of "destruction" is frequently used in the NT to refer to the ultimate fate of sinful human beings. Most scholars correctly resist the conclusion that this language points to the doctrine of annihilationism. Therefore, just as the "destruction of the ungodly" in 2 Peter 3:7 need not mean the annihilation of these sinners, neither need the "destruction" of the universe in 2 Peter 3:10-12 mean that it is annihilated. The parallel with what God did when he "destroyed" the first world in the Flood of Noah suggests that God will destroy this world not by annihilating it but by radically transforming it into a place fit for resurrected saints to live in forever.

We must not minimize the strength of the language in Revelation 20–21 and 2 Peter 3: both texts indicate a radical and thoroughgoing renovation of the world as we now know it. But I do not think the texts require us to believe that this world will be destroyed and replaced. And, as we have pointed out all along, two other considerations point strongly to the idea of renovation rather than replacement. First is the teaching of Romans 8 about the liberation of the cosmos. Second is the doctrine of the resurrection of the body, which demands a significant continuity of some kind between this world and the next. In fact, the analogy of the human body, as many interpreters have suggested, may offer the best way to resolve the tension between destruction and transformation with respect to the universe. Here also we find a puzzling combination of continuity and discontinuity. Jesus' resurrection body is able, apparently, to dematerialize and materialize again; it is not always recognizable; it is, as Paul puts in with respect to the resurrection body in general, a new kind of body, suited for existence in the spirit-dominated eternal kingdom (1 Cor 15:35-54). Yet there is continuity in the body: in some sense, the body that was in the grave is the same as the body that appears to the disciples after the resurrection. This "transformation within continuity," as Colin Gunton puts it, furnishes an apt parallel to the future of the cosmos.[19] Perhaps the word *renewal* best captures this combination of continuity and discontinuity.

---

[19]Colin E. Gunton, *Christ and Creation* (Grand Rapids: Eerdmans, 1992), p. 31. See also Murray J. Harris, *Raised Immortal: Resurrection and Immortality in the New Testament* (Grand Rapids: Eerdmans, 1983), pp. 168-70.

THE PRESENT STATE OF NATURE: THE "ALREADY"
OF ESCHATOLOGICAL FULFILLMENT

Colossians 1:20. If Romans 8:19-22 is the most frequently cited "environmental" text on the "not yet" side of the eschatological tension, Colossians 1:20 certainly deserves the honor on the "already" side of the tension. Verses 19-20 read, in the TNIV, "For God was pleased to have all his fullness dwell in him, and through him to reconcile to himself all things, whether things on earth or things in heaven, by making peace through his blood, shed on the cross." Ray van Leeuwen aptly states a typical claim made for this verse in biblical-theological studies of the environment: "All of reality is Christ's good creation, all of reality is redeemed by him; therefore, all of reality is the responsibility of God's people."[20] Yet those who make such claims rarely acknowledge the complex and debated interpretational issues surrounding Colossians 1:20. It can hardly be cited in support of any view without at least supportive argumentation.

Colossians 1:20 concludes what is generally thought to be an early christological "hymn" (Col 1:15-20). The entire hymn focuses on the universality of Christ, and verse 20 has a similar universal focus. Some interpreters, indeed, think that the "reconciliation" of verse 20 is restricted to human beings. This is what Paul talks about in Colossians 1:21-23, and Paul elsewhere confines reconciliation language to the new relationship offered to humans through the sacrifice of Christ.[21] But this restriction on the scope of reconciliation in verse 20 fails to reckon seriously with the intent of Colossians 1:15-20. The Greek word for "all things" in verse 20 occurs five other times in the immediate context, and in each case it refers to the whole created universe. The scope of the word is especially clear from the reference to "things on earth or things in heaven" in Colossians 1:20. As Colossians 1:16 reveals, "things in heaven" include (though they are not necessarily lim-

---

[20]Raymond C. van Leeuwen, "Christ's Resurrection and the Creation's Vindication," in *The Environment and the Christian: What Does the New Testament Say About the Environment?* ed. Calvin DeWitt (Grand Rapids: Baker Academic, 1991), p. 62.

[21]See Rom 5:10 (twice); Rom 5:11; 11:15; 2 Cor 5:18-19; Col 1:22 and Eph 2:16. Paul uses the verb "reconcile" once in a non-theological sense to refer to reconciliation between marriage partners (1 Cor 7:11).

ited to) the spiritual beings that play so prominent a role in the background of the Colossian controversy (cf. Col 2:10, 14-15). The context therefore requires that "all things" be unlimited in its scope. In Colossians 1:21-23, then, Paul does not limit the referent of Colossians 1:20 but emphasizes the application of the general reconciliation (Col 1:20) to the Colossian Christians.

If, however, Colossians 1:20 does indeed claim that the entire created universe has been reconciled to God in Christ, what is the nature of that reconciliation? Since at least the time of Origen, some interpreters have used this verse to argue for universal salvation: in the end, God will not (and often, it is suggested, *can*not) allow anything to fall outside the scope of his saving love in Christ. Universal salvation is a doctrine very congenial to our age, and it is not therefore surprising that this verse, along with several others in Paul, are regularly cited to argue for this belief. This is not the place to refute this doctrine, which, we briefly note, cannot be reconciled with clear NT teaching about the reality and eternality of hell. Therefore in order to do justice to both (1) the universal scope of "all things" and (2) the explicit limitation on the scope of God's saving work in Christ both in Colossians and in the rest of the NT, "reconcile" in Colossians 1:20 must mean something like "pacify."[22] Through the work of Christ on the cross, God has brought his entire rebellious creation back under the rule of his sovereign power. It is because of this work of universal pacification that God will one day indeed be "all in all" (1 Cor 15:28) and that "at the name of Jesus every knee should bow, in heaven and on earth and under the earth, and every tongue acknowledge that Jesus Christ is Lord, to the glory of God the Father" (Phil 2:10-11).

What Colossians 1:20 teaches, then, is not cosmic salvation or even cosmic redemption, but "cosmic restoration" or "renewal." Again, Paul is indebted to a broad OT theme for his teaching here. The "peace" of verse 20 reflects the widespread OT prediction that in the last day God would establish universal *šālôm*, "peace," or "well-being."[23] The

---

[22]For this view see, e.g., F. F. Bruce, *The Epistles to the Colossians, to Philemon, and to the Ephesians*, NICNT (Grand Rapids: Eerdmans, 1984), pp. 74-76; Peter T. O'Brien, *Colossians, Philemon*, WBC 44 (Waco, Tex.: Word, 1982), pp. 52-57.

[23]In light of our conclusions earlier about the Old Testament background to Rom 8:19-22, it is worth noting that the establishing of "peace" is an important theme in Is 24–27 (see Is 26:3, 12;

OT prophets focus, naturally enough, on the way this peace would bring security and blessing to Israel as the people live in the land God gave them. In a manner typical of NT fulfillment, Paul proclaims that this peace has now been established in Christ and enables God's new covenant people to live in a still dangerous and hostile world with new confidence and freedom from anxiety. They need not fear the spiritual powers that were believed in Paul's day to be so determinative of one's destiny. Of course, this peace is not yet fully established. The "already/not yet" pattern of NT eschatology must be applied to Colossians 1:20. While secured in principle by Christ's crucifixion and available in preliminary form to believers, universal peace is not yet fully realized.

The natural world must, of course, be included in this universal reconciliation, or peace. But what will this reconciliation look like? God's people will be brought back into a relation of harmony with their creator; evil will be judged and banished; the earth itself will be "liberated from its bondage to decay" (Rom 8:21). Furthermore, while the vertical dimension of reconciliation is clearly to the fore in Colossians 1:20— God has reconciled all things "to himself"—a horizontal aspect is probably included as well. This is because the pacification of spiritual beings has specific implications for Christians' relationship to them: because God has subjugated them to himself, they have been disarmed; they no longer have the power to determine the destiny of God's people. Therefore, we might suggest that the reconciliation secured by Christ means that nature is "already" restored in principle to that condition in which it can fulfill the purpose for which God created it and thereby praise its Creator (cf. Rev 5:13). At the same time, reconciliation may also imply that Christians, renewed in the image of God (see below), are both themselves brought into harmony with creation and, in light of the "not yet" side of reconciliation, are to work toward the goal of creation's final transformation.

New Creation. The language of "new creation" as such occurs only twice in the NT, both times in Paul:

27:5). See also *inter alios*, Is 9:7; 52:7; 55:12; 66:12; Jer 30:10; 33:6, 9; 46:27; Ezek 34:29; 37:26; Mic 5:5; Hag 2:9; Zech 9:10.

2 Corinthians 5:17: "Therefore, if anyone is in Christ, the new creation has come: The old has gone, the new is here!"

Galatians 6:15: "Neither circumcision nor uncircumcision means anything; what counts is a new creation."

Both occurrences are often given a strictly anthropological reference: the Christian transformed by God's grace is the "new creation" or "new creature."[24] Context would appear to support this interpretation, since in both passages Paul is drawing out the implications of the new realm of grace for believers. Galatians 6:15 is a final decisive reminder that God in Christ has inaugurated a radically new era in which the old covenant markers of identity are simply no longer relevant. And it is the reconciliation of the world of human beings that Paul seems to have in mind in 2 Corinthians (see 2 Cor 5:19). Moreover, the logic of 2 Corinthians 5:17 would also seem to limit the reference to human beings, since the existence of the "new creation" appears to hinge on a person's belonging to Christ. However, there are also indications that, while *applied* to the new state of believers, the new creation language *refers to* the entire new state of affairs that Christ's coming has inaugurated.

First, the abruptness with which Paul introduces the new creation in 2 Corinthians 5:17 renders uncertain the precise logical connection in the verse. Many English versions follow the pattern found, for instance, in the ESV: "if anyone is in Christ, he is a new creation." But perhaps the abruptness of the construction favors a rendering such as is found in the TNIV (quoted above), or even "if anyone is in Christ, they belong to a new creation." Roughly the same situation obtains in Galatians 6:15, where "new creation" is again used absolutely. Second, it is worth noting that most modern versions have chosen the translation *creation* rather than *creature* in both passages—a move justified, as noted earlier, by the general use of the word *creation* in the NT. Third, while the phrase *new creation* is not found in the OT, it is generally agreed that Paul's phrase refers to the hope of a worldwide, even cosmic, renewal that is so widespread in the last part of Isaiah. Isaiah 40–55 often por-

---

[24]The anthropological side is stressed by, e.g., Moyer Hubbard, *New Creation in Paul's Letters and Thought*, SNTSMS 119 (Cambridge: Cambridge University Press, 2002).

trays the return of Israel from exile in creation language. As Greg Beale has pointed out, Paul's proclamation of a new creation—and the reconciliation that is part of it—is the fulfillment of these prophecies in Isaiah.[25] Jewish writers also used new creation language, probably in most cases depending on Isaiah, to depict God's new work for his people Israel. Paul's phrase *new creation* therefore appears to be his way of summarizing the new state of affairs that has been inaugurated at Christ's first coming and is to be consummated at this second. As Ralph Martin summarizes, "with Christ's coming a whole new chapter in cosmic relationship to God opened and reversed the catastrophic effect of Adam's fall which began the old creation."[26]

In this age, the focus of God's new creation work is the transformation of human beings—in their relationship to God, first of all, and then also in their relationship to each other. But, as we have seen, Paul includes the transformation of the natural world in his presentation of the eschatological program—explicitly in the consummation (Rom 8:19-22) and implicitly in the present (Col 1:20). We would therefore expect that the relation of human beings to their natural environment is included in God's present work of new creation and that the climax of God's new creation work will include the transformation of the natural world.

CONCLUSION: FROM ESCHATOLOGY TO ETHICS

As will be all too evident by this point, the preceding analysis is more in the nature of an initial probe than of a thorough study. Each text and issue deserves more careful treatment, and many other texts and issues need to be brought into the discussion. But, preliminary though it is, this study suggests that the world of nature is by no means absent from the eschatological program set out in the NT. While rarely rising to the level of an explicit emphasis, the world of nature is an integral component of God's new creation work. The cross of Jesus Christ has *already* provided the basis for the restoration of nature to its intended place in

---

[25]G. K. Beale, "The Old Testament Background of Reconciliation in 2 Corinthians 5–7 and Its Bearing on the Literary Problem of 2 Corinthians 6:14-7:1," *NTS* 35 (1989): 551-57.
[26]Ralph P. Martin, *2 Corinthians*, WBC 40 (Waco, Tex.: Word, 1986), p. 152.

the plan of God, though *not yet* do we see that restoration actually accomplished. In a few altogether too brief and superficial concluding remarks, I will explore the ethical implications of this eschatology. I will begin with implications of the futurist side of eschatology.

First, a negative point. Eschatology in the narrow and popular sense of the world is often cited as a reason why Christians are not (and should not be!) concerned about the environment. Al Truesdale is quite forthright, laying the blame for ethical quietism squarely at the door of dispensational premillennialism and arguing that evangelicals must rid themselves of such an eschatology if they are truly to commit themselves to environmental concern. As he puts it, "Until evangelicals purge from their vision of the Christian faith the wine of pessimistic dispensationalist premillennialism, the Judeo-Christian doctrine of creation and the biblical image of stewardship will be orphans in their midst."[27] The charge that a robust futurist eschatology undercuts concerted attention to the needs of this world is, of course, an old one—and needs to be dismissed. True, Christians have sometimes used eschatology as an excuse for not involving themselves in the needs of this world. One hears far too often an unconcern for this world justified by the slogan, "it is all going to burn anyway": since only the human soul will survive the fires of judgment, only the human soul is really worth bothering about. But even if one holds the view that this world is destined for nothing but destruction, the biblical mandate for Christians to be involved in meeting the needs of the world in which we now live is clear and uncompromising. I may believe that the body I now have is destined for radical transformation; but I am not for that reason unconcerned about what I eat or how much I exercise.

On the other hand, it must be said that the conviction that this world is destined for renewal rather than destruction, as I have argued in this paper, does provide a more substantial basis for a Christian environmental ethic. New Testament eschatology is not intended to foster

---

[27]Al Truesdale, "Last Things First: The Impact of Eschatology on Ecology," *Perspectives on Science and Christian Faith* 46 (1994): 118 [116-20]. For a brief response to Truesdale from a premillennial environmentalist, see R. S. Beal Jr., "Can a Premillennialist Consistently Entertain a Concern for the Environment? A Rejoinder to Al Truesdale," *Perspectives on Science and Christian Faith* 46 (1994): 173-78.

Christian passivity but to encourage God's people actively and vigorously to align their values and behavior with what it is that God is planning to do.[28] When we recognize that God plans to restore his creation, we should be motivated to "work for the renewal of God's creation and for justice within God's creation."[29] Just as, then, believers should be working to bring as many human beings as possible within the scope of God's reconciling act, so they should be working to bring the created world as close to that perfect restoration for which God has destined it. The "not yet" of a restored creation demands an "already" ethical commitment to that creation now among God's people. To be sure, our efforts must always be tempered by the realization that it is finally God himself, in a future act of sovereign power, who will transform creation. And we encounter here the positive side of a robust eschatology. Christians must avoid the humanistic "Green utopianism" that characterizes much of the environmental movement. We will not by our own efforts end the "groaning" of the earth. But this realism about our ultimate success should not deter our enthusiasm to be involved in working toward those ends that God will finally secure through his own sovereign intervention.

If the "not yet" side of eschatology should stimulate us to work hard to bring the condition of the earth into that state for which God has destined it, the "already" side should remind us that our work, though always imperfect, is not in vain. As Francis Shaeffer argued in his pioneering *Pollution and the Death of Man*, inaugurated eschatology enables us to insist that "substantial healing can be a reality here and now."[30] Evangelicals generally recognize that, while the "healing" we offer the world is, above all, spiritual in focus, offering eternal life to sinful human beings, it also includes physical healing and social justice. To these, we contend, needs to be added environmental healing. Realism about the continued fallen state of this world reminds us that we will not erase illness and death from the world, that we will not

---

[28]Michael S. Northcott, *The Environment and Christian Ethics*, New Studies in Christian Ethics (Cambridge: Cambridge University Press, 1996), p. 198.
[29]N. T. Wright, *New Heavens, New Earth* (London: Grove Books, 2003), p. 22.
[30]Francis Schaeffer, *Pollution and the Death of Man* (Wheaton, Ill.: Crossway, 1992), p. 67.

eradicate poverty and injustice, and that we will not restore the earth to its pristine condition. But the realism stemming from the "not yet" side of eschatology should in no way deter us from vigorously pursuing each of these goals, motivated and empowered by the "already" of kingdom realization.

PART TWO

CITIES AND THE WORLD

2

CITIES AND THE GLOBAL ENVIRONMENT

Noah J. Toly

IN HIS 1991 BOOK, *Nature's Metropolis: Chicago and the Great West*, William Cronon, widely regarded as the most significant environmental historian of his time, chronicles the relationship between the middle of the North American continent and what was once America's most dynamic city.[1] "No city," he writes, "played a more important role in shaping the landscape and economy of the midcontinent during the second half of the nineteenth century than Chicago."[2] The birth and growth of the United States' "second city" was the single greatest contemporary influence upon the landscape between the Great Lakes and the Rocky Mountains. The Great West became a sort of *ex situ* urban landscape shaped more by Chicago's urban dynamic than by developments in territories west of the city.

Few texts have been as influential as *Nature's Metropolis* in informing responsible consideration of the relationship between a city and its hinterland—a relationship of mutual and multivalent influence that, in the latter half of the nineteenth century, expanded to nearly continental

---

[1]I would like to thank Daniel I. Block and Hillary Waters for their insightful comments on earlier drafts. Special thanks are due to Erin Olson and Ben Gibson, whose assistance with this chapter made it a better one, to Project Teacher, a faculty development initiative of Wheaton College, which provided a Mentor Guided Scholarship Stipend to facilitate Erin's work, and to the G. W. Aldeen Fund, which provided a grant to facilitate Erin's and Ben's work.
[2]William Cronon, *Nature's Metropolis: Chicago and the Great West* (New York: W. W. Norton, 1991), p. xv.

proportions. The environmental impact of this relationship was re-markable. "During the second half of the nineteenth century," Cronon writes, "the American landscape was transformed in ways that antici-pated many of the environmental problems we face today: large-scale deforestation, threats of species extinction, unsustainable exploitation of natural resources, widespread destruction of habitat."[3] Since then, the relationship between cities and the environment has expanded to global proportions. In his epilogue, Cronon writes, "The city-country relations I have described in this book now involve the entire planet. . . . We all live in the city."[4] In the first decade of the twenty-first century, the truth of Cronon's statement is evident. Rapid urbanization—in-creases in both the population of existing urban areas and in the num-ber of urban settlements—has an impact on the global environment. The birth and growth of metropolises and megalopolises (megacities of more than ten million inhabitants) are among the greatest contempo-rary influences upon the global landscape.

Environments and ecologically-mediated social relations the world over constitute an *ex situ* urbanism, a global landscape shaped by urban dynamics both proximate and distant. For example, marine layer air pollution on the west coast of North America can be traced to its ori-gins in Shanghai's manufacturing districts, which are busy producing exports bound for Los Angeles.[5] At the same time, e-waste (or elec-tronic waste, the fastest growing waste stream in the world, including household appliances, cell phones, fluorescent light bulbs and comput-ers) from urban centers of high technology in the United States and elsewhere "follows the 'path of least resistance' and finds its way into

---

[3]Ibid.
[4]Ibid., pp. 384-85. Emphasis added.
[5]Leonard Levin, "Global Impacts: Atmospheric Long-Range Transport of Urban Pollutants," in *Urbanization, Energy, and Air Pollution in China: The Challenges Ahead—Proceedings of a Sym-posium*, ed. Jack J. Fritz (Washington, D.C.: National Academies Press, 2004). Chinese urban politics has been characterized as "global environmental politics": Hans Bruyninckx, "China's Domestic Environmental Politics as 'Global' Environmental Governance," paper presented at the 49th Annual Convention of the International Studies Association (San Francisco, 2008). See also a recent report by NASA and the National Oceanic and Atmospheric Organization indicating that air pollutants originating in Asia—and, specifically, in cities of the world's fast-est urbanizing region—currently affect air temperatures over the North American heartland and will likely have dramatic local warming influences in the future.

nations that are poor and largely populated by non-European peoples."[6] New York City has famously globalized garbage; as Robert Fitch wrote of the Big Apple, "the rest of the world sends us cars, bananas, cocoa, electronic goods, all manner of ingeniously made and rare commodities. We ship back waste paper."[7] The idiosyncratic functions of urban centers throughout the world—whether export manufacturing in China, the production and consumption of Silicon Valley's high-tech industry, or the vast paper ecology of New York's commercial economy—affect global and distant local environments.

At the same time, *in situ* urban environments—urban landscapes, proper—throughout the world are among the most toxic, polluted, hazardous, and otherwise unhealthy and inhospitable inhabited landscapes. Many of the world's 3.2 billion city-dwellers experience the vulnerability of the city to the environmental hazards of the global political economy. For example, in his book *Heat Wave*, Eric Klinenberg narrates the role of global restructuring and deindustrialization in producing the vulnerabilities that left over seven hundred people dead in the wake of Chicago's severe summer weather of 1995.[8] As a rule, those on the margins of society, including more than 1 billion urban and peri-urban slum dwellers, suffer these ills first and worst.

This chapter argues that the relationship between cities and the world is an ethically considerable dimension of global environmental concern, deserving thoughtful and careful consideration of biblical

[6]David Naguib Pellow, "Transnational Alliances and Global Politics: New Geographies of Urban Environmental Justice Struggles," in *In the Nature of Cities: Urban Political Ecology and the Politics of Urban Metabolism*, ed. Nik Heynen, Maria Kaika and Erik Swyngedouw (New York: Routledge, 2006), p. 226; see also David Naguib Pellow, *Resisting Global Toxics: Transnational Movements for Environmental Justice*, Urban and Industrial Environments (Cambridge, Mass.: MIT Press, 2007).

[7]Robert Fitch, *The Assassination of New York* (New York: Verso, 1993), p. 259. See also Julie Sze, "The Racial Geography of New York City Garbage: Local and Global Trash Politics," in *Noxious New York: Racial Politics of Urban Health and Environmental Justice* (Cambridge, Mass.: MIT Press, 2007), pp. 109-42.

[8]Eric Klinenberg, *Heat Wave: A Social Autopsy of Disaster in Chicago* (Chicago: University of Chicago Press, 2002). While Mitchell Duneier argues that Klinenberg errs according to the ecological fallacy, he agrees that conditions produced or exacerbated by deindustrialization, such as abandoned buildings, open spaces and commercial depletion, among others, can increase vulnerability. Mitchell Duneier, "Ethnography, the Ecosycal Fallacy, and the 1995 Chicago Heat Wave," *American Sociological Review*, no. 71 (2006): 679-88.

warrant (to say nothing of pragmatic warrant) for extended ethical de-liberation. After conceptualizing cities as both environmental and global sites, the chapter explores several issues at the intersection of urbanism and the global environment.

CITIES AND THE WORLD

The word *city* is marked by significant ambiguity and elasticity. Such confusion often stems from an inclination to assign the urban phenom-enon to one of two categories: natural or cultural, local or global.[9] This section first briefly describes the city and then briefly establishes its environmental and global credentials.

Describing the city. Cities have marked discursive and cultural land-scapes since Cain named the proto-historical city after his son, Enoch.[10] Since then, we have not lacked fascination with, description of, nor definition of the city. While some have defined the city in strictly spa-tial or territorial terms, Jane Jacobs and other urbanist luminaries em-phasize its social dimensions. At the beginning of his National Book

---

[9]For excellent and concise book-length discussions of these ambiguities, see Phil Hubbard, *City*, Key Ideas in Geography (New York: Routledge, 2006); Noel Castree, *Nature*, Key Ideas in Geography (New York: Routledge, 2005); Georgina Endfield, *Environment*, Key Ideas in Geography (New York: Routledge, 2006). Much of the confusion surrounding our concep-tions of city and environment emerge from dualisms written deeply into what Bruno Latour would call the "modern constitution," which, he would suggest, consists of separating subject from object, nature from culture, and all of the above from a transcendent God. Bruno Latour, *We Have Never Been Modern*, trans. Catherine Porter (Cambridge, Mass.: Harvard University Press, 1993). The city is a "thing" (Latour emphasizes the suitability of this inelegant word to describe what he calls collectives, hybrids, networks and nature-cultures) that defies modern dualisms. In fact, the city can be understood as a product of our false dualisms; acting as though our misunderstood dichotomies represent ontological reality has produced a prolifera-tion of hybrid subject-objects, including the urban landscape. Our ontological and epistemo-logical reductionism has created a superficial legibility by which we know just enough to get ourselves in trouble. For further study, please see Bruno Latour, *Politics of Nature: How to Bring the Sciences into Democracy*, trans. Catherine Porter (Boston: Harvard University Press, 2004); Clarence J. Glacken, *Traces on the Rhodian Shore: Nature and Culture in Western Thought from Ancient Times to the End of the Eighteenth Century* (Berkeley: University of California Press, 1967). With specific regard for cities and nature, see, again, Cronon, *Nature's Metropolis*.

[10]Gen 4:17. Important discussions of this point include Jacques Ellul's take on the matter in *The Meaning of the City* and Manuel Ortiz and Harvie Conn's in *Urban Ministry*. A discussion of a biblical theology of the city, by M. Daniel Carroll R. follows in chapter 3 of this volume. Jacques Ellul, *The Meaning of the City* (Grand Rapids: Eerdmans, 1993); Harvie M. Conn and Manuel Ortiz, *Urban Ministry: The Kingdom, the City and the People of God* (Downers Grove, Ill.: InterVarsity Press, 2001).

Award–winning volume, *The City in History*, Lewis Mumford—urbanist, critic of technology, editor, public intellectual and recipient of the Presidential Medal of Freedom—writes, "No single definition will apply to all its manifestations and no single description will cover all its transformations, from the embryonic social nucleus to the complex forms of its maturity and the corporeal disintegration of its old age."[11] Despite his own reservations about our incapacity to define the city while doing justice to all of its forms, in an earlier contribution to *Architectural Record*, Mumford described the city as

> a related collection of primary groups and purposive associations. . . . These varied groups support themselves through economic organizations that are likewise of a more or less corporate, or at least publicly regulated, character; and they are all housed in permanent structures, within a relatively limited area. The essential physical means of a city's existence are the fixed site, the durable shelter, the permanent facilities for assembly, interchange, and storage; the essential social means are the social division of labor, which serves not merely the economic life, but the cultural processes. The city in its complete sense, then, is a geographic plexus, an economic organization, an institutional process, a theater of social action, and an aesthetic symbol of collective unity. . . . It is in the city, the city as theater, that man's more purposive activities are focused, and work out, through conflicting and cooperating personalities, events, groups, into more significant culminations.[12]

In short, the city is a social form greater than the sum of its material and immaterial parts.[13]

---

[11]Lewis Mumford, *The City in History: Its Origins, Its Transformations, and Its Prospects* (New York: Harcourt Brace Jovanovich, 1961), p. 3.

[12]Idem, "What Is a City," *Architectural Record* 82 (1937): 58-62.

[13]Recent definitions of the city by prominent urbanists have taken a more political turn. In the 1970s, Manuel Castells and David Harvey reinvigorated questions regarding the character of the city, each of them concerned with what generates the contemporary city and what the contemporary city generates. While Mumford framed an investigation into the essence of the city, Harvey and Castells were (and remain) more interested in the causes and consequences of a historically contingent urbanism. Manuel Castells, *The Rise of the Network Society*, The Information Age: Economy, Society, and Culture (Cambridge, Mass.: Blackwell, 1996); David Harvey, *Social Justice and the City* (New York: Blackwell, 1973); see also idem, *Justice, Nature, and the Geography of Difference*, ed. Anonymous (Oxford: Blackwell, 1996), and *Spaces of Hope* (Berkeley: University of California Press, 2000).

And the city's parts are greater today than at any other point in human history. The world's 3.2 billion city-dwellers represent more than half of humanity, exceed the urban population of 1950 by more than four times, and exceed the urban population of 1900 by more than fifteen times.[14] The world's 3.2 billion city-dwellers exceed the population of the European Union by 2.8 billion, and the population of Scandinavia by more than 3.1 billion. These staggering population statistics are matched by astounding rates of urbanization. Fueled by migration to existing cities and the construction of new cities seemingly from whole cloth, the urban population is growing faster than any other population segment. But population and urbanization alone cannot account for the city's important place among global environmental concerns. The city, conventionally regarded as un-natural and local, defies facile dichotomies.

The nature of the city. "Urban metabolism" transcends the nature-culture dichotomy. As Erik Swyngedouw notes, "Circulatory conduits of water, foodstuffs, cars, fumes, money, labour, etc., move in and out of the city, transform the city, and produce the urban as a continuously changing socio-ecological landscape."[15] These circulatory flows reveal "the social appropriation and transformation of nature, [which] produce historically specific social and physical natures," including the cities we know.[16] As Karl Marx suggested, the interruption of this metabolism for even a year would cause "an enormous change in the natural world. . . . Soon the whole world of men and his own perceptive faculty, nay his own existence, were missing."[17] Some speculate that great ancient cities collapsed because of malfunctioning urban metabolisms. Their populations could not sustain the metabolism necessary to prevent "un-socialized" nature from overrunning the city. Contemporary decline or reversal of this metabolism has provided the context of

[14]United Nations Department of Economic and Social Affairs Population Division, *World Urbanization Prospects: The 2007 Revision* (New York: United Nations, 2008).
[15]Erik Swyngedouw, "Metabolic Urbanization: The Making of Cyborg Cities," in *In the Nature of Cities*, p. 21.
[16]Nik Heynen, Maria Kaika and Erik Swyngedouw, "Urban Political Ecology: Politicizing the Production of Urban Natures," in *In the Nature of Cities*, p. 7.
[17]Cited in Neil Smith, "Foreword," in *In the Nature of Cities*, p. xiii.

recent films and has been the subject of recent television dramatizations.[18] 2007's *I Am Legend*[19] was set in a largely depopulated Manhattan, the metabolism of which had been shut down or at least considerably slowed by depopulation due to an out-of control virus-based vaccine. And in January 2008, the History Channel premiered *Life After People*, inspired by the circumstances of Pripyat, Ukraine, abandoned since the 1986 Chernobyl nuclear plant disaster. Without constant attendance to the urban metabolism, the city succumbs to the influences of time and non-human nature.

Superficially, this may seem to indicate the city's status as human triumph over nature, as human achievement par excellence. According to Cronon, this perspective was among the two most common ways of conceiving the relationship between the city and the environment during the early industrial period. While some considered Chicago, then the fastest growing and second largest city in the United States, the evident triumph of humanity over nature, others conceived the city as *Nature's Metropolis*, the settlement that could not but have emerged from the physical geography of its location, privileged as it was by access to the Great Lakes and the Mississippi River.[20] Both conceptions were consistent with our modern dualisms. Neither was sustainable in the face of reality. The thoroughgoing penetration of the seemingly natural into the seemingly social, and vice versa, demonstrates the city's transcendence of the nature-culture dichotomy.

The city as a global site. Understanding the city as a *global* environmental concern requires rethinking notions of scale. Just as urban issues have long been mistakenly regarded as strictly social, the city has long been mistakenly regarded as strictly provincial. In fact, throughout history, cities have exercised a great deal of extra-territorial influence. What we know as the city, or the *polis*, was the primary locus of ancient

---

[18]Marianne Torgovnick has suggested that such representations are consistent with a broader fascination with urban destruction. Marianna Torgovnick, "The Lure of Urban Destruction," *The Chronicle of Higher Education* 54, no. 35 (2008), <http://chronicle.com/weekly/v54/i35/35b01801.htm>.

[19]*I Am Legend* is based on the 1954 Richard Matheson novel of the same title, which was earlier adapted as *The Last Man on Earth* (1964) and *Omega Man* (1971). Richard Matheson, *I Am Legend* (New York: Fawcett Gold Medal, 1954).

[20]Cronon, *Nature's Metropolis*.

political reflection, providing an important context for the work of
Thucydides, Socrates, Plato and Aristotle, among others. City-states,
such as Sparta and Athens, were sites of both local political practice
and projection of extra-territorial influence. The primacy of the city
lasted roughly until the Enlightenment, and some cities formally abet-
ted the establishment of principles—including territorial sovereignty—
upon which the "national assemblage" was founded.[21] Several cities
were signatories to the Peace of Westphalia in 1648, formalizing mu-
nicipally centralized authority over Western Europe's regional hinterlands and moving away from a system of overlapping spheres of influence centered in urban settlements.[22] The post-Westphalian political
landscape witnessed both an increase in urbanization *and* the eclipse of
the city-state by the nation-state. At the same time, the national assemblage ironically prepared the way for the contemporary resurgence
of urban importance. Nation states proliferated novel capabilities, dif-
fusing these across disparate non-state actors at various scales, setting
the stage for sub-national sites to emerge as globally significant players
in a profoundly territorial world economy. [23]

Long understood as places for the instantiation of global politics or
loci of strictly centripetal forces, sub-national sites and actors, including cities, are now "redeploying the physics of globalization," establishing significant centrifugal relationships with the world.[24] This is
reflected, in part, by the increasing practice of municipal foreign policy in areas such as nuclear disarmament, fair trade and immigration.[25]
Apart from formal jurisdictional mechanisms, cities also diffuse best
practices, governance capacity, policies, and norms both horizontally

---

[21]"National assemblage," referring to the development of organizing by nations as opposed to
city-states, is a term coined by Saskia Sassen, in *Territory, Authority, Rights: From Medieval to
Global Assemblages* (Princeton, N.J.: Princeton University Press, 2006).

[22]Ibid.

[23]Ibid.

[24]Arjun Appadurai, "Deep Democracy," *Public Culture* 14, no. 1 (2002): 3.

[25]See, for example, David C. Earnest, "From Alien to Elector: Citizenship and Belonging in
the City," *Globalizations* 4, no. 2 (2007): 137-55; W. E. Hewitt, "Municipalities and the New
Internationalism: Cautionary Notes from Canada," *Cities* 16, no. 6 (1999): 435-44; Heidi H.
Hobbs, *City Hall Goes Abroad: The Foreign Policy of Local Politics* (New York: Sage Publications,
1994); John M. Kline, "Continuing Controversies over State and Local Foreign Policy Sanc-
tions in the United States," *Journal of Federalism* 29, no. 2 (1999): 111-34.

and vertically, that is, within networks of cities and with actors on other scales.[26]

As an expression of (re)emergent extra-territorial capabilities and a centrifugal organizing logic,[27] we now witness what Julie-Anne Boudreau describes as the urbanization of global politics.[28] Boudreau writes of "the centrality of urban politics in a global era," citing four forces that have "urbanized" the global political process: (1) decentralization and increased intergovernmental relations; (2) conventionally municipal policy interests moving to the national and global scales and conventionally national and global policy interests moving to the local scale; (3) the re-scaling of civil society activities; and (4) the continued territorialization of the policy-making process.[29] Cities are important subnational sites in the shifting architecture of globalization.

Two decades of scholarship on global, or world, cities have found that cities are "strategic to economic globalization because they are command points, global marketplaces and production sites for the information economy."[30] Cities concentrate globally networked institutions with significant influence upon a wide range of global possibilities. For example, more than 90 percent of all foreign exchange transactions occur in fewer than ten cities. Just four cities—New York, London, Hong Kong and Tokyo—account for more than 75 percent of such transactions. Even in rural areas and in remaining margins of the cash economy, purchasing power is largely mediated by urban transactions. Everyone lives under the sway of cities; global networks of urban nodes construct and constrain, potentiate and limit, both global and local possibilities.

Cities exist in mutually but highly differentially influential relationships with the non-urban world. While the world spins things into the urban landscape, the city spins things into the global landscape. Cities

---

[26]Noah J. Toly, "Transnational Municipal Networks and Climate Change: From Global Governance to Global Politics," *Globalizations* 5, no. 3 (2008): 341-56.

[27]Sassen, *Territory, Authority, Rights.*

[28]Julie-Anne Boudreau, "The Centrality of Urban Politics in a Global Era: A Paper Presented at the 2007 Annual Meeting of the American Political Science Association" (2007).

[29]Ibid.

[30]Saskia Sassen, *Cities in a World Economy,* Sociology for a New Century Series (Thousand Oaks, Calif.: Pine Forge Press, 2006), p. 7.

transcend the global/local dichotomy. Cities make the world.

Urban metabolisms, coupled with the re-emergence of significant extra-territorial capabilities, endow cities with astonishing potential to shape the global environment for good or ill. At the same time, cities are vulnerable to the environmental impact of global dynamics and processes.

LOCAL IMPACTS OF GLOBAL DYNAMICS

In situ, or territorial, urbanism—that urbanism we typically consider part of the city, proper—represents one aspect of urban environmental concern. Patterns of global production, distribution, and consumption shape urban distributions of environmental goods and ills, especially risks, in cities. With regard to global cities, Roger Keil describes this relationship as the "environmental problematic," referring to a "specific urban ecology which emerges from a world city's relationship to the global economy and to other world cities."[31] Not limited to world cities, this relationship is typical of contemporary urbanism. Most conventionally urban environmental issues can be construed as part of this environmental problematic. Brownfields and air pollution are among the challenges best understood in this fashion, highlighting the need to consider the local urban impacts of various global processes.[32]

Brownfields. The Environmental Protection Agency (EPA) defines brownfields as "real property, the expansion, redevelopment, or reuse of which may be complicated by the presence or potential presence of a hazardous substance, pollutant, or contaminant."[33] Primary brownfield contaminants include lead, PCBs, nickel, chromium, copper compounds, iron compounds, phthalates, TDI, naphthalene, benzene, cad-

---

[31]Roger Keil, "The Environmental Problematic in World Cities," in *World Cities in a World System*, ed. Paul L. Knox and Peter J. Taylor (Cambridge: Cambridge University Press, 1995), p. 280.

[32]Appropriation and distribution of environmental services through electricity and water utilities could also be included in this section. Privatization and deregulation of utilities, especially in poorer countries and often according to the requirements of structural adjustment programs, has sometimes led to more efficient service provision, but has often led to extremely inequitable appropriation and distribution of environmental services according to willingness and ability to pay.

[33]Environmental Protection Agency, "Brownfields Definition," Environmental Protection Agency, <www.epa.gov/brownfields/overview/glossary.htm>.

mium, ethylene oxide, pentachlorophenol, acryllonitrile, beryllium, creosote and arsenic.[34] Most brownfield sites are abandoned, idled, or underused industrial and commercial facilities, the historic uses of which include, but are not limited to, the following: shipyards, tanneries, railroad operations, chemical plants, petroleum refining and storage, landfills, power plants and contaminated fill of wetlands. Many studies find dramatically increased morbidity and mortality rates in neighborhoods with high concentrations of brownfield sites, even while controlling for other risk factors. In a study of Southeast Baltimore, Jill Litt, Nga L. Tran and Thomas A. Burke find statistically significant increases in cancer mortality rates, incidence of lung cancer, respiratory diseases and other major causes of death.[35]

While brownfields are not limited to the urban landscape, they are primarily an urban environmental issue and threaten poor and otherwise vulnerable populations most directly. As the National Environmental Justice Advisory Council writes,

> [Brownfields] dot the urban landscape [and] are overwhelmingly concentrated among people of color and low-income, indigenous peoples, and otherwise marginalized communities. By their very nature, brownfields are inseparable from issues of social inequity, racial discrimination and urban decay.[36]

Brownfields are largely the result of the partial deindustrialization of specific localities and the restructuring of the global economy.[37] Given the emergence of a global service economy, and facilitated by trade liberalization, many industries have fled cities of the Global

---

[34]Jill S. Litt, Nga L. Tran and Thomas A. Burke, "Examining Urban Brownfields through the Public Health 'Macroscope'" in *Urban Health: Readings in the Social, Built, and Physical Environments of U.S. Cities*, ed. H. Patricia Hynes and Russ Lopez (Sudbury, Mass.: Jones and Bartlett, 2009), pp. 217-36.

[35]Litt, Tran and Burke, "Examining Urban Brownfields."

[36]National Environmental Justice Advisory Council, "Environmental Justice, Urban Revitalization, and Brownfields: The Search for Authentic Signs of Hope (a Report on The 'Public Dialogues on Urban Revitalization and Brownfields: Envisioning Healthy and Sustainable Communities')" (Washington, D.C.: National Environmental Justice Advisory Council, 1996), p. 18.

[37]Lisa Benton-Short and John Rennie Short, *Cities and Nature* (New York: Routledge, 2008), pp. 65-96.

North, where high wages, labor standards and environmental regulations make for expensive business. Some of these have left behind abandoned or underutilized, polluted sites in marginalized neighborhoods.
Indeed, brownfields disproportionately affect poor, working class and
minority communities.[38]

At worst, these sites are extremely hazardous. At best, these sites are
problematic—and expensive—for redevelopment. Brownfield site remediation and redevelopment is important to a range of community
development concerns, including education, employment and housing.
It is difficult to be in school consistently when ill. It is difficult to retain
a job when ill. And it is difficult to build affordable housing on sites
that require expensive remediation. But as Litt, Tran and Burke write,
even redevelopment can be problematic:

> At first glance, the prospects of cleanup and concomitant redevelop-
> ment may be tantalizing given the promised economic benefits. At sec-
> ond glance, however, expedited cleanup and redevelopment may come
> at the community's expense—environmental, social, economic, and
> public health harm—given the environmental unknowns of brownfields
> and the sensitive populations living in affected areas.[39]

The effects of global political economic upheaval persist even into remediation and redevelopment of contaminated sites.

Air pollution. Air pollution is among the most significant of urban
hazards. Ozone (O_3), sulfur oxides (SO_x), nitrogen oxides (NO_x) and
particulate matter, among other pollutants, have ill effects upon non-
human populations and upon human health in urban areas.[40] Such pollution is "linked with a broad range of health effects, including mortality and morbidity from heart and lung disease, impaired lung function
and lung cancer," as well as birth defects.[41] But it is not as if air pollu-

---

[38]Litt, Tran and Burke, "Examining Urban Brownfields."

[39]Ibid., p. 218.

[40]R. T. Forman, D. Sperling and J. A. Bissonette, *Road Ecology: Science and Solutions* (Washington, D.C.: Island Press, 2003).

[41]Marie S. O'Neill, Micheal Jerrett, Ichiro Kawachi, Jonathan I. Levy, Aaron J. Cohen, Nelson
Gouveia, Paul Wilkinson, Tony Fletcher, Luis Cifuentes and Joel Schwartz, "Health, Wealth,
and Air Pollution: Advancing Theory and Methods," in *Urban Health: Readings in the Social,
Built, and Physical Environments of U.S. Cities*, ed. H. Patricia Hynes and Russ Lopez (Sudbury, Mass.: Jones and Bartlett, 2009), p. 191.

tion is an equal opportunity hazard. Some places in the urban environment are more polluted than others. Some populations suffer more intense air pollution problems than others. This overexposure, coupled with higher levels of susceptibility, leads to more pernicious air pollution effects for urban populations of lower socioeconomic status.[42]

The preponderance of air pollutants in urban places can be construed as the result of the city's function in the world economy. People and goods flow through urban areas on transportation infrastructure meant to support global economic growth. As everything has been made faster and more efficient for the sake of global economic growth, cities have served as nodes in transportation networks meant to advance this purpose and, at the same time, have grown more polluted. Planes, trains and automobiles congest these urban networks and pollute the air. Airports are often sited near marginalized and vulnerable populations without the resources or relationships to effectively oppose the siting. Large trucks are often routed through the poorest and most vulnerable communities. The dromological[43] imperatives of global political economy—including the acceleration of wealth accumulation—have differential implications in the urban landscape.

Not all urban air pollution is related to transportation. Much is related to energy use in industrial and commercial sectors. Perhaps no example is more striking than that of China's urban air pollution. The astounding urbanization of China, as well as its environmental crisis, can be linked to the country's increasing function as a major manufacturing exporter in the world economy since the end of the Cultural Revolution and the beginnings of economic reform in the late 1970s.[44] The past sixteen years, especially, have seen dramatic increases in the

---

[42]Ibid.

[43]Paul Virilio has pioneered dromology, including the study of multiple intersecting and accelerating velocities of globalization. See Paul Virilio, *The Art of the Motor* (Minneapolis: University of Minnesota Press, 1995); idem, *Open Sky* (New York: Verso, 1997), and *The Information Bomb* (New York: Verso, 2000).

[44]Elizabeth Economy, *The River Runs Black: The Environmental Challenge to China's Future* (Ithaca, N.Y.: Cornell University Press, 2004), p. 72. For more on the origins and implications of China's rapid and continuing urbanization, see Thomas J. Campanella, *The Concrete Dragon: China's Urban Revolution and What It Means for the World* (New York: Princeton Architectural Press, 2008) and John Friedmann, *China's Urban Transition* (Minneapolis: University of Minnesota Press, 2005).

country's urban population. Since 1992, 46 Chinese cities have passed the one million-inhabitant threshold, and the country now has 102 such metropolises.[45] As was famously publicized in anticipation of the 2008 Summer Olympic Games in Beijing, Chinese cities suffer from extreme air pollution. Of the twenty cities in the world with the most severe air pollution problems, sixteen are in China.[46] While a great deal of this pollution can be attributed to China's continued dependence upon coal and other relatively dirty fuels, much can be attributed to the sometimes perverse efficiencies of the world economy. As Elizabeth Economy writes,

> China's integration into the world economy has been a dual-edged sword with regard to the country's air quality. . . . While many multinationals have significantly elevated the level of environmental technology employed in Chinese enterprises, others, with the complicity of local officials, have taken advantage of China's weaker laws and enforcement capacity to relocate their most polluting enterprises.[47]

Economy notes the relocation of Taiwanese and South Korean businesses to urban China in order to avoid the costs of domestic environmental regulations.[48] Like brownfields in Baltimore, urban air pollution in China is largely the result of a restructured and partially deindustrialized global economy in which polluting industries relocate in order to lower costs. While much of this relocation is international, some is domestic. For example, Hong Kong businesses have been known to relocate polluting industries to urban centers in Guangdong province in order to avoid the island city's ban on the industrial use of sulfur-heavy fuels. But, as Economy writes, "Hong Kong itself has begun to pay the price for shipping these factories across the Pearl River," suffering some ill effects of the externalized pollution and anticipating the even farther-reaching effects of urban metabolisms that are the subject of the next section.[49]

---

[45]Campanella, *The Concrete Dragon*, p. 14.
[46]Economy, *The River Runs Black: The Environmental Challenge to China's Future*, p. 72.
[47]Ibid., p. 73.
[48]Ibid.
[49]Ibid.

GLOBAL IMPACTS OF LOCAL DYNAMICS

Just as global dynamics affect environmental quality in the city, urban dynamics shape the global environment. Both incidental and purposeful displacement of the costs of urban metabolism onto hinterland environments and populations shape a global *ex situ* urbanism. As Timothy Luke states,

> Today's "global cities," then, are entirely new built environments tied to several complex layers of technological systems whose logistical grids are knit into other networks for the production, consumption, circulation and accumulation of commodities. . . . As a planetary system of material production and consumption, these built environments constitute much of the worldwide webs of logistical flows which swamp over the conventional boundaries between the human and the natural with a new biopolitics of urbanism.[50]

In an expression of mutual influence, the generative capacities of cities extend to the global environment while the global environment constrains urban possibilities. On one hand, cities are globalizing resource depletion and risk. On the other hand, cities are globalizing technical and normative responses to global environmental challenges.[51]

Resource depletion. In many ways, cities have a parasitic relationship with their hinterlands, extracting resources. One contemporary indicator of such relationships is the increasing (and increasingly urban) ecological footprint.[52] Such a measurement recognizes that the hinterland is now global, with global urban consumption driving global hinterland resource extraction to unsustainable paces.[53] Cities of the Global North

---

[50]Timothy Luke, "'Global Cities' vs. 'Global Cities': Rethinking Contemporary Urbanism as Public Ecology," *Studies in Political Economy* 70 (2003): 13.

[51]An extended and differently contextualized description of these three issues appears in Toly, "Transnational Municipal Networks and Climate Change."

[52]Matthias Wackernagel and William E. Rees, *Our Ecological Footprint: Reducing Human Impact on the Earth* (Gabriola Island, B.C.: New Society Publishers, 1996).

[53]This is not to suggest that urban consumption was not previously global in character. Many regard colonialism as among the earliest forms of globalization, and it is certain that expanding urban populations and changing urban consumption drove European ships to continental hinterlands in search of goods and raw materials. Many scholars have noted the continuity of this relationship with the present. As Joan Martinez Alier writes, "In this sense, Europe has never been so colonial as today. Gasoline stations on German motorways should have signs reading '*Kolonialwaren*.'" Joan Martinez-Alier, "Energy, Economy, and Poverty: The Past and

have an average footprint of almost four times an equitable level. While footprint and other such measures emphasize the spatial dimension of the relationship between urban human settlement and global resource extraction, some have explored the temporal dimensions of the hinterlands. Cities consuming resources at unsustainable rates essentially foreclose on future options.[54]

Thus, cities are globalizing resource depletion, rather than simply resource extraction. Contemporary urbanism is depleting water resources, biodiversity and energy resources. The urbanization of hinterland water supplies creates problems of both sustainability and equity. The southwestern United States and, increasingly, the southeastern United States, are examples of this phenomenon, an ecological imperialism that shapes far-off landscapes by internalizing the benefits of distant resources. From Las Vegas to Los Angeles, industrial and post-industrial lifestyles can only be maintained by the unsustainable appropriation of energy and water resources from the region's rivers. And urbanization daily encroaches upon biodiverse landscapes, especially in Africa, Asia and Latin America. High levels of energy consumption and low levels of technology ensure masses of peri-urban foragers collecting biomass for charcoal stoves. But such marginal uses are hardly among the most environmentally deleterious urban energy consumption. Industrial and post-industrial urban metabolisms require significant amounts of energy delivered in the form of electricity—produced by the combustion of fossil fuels, through nuclear technology or by alternative or renewable sources—heat, and fuel for transportation. Sustaining contemporary urban agglomerations requires not only the depletion of non-renewable energy sources, but also the appropriation of such sources from distant and vulnerable landscapes and communities. As Luke writes, "'global cities' leave very destructive environ-

---

Present Debate," in *Transforming Power: Energy, Environment, and Society in Conflict*, ed. John Byrne, Noah J. Toly and Leigh Glover (New Brunswick, N.J.: Transaction Publishers, 2006).

[54]Leigh Glover, Research Fellow at the Australasian Centre for the Governance and Management of Urban Transport, has been especially helpful to me in understanding this, noting unsustainable urban consumption of the past (citing Jeffrey S. Dukes, "Burning Buried Sunshine: Human Consumption of Ancient Solar Energy," *Climatic Change*, no. 61 [2003]) as well as the future.

mental footprints as their inhabitants reach out into markets around the world for material inputs to survive, but the transactions of this new political ecology also are the root causes of global ecological decline."[55]

Pollution and risk. Cities are not only globalizing resource depletion, but are also globalizing pollution and risk, exercising forms of spatial and temporal externalization.[56] This globalization of risk most clearly highlights the extra-urban "spatial fix" associated with urban development.[57] For example, urban areas account for the vast majority of electricity consumption, including that from nuclear power. But, generally, neither the risky mining operations, nor the risky generation facilities, nor the risky waste is located in urban areas. Apart from prospects for extended power outage, which are exacerbated by the presence of nuclear facilities, and the prospects of terrorist attacks, using nuclear fuel to construct a nuclear weapon or weaponizing nuclear waste to construct a "dirty bomb," cities externalize the radioactive risks of their energy habits. Nevertheless, potential "blowback" frustrates the presumptive safety of "Not in My Backyard" (NIMBY) approaches to pollution and risk.

But the return of some risk is more than prospective. For example, those manufacturing activities relocated from Hong Kong to the Guangdong province now have an impact on water quality on and produce "toxic cloudbanks" that drift over Hong Kong itself from October to April.[58] Economy notes one Chinese engineer's insight into the relationship between Hong Kong and the mainland: "Hong Kong companies use us to make money, but in the end what they do goes back to haunt them."[59] Hong Kong companies have increased profits by operating polluting industries on the mainland and externalizing environmental degradation and its risks, rather than absorbing these costs through compliance with stricter laws in the city. It so happens, now,

---

[55]Luke, "'Global Cities' vs. 'Global Cities,'" p. 30.

[56]Of course, this argument falls short if extraction itself has a net negative impact upon distant ecologies and communities.

[57]Harvey, *Justice, Nature, and the Geography of Difference;* idem, *Spaces of Hope,* and "The Spatial Fix: Hegel, Von Thunen, and Marx," in *Spaces of Capital: Towards a Critical Geography* (New York: Routledge, 2001).

[58]Economy, *The River Runs Black,* p. 73.

[59]Ibid.

that these risks are coming home to roost.

The relationship between Hong Kong and its mainland hinterland is microcosmic for the relationship of cities to the global environment. Especially with the prospective hazards and consequences of anthropogenic climate change, the immediate causes of which—greenhouse gas emissions and land use change—are attributable to a great extent to urban consumption, cities globalize risk. Cities account for roughly 80 percent of anthropogenic greenhouse gas (GHG) emissions even as urban expansion and urban demands for raw materials exert significant influence on land use in peri-urban and wild areas of the global hinterland.

Climate change is the most significant global environmental threat of our time.[60] Its ecological impact is substantial; many suggest that it is the primary cause of extinctions. And its affects on human beings are overwhelming. Extreme weather, sea level rise, changes in food production, the spread of disease, and destabilized social, political and economic conditions threaten catastrophe for millions. A 2005 study by the Harvard Center for Health and the Global Environment suggested that as many as 160,000 people per year were already dying of the effects of climate change.[61] For a number of reasons, urban populations are particularly vulnerable to many of the projected ill effects of climate change. Cities are, in effect, fouling their own nests.

Best practices and norms for global environmental governance. Recognizing significant responsibility and vulnerability, many cities have undertaken strategies for climate stabilization. Some are engaged in GHG emissions abatement measures, others in measures for GHG sequestration and climate change adaptation—some related to land use, land use change and forestry—and still others in measures designed to reap the "triple benefits" of emissions abatement, biodiversity conservation and community development. Many cities exercise significant control over the environment through planning, zoning and other land use policies. For example, municipalities often have the latitude to ef-

---

[60]For a concise treatment of climate change, see chapter 8.
[61]A. J. McMichael, D. H. Campbell-Lendrum, C. F. Corvalan, K. L. Ebi, A. Githelo, J. D. Scheraga and A. Woodward, eds., *Climate Change and Human Health: Risks and Responses* (Geneva: World Health Organization, 2003), p. 276.

fect policy measures for efficiency and conservation in building and transportation. Such a variety of policy instruments also lends cities the flexibility to introduce co-benefits in ways that are more difficult at larger scales.

Municipal capacities are augmented by the formation of inter-municipal networks. Transcending municipal, and often regional and national, boundaries, a number of initiatives have emerged to take advantage of urban connectivity, stimulating inter-municipal dialogue while leveraging global influence. These include the United States Conference of Mayors' Climate Protection Agreement, the International Council for Local Environmental Initiative's Cities for Climate Protection (CCP) program, and the International Solar Cities Initiative (ISCI). The emissions of cities involved in such programs are considerable. Almost seven hundred municipal governments from over thirty countries participate in CCP, accounting for more than 15 percent of global anthropogenic greenhouse gas emissions. These cities commit to a program of five milestones—emissions inventory and forecasting, emissions reduction targeting, development of a local action plan, implementation of policies and measures, and monitoring and verification of outcomes. The direct effects of CCP and programs like it may be important to achieving a climate-stable future.

Perhaps as important as emissions reductions and other direct effects upon the global environment are the indirect effects constituted by contributions to global environmental politics. ISCI cities are fewer—less than two dozen—and represent a much smaller portion of anthropogenic greenhouse gas emissions. ISCI favors commitments to a per capita approach to emissions targets, recognizing the vast disparities between the responsibilities of cities in the Global South, where per capita emissions are often at sustainable levels, and cities in the Global North, where per capita emissions may be orders of magnitude higher than sustainable levels. Such approaches, also advocated by organizations such as the Alliance of Small Island States, are marginalized by international climate governance regimes, which are generally driven by concerns for economically efficient governance mechanisms. Cities, on the other hand, are places of bundled concerns, where the economic, the environmental, the social, the cultural and the political cannot be easily dissected.[62] Cities and other sub-national actors, especially those party to transnationally networked initiatives such as ISCI, participate in multiscalar and partly denationalized governance of global environmental issues, possibly proliferating norms oriented toward an equitable, as well as sustainable, climate stabilization regime. Cities may be globalizing resource depletion, pollution and risk, but they are also globalizing best practices and norms for global environmental governance. Urban responsibility for and vulnerability to anthropogenic climate change may undermine prospects for a future world city hierarchy practicing NIMBY environmental politics of externalization, in favor of global network of urban nodes introducing progressive norms.[63]

CONCLUSION: QUESTIONS OF STEWARDSHIP AND JUSTICE

In his epilogue to *Nature's Metropolis*, Cronon notes the ways in which rightly understanding the relationship between cities and the environment highlights moral responsibilities:

> The urban and rural landscapes I have been describing are not two places, but one. They created each other, they transformed each others' environments and economies, and they now depend on each other for their very survival. To see them separately is to misunderstand where they came from and where they might go in the future. Worse, to ignore the nearly infinite ways they affect one another is to miss our moral responsibility for the ways they shape each other's landscapes and alter the lives of people and organisms within their bounds.[64]

Where creation care is concerned with the global environment, it must be concerned with the city. From Mumbai to Moscow, Nairobi to New York, La Paz to Los Angeles, cities affect the global environment.

---

[62]This is not to say that these concerns are never perversely dissected by cities. But they are more transparently intertwined at the local level.

[63]For an argument that cities are, indeed, part of an emerging architecture that challenges the unsustainability of global political economy, but one that practices NIMBY politics, see Peter J. Taylor, "World Cities and Territorial States: The Rise and Fall of Their Mutuality," in *World Cities in a World System*, ed. Paul Knox and Peter J. Taylor (Cambridge: Cambridge University Press, 1996).

[64]Cronon, *Nature's Metropolis*, pp. 384-85.

The environments of these same cities and their rapidly growing populations are affected by global political, economic and social dynamics.

For the first time in human history, more than 50 percent of the world's population lives in urban areas,[65] experiencing the tragedy and triumph of urban landscapes. Approximately 1.5 billion people, including more than 40 percent of the world's children, live in polluted urban areas.[66] The impact of global dynamics upon these urban populations must be among the concerns of global environmental ethics and the expression of these ethics in politics, policy and management. By 2050, more than 70 percent of the world population is projected to live in cities, with the entire net population growth of the world absorbed by cities. No less than 90 percent of the world population increase is project to be absorbed by cities of the Majority World.[67] That the most rapidly urbanizing regions of the world are also marked by desperate poverty despite creative and resilient adaptations by one billion urban and peri-urban slum dwellers, reveals the gravity of current urban insecurities.[68]

Whether we choose to locate ourselves in Antarctica or rural Africa, we live in an urban world. The profound effects of urban metabolisms upon the global environment make cities critical sites of global environmental governance. The future of the planet is at stake in the ways in which cities transform the hinterland. And the disparities in human dimensions—both origins and implications—of environmental change, make such a relationship a concern for those preoccupied with inequitable distribution of environmental goods and ills across space and according to gender, ethnicity, class and other characteristics. Both global sustainability and global environmental justice are at stake in our urban engagements. The fate of the earth is intimately related to the fate of our cities.

[65]United Nations Department of Economic and Social Affairs Population Division, *World Urbanization Prospects: The 2007 Revision* (New York: United Nations, 2008).

[66]World Health Organization, *Air Quality Guidelines for Europe* (Copenhagen: World Health Organization, 2000). Cited in O'Neill et al., "Health, Wealth, and Air Pollution," p. 1870.

[67]United Nations Department of Economic and Social Affairs Population Division, *World Urbanization Prospects: The 2007 Revision* (New York: United Nations, 2008).

[68]Mike Davis, *Planet of Slums* (New York: Verso, 2007), Robert Neuwirth, *Shadow Cities: A Billion Squatters, a New Urban World* (New York: Routledge, 2006).

This relationship between cities and the global environment is clearly one of great consequence, demanding the attention of our capacities for ethical reasoning. Many biblical-theological themes and motifs might inform this reasoning. We might wonder, though, whether Scripture speaks in a normative fashion regarding the relationship between human settlements and surrounding environs. In the following chapter, M. Daniel Carroll R. closely examines this theme.

3

A BIBLICAL THEOLOGY OF
THE CITY AND THE ENVIRONMENT

Human Community in the Created Order

M. Daniel Carroll R.

> *In very general terms it has to be said that one of the main foci of the Hebrew Bible is its focus on "cities" or, if you prefer, "the city." From city-builder Qain to Qoheleth (Eccl. 9.13-16) or from Gen. 4.17 to 2 Chron. 36.23—that is the aleph (alpha) and taw (omega) of the Hebrew Bible—the city is one of the great focalizations of the Bible.*

R. P. CARROLL,
"CITY OF CHAOS, CITY OF STONE, CITY OF FLESH:
URBANSCAPES IN PROPHETIC DISCOURSES"

THE WORDS IN THE EPIGRAPH ABOVE express the importance of the city in the Old Testament, and a similar judgment could be made in regards to the New Testament. The Bible begins and ends with a city. The first city appears in the opening chapters of Genesis (Gen 4:17), while a glorious, eternal city closes the canon (Rev 21–22).

THE CITY IN THE BIBLE: PRELIMINARY CONSIDERATIONS
How prominent is the city in the Bible, truly? One measure of its importance is the number of times terms for "city" appear. In biblical He-

brew the primary word is ʿir, which occurs almost 1100 times.[1] The New Testament's key term is *polis*, which is used 161 times.[2] The data suggest that the city occupies a weighty place. This statistical fact, however, begs several questions. One is a matter of definition: What is a city? The second is one of significance: What import does the city have in the divine scheme of human history? The answer to the first question continues to be debated in social science literature. The second question is the focus of this essay.

Defining the essence of the city is difficult. A complicating factor is that the shape and role of cities have changed over time and vary from place to place. Today an increasing number of metropolises—especially in the Majority World—dominate societies, and we tend to think of biblical cities in these terms. The percentage of urban dwellers continues to grow and is surpassing those who live in rural areas. This was not the case in the past. Generally speaking, cities existed within an agrarian world. They were smaller and had a different purpose than they do now.[3]

Biblical scholars use archaeology and social sciences to gain a clearer grasp of urban life in biblical times.[4] These inform our understanding, for instance, of population densities, the placement of communities vis-à-vis trade routes and strategic military potential, the impact of soil quality and rainfall, social organization, and the role of temples in eco-

---

[1]*HALOT* 821-22; *TDOT* 11:51-67; *NIDOTTE* 3:396-99. Another term is *qiryâ* (*HALOT* 1142-43). According to M. V. VanPelt and G. D. Pratico, only about a dozen other nouns appear more often in the Old Testament (*The Vocabulary Guide to Biblical Hebrew* [Grand Rapids: Zondervan, 2003], pp. 2-3).

[2]*BDAG* 691-92; *TDNT* 6:522-29; *NIDNTT* 2:801-5.

[3]C. E. Carter, *The Emergence of Yehud in the Persian Period: A Social and Demographic Study* JSOTSup 294 (Sheffield, U.K.: Sheffield Academic Press, 1999), pp. 172-213; J. D. Schloen, *The House and the Father as Fact and Symbol: Patrimonialism in Ugarit and the Ancient Near East*, Studies in the Archaeology and History of the Levant (Winona Lake, Ind.: Eisenbrauns, 2001), pp. 135-83; cf. M. P. O'Connor, "The Biblical Notion of the City," in *Constructions of Space II: The Biblical City and Other Imagined Spaces*, ed. Jon L. Berquist and Claudia V. Camp, LHB/OTS 490 (New York: T & T Clark, 2008), pp. 18-39.

[4]F. S. Frick, *The City in Ancient Israel*, SBLDS 36 (Missoula, Mont.: Scholars Press 1977), pp. 1-23; D. B. Mackay, "A View from the Outskirts: Realignments from Modern to Postmodern in the Archeological Study of Urbanism," in *Urbanism in Antiquity: From Mesopotamia to Crete*, ed. W. E. Aufrecht, N. A. Mirau and S. W. Gauley, JSOTSup 244 (Sheffield, U.K.: Sheffield Academic Press, 1997), pp. 278-85; L. L. Grabbe, "Sup-Urbs or Hyp-Urbs? Prophets and Populations in Ancient Israel and Socio-Historical Method," in *'Every City Shall Be Forsaken': Urbanism and Prophecy in Ancient Israel and the Near East*, ed. idem and R. D. Haak, JSOTSup 330 (Sheffield, U.K.: Sheffield Academic Press, 2001), pp. 97-112 [95-123].

nomic and political life. Studies of ancient town planning examine the nature of defense systems,[5] the relationships with adjoining farm lands, the layout of streets, housing styles and residential districts, the storage of water, diet, the treatment of garbage and sewage systems, the care of the dead, and the rise of industry.[6] The same sorts of concerns, and others appropriate to that later context, are topics of New Testament research into Greco-Roman cities and first century Palestine.[7]

This information is necessary for appreciating the urban scenes described in Scripture. Yet, how do we move from an examination of the mundane to *a theology of the city* that can guide *us* in the twenty-first century? Two initial comments are needful. On the one hand, it is important to avoid an exaggerated moral dichotomy between the urban and the rural. This approach has had a number of proponents in the past, and a few continue to lean toward this easy bifurcation. According to this perspective, the prophets condemned the human city *qua* city and championed the more nomadic existence of the earlier desert or agrarian phase of Israel's history before the establishment of the monarchy and the rise of urban centers.[8] On the New Testament side, some defend the portrayal of a peasant Jesus, who incarnated a simpler lifestyle and condemned those who controlled the socio-economic, political and religious world at that time.[9]

It also is necessary to admit that the Bible speaks to the contempo-

---

[5]In the ancient world a distinguishing difference between a town or city and a village often was the presence of protective walls (Deut 3:5; 1 Sam 6:18). Cities could have a group of nearby related villages that were called their "daughters" (for example, Num 21:25, 32; 32:42; Josh 15:45, 47).

[6]Frick, *City in Ancient Israel*, pp. 77-170; V. Fritz, *The City in Ancient Israel* (Sheffield, U.K.: Sheffield Academic Press. 1995); C. H. J. de Geus, *Towns in Ancient Israel and in the Southern Levant*, Palaestina Antiqua 10 (Leuven: Peeters, 2003).

[7]J. E. Stambaugh and D. L. Balch, *The New Testament in Its Social Environment*, Library of Early Christianity 2 (Louisville, Ky.: Westminster John Knox, 1986); J. S. Jeffers, *The Greco-Roman World of the New Testament Era: Exploring the Background of Early Christianity* (Downers Grove, Ill.: InterVarsity Press 1999); W. Meeks, *The First Urban Christians: The Social World of the Apostle Paul*, 2nd ed. (New Haven, Conn.: Yale University Press, 2003).

[8]J. Lindblom, *Prophecy in Ancient Israel* (Philadelphia: Fortress, 1962), pp. 343-46; more recently, J. Blenkinsopp, "Cityscape to Landscape: The 'Back to Nature' Theme in Isaiah 1-35," in *'Every City Shall Be Forsaken'*, pp. 35-44.

[9]For example, J. D. Crossan's *God and Empire: Jesus Against Rome, Then and Now* (San Francisco: Harper, 2007). This is not to suggest that Crossan would lend his theory to certain positions in ecological debates.

rary city only indirectly. Issues facing ancient cities were not of the same magnitude as those facing contemporary urban areas, and some modern problems simply did not present themselves. Equally, many challenges of ancient times no longer exist. Regarding cities and the environment, there is no sustained discourse within the text that provides a theology of the city and its relationship to the created order. One must be careful not to superimpose contemporary convictions about the environment onto the biblical material and then engage in proof-texting that does not reflect properly what is actually available in the Bible. The task that lies before us is to probe relevant dimensions of the biblical revelation and then craft a position that is faithful to the heart of that material.

As Chris Wright argues, while ancient Israelites did not appreciate environmental realities in the same manner or degree that we do today, the Old Testament can contribute to our answers to current ecological questions.

> Ancient Israel may not have been anxious or fearful about the plight of the physical planet in the way that we are, for the very good reason that we have made a far greater mess of it than the ancient world ever did. So to that extent many aspects of what we would now regard as urgent ecological ethical issues were not explicitly addressed within the Old Testament. Nevertheless, the theological principles and ethical implications that they *did* articulate regarding creation do have a far-reaching impact on how biblically sensitive Christians will want to frame their ecological ethics today.[10]

The following discussion is divided into three parts. The first section rehearses the Genesis account of the origins of the city. The second explores how this framework impacts the depiction and evaluation of urban realities in the rest of the Bible. The third looks at the hope for the city and the cosmic order in the Bible.

---

[10]Christopher J. H. Wright, *Old Testament Ethics for the People of God* (Downers Grove, Ill.: InterVarsity Press, 2004), p. 144. He is responding, in part, to C. S. Rodd, *Glimpses of a Strange Land: Studies in Old Testament Ethics*, Old Testament Studies (Edinburgh: T & T Clark, 2001), pp. 207-49; cf. E. F. Davis, *Scripture, Culture, and Agriculture: An Agrarian Reading of the Bible* (New York: Cambridge University Press, 2009).

THE FIRST CITY AND ITS SIGNIFICANCE

Genesis 4 describes the beginning of the spread of sin outside of paradise. Cain kills Abel and is condemned by God (Gen 4:3-16), and the words of this divine curse resonate with those of chapter 3: difficulties in tilling the soil (Gen 3:17-19; 4:12) and the destiny to wander east of Eden (Gen 3:22-24; 4:16). Yet, even as he had been gracious to cover the shame of Cain's parents (Gen 3:21), God gives Cain a mark to guard him from others (Gen 4:15). There is, then, continuity between the accounts of Adam and Eve and Cain. He, too, is representative of humanity.

What is most pertinent is the statement in Genesis 4:17 concerning the building of the first city. Scholars debate the meaning of this verse. Was Cain the founder, and was this project another example of rebellion against Yahweh? Does it signify his refusal to keep moving and to provide his own protection apart from God? If so, then the city has as its father the first murderer. If the city is by definition a defensive response to external threats, its founding represents insecurity and lack of faith.[11]

Even if the verse is understood as saying that Enoch was the builder,[12] there is a connection to Cain through this descendent. The chain of hostility escalates with Lamech, whose boast of vengeance is juxtaposed to the achievements of his children (Gen 4:19-24). The reappearance of Cain in Genesis 4:25 is a reminder that all that has transpired is inseparable from that original violence.[13] This chapter underscores the fundamental irony for all cities and civilizations: tremendous creative potential of humanity marred by cruelty and exploitation. This association between cities and violence resurfaces in Genesis 10. The so-called Table of Nations mentions Nimrod (Genesis 10:8-12) and de-

---

[11]V. P. Hamilton, *The Book of Genesis, Chapters 1-17*, NICOT (Grand Rapids: Eerdmans, 1990), pp. 237-38; cf. W. P. Brown, *The Ethos of the Cosmos: The Genesis of the Moral Imagination in the Bible* (Grand Rapids: Eerdmans, 1999), pp. 164-74; Jacques Ellul, *The Meaning of the City* (Grand Rapids: Eerdmans, 1993), pp. 1-9.

[12]This interpretation requires a different reading of the Hebrew text. See C. Westermann, *Genesis 1-11*, trans. J. J. Scullion, Continental Commentary (Minneapolis: Fortress, 1984), pp. 326-27; Gordon J. Wenham, *Genesis 1-15*, WBC 1 (Waco, Tex.: Word, 1987), p. 111.

[13]Wenham, *Genesis 1-15*, p. 111.

clares him to be "a mighty warrior" or "hunter."[14] He built the great cities of empires that would conquer the world, Babylonia and Assyria. Both figure prominently in the history of Israel.

The mention of Shinar and Babel in Genesis 10:10 anticipates the story in Genesis 11. Again rebellion lies at the root of the effort to build a city, and the continued progress eastward suggests further removal from God (Gen 11:2). Humankind wishes to make a "name" for itself.[15] The objective appears to be to supplant God, who alone is worthy of singular renown (for example, Ps 8:1, 9; Jer 32:20). They desire to construct a tower that reaches to the heavens, thereby connecting the city with celestial realms (Gen 11:4). This reminds the reader of the temptation to be like God in Genesis 3:5. The transgression is compounded further by the effort to not be scattered, contrary to the commission of Genesis 1:28 (cf. Gen 9:1).

What from a human point of view was grand is so small that God must come down to find it (Gen 11:5)! With sinful humankind united, the possibilities for evil are limitless (Gen 11:6). The city of Babel is at once the (failed) gateway to the gods[16] and represents the refusal to live within the proper boundaries set for humanity by Yahweh.[17] Here languages have their start (Gen 11:8-9), and these languages identify the nations of the world (Gen 10:5, 20, 31). In a sense, then, the nations are born at Babel; her spirit of ambition resides in the heart of all peoples.

This characterization of the sinful conceit of Babel/Babylon continues throughout the Bible. In Isaiah, Babylon fittingly stands at the head of the Oracles against the Nations (Is 13–14; cf. 47). The most powerful city on earth is pitiless in its treatment of others, and its king aspires to deity (Is 14:4-6, 12-14). Yet defeat is in its future, and a humiliating death will be the fate of its leader (Is 13:14-22; 14:3-23). The judgment on the pride of nations, even Judah, is a key theme in Isaiah (for ex-

---

[14]"Mighty warrior" (Gen 10:8) is *gibbōr*, which is used of the "sons of God" in Gen 6:4. It could have a negative connotation here, too.

[15]Genesis 11:4 also echoes Gen 6:4 concerning those "sons of God," those "warriors of renown (lit. 'men of the name')."

[16]The Babylonians understood the name to mean "the gate of the god," but Gen 11:9 links Babel to *bll*, which is "confuse" (*HALOT* 107-8, 134).

[17]Cf. Westermann, *Genesis 1–11*, pp. 551-52, 554-55; W. Brueggemann, *Genesis*, Interpretation (Louisville, Ky.: Westminster John Knox, 1982), pp. 97-104.

ample, Is 2:12-17; 3:16–4:1; 10:8-19; 16:6; 23:9; 47:7-10). Babylon is the epitome of that deep-seated human character trait.

This hubris recurs in the book of Daniel. The Babylonian king Nebuchadnezzar demands worship and glories over his capital city, Belshazzar utilizes the utensils of the temple of Yahweh for his feasting, and the little horn boasts before the Ancient of Days (Dan 2–7). In 1 Peter, Babylon represents Rome (1 Pet 5:13; cf. 1:1), but apparently without the negative connotations of the Old Testament.[18] In Revelation "Babylon the Great" (cf. Dan 4:30) appears again as the proud city, the harlot that dominates the world and leads rebellion against God (Rev 11; 14; 16–18). The metaphor fits the first century, but it can be applied to cruel empires of every era.[19] From the perspective of the Bible, the history of nations—and the city—begins and ends with Babel. Disobedience and pride intertwined with achievement: these are basic parameters of a biblical theology of the city.

One would hope that it would not be so with the people of God. In Genesis 4, the line of Cain is set off from that of Seth. They would be the first to call on Yahweh, and Abram and his descendents do the same (Gen 4:26; 12:8; 13:4; 21:33; 26:25). Babel sought fame and is judged, but God decrees that Israel's name would be great as it fulfilled the mission of being a blessing to the world (Gen 12:2). The contrast is explicit.

What would be the experience of Israel once it had its own cities? Might their ethos differ from that of Babel/Babylon, that archetype of all cities? Would it stand out in sharp contrast from the harsh bondage of the storage cities in Egypt? The story of the people's entry into the land carries the call to make a choice, a decision connected to life in their cities (Deut 6:10-12). These lines are a window into urban life in ancient times. There are houses, water resources and agriculture adjacent to the settlements (cf. Deut 28:3-6). This passage is imbedded in a

---

[18]This is the consensus among commentators (note the exhortation of 2 Pet 2:13-17). Babylon also might symbolize exile from the land (cf. 1 Pet 1:1). See J. R. Michaels, *1 Peter*, WBC 49 (Waco, Tex.: Word, 1988), p. 311; J. H. Elliott, *1 Peter: A New Translation with Introduction and Commentary*, AB 37B (New York: Doubleday, 2000), pp. 882-87; K. H. Jobes, *1 Peter*, BECNT (Grand Rapids: Baker Academic, 2005), pp. 250-51.

[19]R. Bauckham, *The Theology of the Book of Revelation*, New Testament Theology (Cambridge: Cambridge University Press, 1993), pp. 35-39, 155-56, 160.

longer discourse, which has an exhortation for total commitment to
Yahweh (Deut 6:1-9), a command not to follow other gods (Deut 6:13-
19), and a charge to pass on to future generations the story of their relationship to God (Deut 6:20-25). The ongoing existence of and provision for the cities of Israel were contingent on faithfulness to the laws
of God.

Sadly, the cities during the United Monarchy and after the division
of the kingdom did not exhibit a moral fiber different from that of
other cities. The most stunning example of promise doomed by failure
is found in Solomon. This wisest of all kings (1 Kings 4:29-34; 10:24)
evolves into a pharaonic figure.[20] He accumulates wealth (1 Kings 9:26-
28; 10:14-29) and sustains a court of exorbitant consumption (1 Kings
4:7-28). He launches a building program that includes the construction
of the temple and a palace (1 Kings 5–7) and administrative and military centers (1 Kings 9:15-19). These undertakings required the forced
labor of his people and others (1 Kings 5:13-18 [vv. 27-32 Heb.]; 9:15-
23). This exploitation of Solomon's subjects in work, taxes and provisions in kind would have impacted the livelihood of many and left their
mark on the natural environment, through the use of raw materials and
the centralized management of property and crop yields. The ideology
of kingship that was to distinguish God's people from the other nations
had been turned on its head (Deut 17:14-20; cf. 1 Sam 8:10-18).[21] This
reversal found its most evident expression in the cities—especially Jerusalem—where wealth and power were concentrated.

The portrayal of Jerusalem, as the city both of righteousness and of
injustice, is presented powerfully in Isaiah. This city is a central theme
of the book.[22] Images of corruption are juxtaposed with a different fu-

---

[20]J. D. Hays, "Has the Narrator Come to Praise Solomon or to Bury Him? Narrative Subtlety
in 1 Kings 1-11," *JSOT* 28 (2003): 149-74; cf. K. Lawson Younger Jr. "The Figurative Aspect
and the Contextual Method in the Evaluation of the Solomonic Empire," in *The Bible in Three
Dimensions*, ed. D. J. A. Clines et al., JSOTSup 87 (Sheffield, U.K.: JSOT Press, 1990), pp.
157-75.

[21]J. G. McConville, *God and Earthly Power: An Old Testament Political Theology. Genesis–Kings*,
LHB/OTS 454 (London: T & T Clark, 2006).

[22]B. C. Ollenberger, *Zion—The City of the Great King: A Theological Symbol of the Jerusalem Cult*,
JSOTSup 41 (Sheffield, U.K.: Sheffield Academic Press, 1987), pp. 107-29; Barry G. Webb,
"Zion in Transformation: A Literary Approach to Isaiah," *The Bible in Three Dimensions: Es-
says in Celebration of Forty Years of Biblical Studies in the University of Sheffield*, ed. D. Clines,

ture, where the redeemed city is a beacon to the world (for example, Is 1–4). An interesting literary play occurs in Isaiah 24–27. Diverse referents for the unnamed city have been postulated, but a good option is that it is Jerusalem.[23] In chapter 24 the "earth" (or "land") is cursed because of sin (Is 24:4, 7, 13, 18-19). But, one day Jerusalem will be exalted and characterized by material abundance (Is 25:6-8); it will be a fruitful vineyard (Is 27:2-6). The fact that the city remains anonymous throughout this section suggests that it is a symbol. Jerusalem, like other cities, can be a place of pride and transgression (cf. Mt 23:37 and parallels).

THE CITY, HUMAN ECOLOGY AND THE ENVIRONMENT

For millennia, the world of the Levant was fundamentally agrarian, so the attention given to nature in the Bible is not surprising. The land's widely diverse geographical features and climatic conditions shaped daily life and political history (cf. Deut 11:10-12).[24] The people were acquainted with the soil, seasons, precipitation patterns and the flora and fauna.[25] Material from the New Testament, such as the teachings of Jesus (for example, Mt 6:25-34; 7:15-20; 13:3-32; 21:33-41; 24:14-46; and parallels) and Pauline passages (1 Cor 3:5-9; 9:9-11; Gal 6:7-10), also reflect an awareness of the natural world. Acts and the epistles focus on urban areas because of the early missionary strategy of targeting cities.[26]

Genesis reveals that nature and humanity are interconnected. Even as humans are part of the creation, they are its culmination; only they are made in the image of God (Gen 1:26-31). Because of this relationship and the primacy of humanity, the Fall negatively affected the orig-

---

S. E. Fowl and S. E. Porter, JSOTSup 87 (Sheffield, U.K.: JSOT Press, 1990), pp. 65-84.

[23]J. T. Hibbard, *Intertextuality in Isaiah 24-27*, FAT, sec. series, 16 (Tübingen: Mohr Siebeck, 2006), pp. 20-26; M. E. Biddle, "The City of Chaos and the New Jerusalem: Isaiah 24–27 in Context," *PRSt* 22, no. 1 (1995): 5-12; Carroll, "City of Chaos, City of Stone, City of Flesh."

[24]J. Rogerson, *The New Atlas of the Bible* (London: Macdonald, 1985), pp. 58-213; A. F. Rainey and R. S. Notley, *The Sacred Bridge: Carta's Atlas of the Biblical World* (Jerusalem: Carta, 2006), pp. 36-42.

[25]Davis, *Scripture, Culture, and Agriculture*; O. Borowski, *Agriculture in Iron Age Israel* (Boston: American Schools of Oriental Research, 2002).

[26]Eckhard J. Schnabel, *Early Christian Mission*, vol. 2: *Paul and the Early Church* (Downers Grove, Ill.: InterVarsity Press, 2004).

inal harmony of the environment (Gen 3:17-19, 21). Ecological disaster was a corollary to offenses committed against God and humanity. Accordingly, the transgressions of cities also impinge on nature.

People in the ancient world held the conviction that the moral order was embedded within the created order.[27] To violate this morality or to fail to meet the demands of the deity would bring environmental calamities or other disasters, such as armed conflict. The representative and guarantor of this cosmic order was the king, and so creation motifs weave their way into royal ideologies. The gods were the patrons and protectors of the realm. Wars would be fought and victory assured, crops watered and harvests secured, with their help. The presence of the deities was made visible in the sanctuaries within the sacral precincts of the capital and temple cities, structures designed to mirror the heavens.[28]

Israel, too, believed in a cosmic moral and spiritual order grounded in creation and connected to the national cult.[29] The people honored Jerusalem as the city of Yahweh and Zion as his abode (for example, Ps 76; 87; 132). They supposed that God would defend that city and the land (for example, Ps 46; 48).[30] In his freedom and sovereignty, however, Yahweh transcended the Israelite monarchy and was critical of it.[31] Even David commits sins that yield suffering for his family and the

---

[27]H. H. Schmid, "Creation, Righteousness, and Salvation: 'Creation Theology' as the Broad Horizon of Biblical Theology," in *Creation in the Old Testament*, ed. B. W. Anderson (Philadelphia: Fortress, 1984), pp. 102-17; D. A. Knight, "Cosmogony and Order in the Hebrew Tradition" and H. D. Betz, "Cosmogony and Ethics in the Sermon on the Mount," in *Cosmogony and Ethical Order*, ed. R. W. Lovin and F. E. Reynolds (Chicago: University of Chicago Press, 1985), pp. 133-57 and 158-76, respectively. Cf. Brown, *The Ethos of the Cosmos*, pp. 35-132; T. E. Fretheim, *God and World in the Old Testament* (Nashville: Abingdon, 2005).

[28]M. Nissinen, "City as Lofty as Heaven: Arbela and Other Cities in Neo-Assyrian Prophecy," in *'Every City Shall Be Forsaken'*, pp. 172-209; G. W. Ahlström, *Royal Administration and National Religion in Ancient Palestine*, SHANE 1 (Leiden: Brill, 1982), pp. 1-26.

[29]S. E. Balentine, *The Torah's Vision of Worship*, Overtures to Biblical Theology (Minneapolis: Fortress, 1999), pp. 59-118; cf. G. K. Beale, *The Temple and the Church's Mission: A Biblical Theology of the Dwelling Place of God*, NSBT 17 (Downers Grove, Ill.: InterVarsity Press, 2004), pp. 29-121.

[30]Ahlström, *Royal Administration and National Religion in Ancient Palestine*, pp. 27-81; J. J. M. Roberts, "Zion in the Theology of the Davidic-Solomonic Empire," in *Studies in the Period of David and Solomon and Other Essays*, ed. T. Ishida (Winona Lake, Ind.: Eisenbrauns, 1982), pp. 93-108; Ollenberger, *Zion—The City of the Great King*.

[31]Some claim a strong link between creation theology and the royal ideology of the status quo. See, for example, N. C. Habel, *The Land Is Mine: Six Biblical Land Ideologies*, OBT (Min-

nation (for example, 2 Sam 12:7-14; 24:15-17). Jeremiah announces that Judah and Jerusalem would suffer at the hands of Babylon (Jer 11–12; 16; 20; 26; 36–38), and Ezekiel recounts the departure of Yahweh from Jerusalem (Ezek 10–11). Violations of the divine norms in any sphere affected the natural realm.

The devastation of war. The blessings and curses of Deuteronomy 28 presents the two ways that lie before Israel, the road of obedience and that of sin. The decision would have consequences for both "the city" and "the field" (Deut 28:1-3, 15-16). Blessings include agricultural abundance—ecological bliss, as it were—for urban centers and rural areas alike (Deut 28:4-14). On the other hand, waywardness guaranteed disaster (Deut 28:15-68).

Many curses in this chapter concern the effects of warfare, specifically of a siege.[32] A lengthy siege could result in starvation within the city (Deut 28:53-57; cf. 2 Kings 6:24–7:20; 18:27-32), as well as bring ruin outside the walls (Deut 28:49-52). In the ancient world, invading armies ate from the land they were occupying, so wars often were waged during the spring, at harvest time. In addition to the despoliation of crops, trees would be cut down to construct siege equipment, such as ramps, battering rams and ladders (cf. Deut 20:19-20; Jer 6:6). To deny the surviving population the opportunity to begin their life anew after the siege nearby orchards would be destroyed. New trees would need to be planted and nurtured to bear fruit, a process that could take years. Land sometimes was sown with salt or stones to make it unproductive (cf. Judg 9:45; 2 Kings 3:19, 25; Jer 7:20; 46:22-23). After the war (or in order to avoid invasion by a powerful neighbor), a vassal state was obligated to pay annual tribute to its suzerain. This tribute could take the form of goods in kind, like olive oil, wine, grains, lumber and other natural resources.

---

neapolis: Fortress, 1995), pp. 17-32; W. Brueggemann, *The Land: Place as Gift, Promise, and Challenge in Biblical Faith*, 2nd ed. (Minneapolis: Fortress, 2002), pp. 67-83; yet, see Brown, *The Ethos of the Cosmos*; Fretheim, *God and World in the Old Testament*.

[32]T. R. Hobbs, *A Time for War: A Study of Warfare in the Old Testament*, OTS 3 (Wilmington, Del.: Michael Glazier, 1989), pp. 70-181; J. L. Wright, "Warfare and Wanton Destruction: A Reexamination of Deuteronomy 20:19-20 in Relation to Ancient Siegecraft," *JBL* 127, no. 3 (2008): 423-58.

The human costs of war also affected the environment. Archaeological data show that the population of Jerusalem and Judah swelled
after Assyria conquered Israel as refugees fled south. New pressures on
food production, housing and labor would have been acute—all of
which would have impacted the land. Lamentations graphically portrays the anguish of those who remained after the sacking of Jerusalem
by the Babylonians in 586 B.C. They endured hunger, thirst and deprivation (Lam 1:11, 19; 2:12, 19; 4:4-5, 9-10; 5:4, 9-17). Surely in the
countryside the situation was similar, due to the loss of hands to work
the fields and the destruction of the environment by the invader.

With defeat could come deportation to distant lands (for example,
Lev 26:33-35; Deut 28:36-37, 41, 64-68; Amos 5:27; 7:11, 17). Many
inhabitants of the Northern Kingdom were taken away by the Assyrians (2 Kings 17:6, 18-20, 23). Others were shipped in from elsewhere
to occupy their cities and work their farms (2 Kings 17:24-40). The
death of large numbers and the displacement and resettlement of populations wreaked havoc, at least for a time, on the cities and surrounding
areas. Scholars debate the impact of the Babylonian invasion on Judah
and the empire's subsequent rule over the region.[33] What might have
been the immediate environmental impact of the defeat of Judah and
conditions during the following decades? The destruction of the Jerusalem and other urban centers meant the loss of markets and city-based
socioeconomic and judicial infrastructures, capital investment and
trained administrators.

The text says that the expulsion of the people provided the land its
neglected Sabbath rest (2 Chron 36:21; cf. Lev 25:1-7; 26:33-35, 43).
Refusal to follow God's ethical demands had led to an environmental
respite of sorts accomplished through external forces. This implies
that to some degree the war-ravished countryside lay neglected or
abandoned. Was there any change under the Persians? A century later
Nehemiah lamented that the walls of Jerusalem still lay in ruins (Neh
1:3; 2:3, 11-18)! Had the rural zones recuperated from their losses? It

---

[33]O. Lipschits and J. Blenkinsopp, eds., *Judah and the Judeans in the Neo-Babylonian Period*
(Winona Lake, Ind.: Eisenbrauns, 2003); O. Lipschits, *The Fall and Rise of Jerusalem: Judah
Under Babylonian Rule* (Winona Lake, Ind.: Eisenbrauns, 2005).

is impossible to say with certainty, but perhaps they had not or at least not fully.

The desolation of poverty. The prophetic literature is scathing in its critique of the ethical realities of the cities of Judah and Israel. Even though it is not possible to reconstruct with absolute certainty the mechanisms of social and economic injustice,[34] the moral indictment is patent. The vocabulary of oppression communicates an underlying violence against the vulnerable of society. The prophet Amos is representative. In the Northern Kingdom, many suffered from hunger and drought (Amos 4:6-9), while others enjoyed abundance (Amos 4:1; 6:3-6). The urban centers do not appear to endure the same lack, and some there survive at the expense of those who do. The text says the defenseless were exploited, burdened by taxes, and were losing their land because of debts and corruption and being sold into debt slavery (Amos 2:6-8; 5:11-12; 8:4-6).

The provision for the tables of the powerful in the urban centers probably came from the king's estates (or from those of the ruling aristocracy) and taxes.[35] What level of misery existed among those who worked those estates or among the smaller landowners and shepherds within the broader economic framework? Were these groups obliged to pay from what they needed to survive in that unpredictable environment, or was there sufficient surplus to fulfill that obligation? Was debt slavery part of a larger process of the growth of large estates (latifundia) (cf. Is 5:8; Mic 2:1-2; 1 Kings 21)? References to debt slavery suggest that there was distress in the countryside, as peasants lost their land, homes, even family members because of loan demands.[36] Increased regional specialization of crops (2 Chron 26:10; cf. 1 Chron 27:25-31)[37]

---

[34]Note the survey of prominent theories in W. Houston, *Contending for Justice: Ideologies and Theologies of Social Justice in the Old Testament*, LHB/OTS 428 (London: T & T Clark, 2006), pp. 18-51.

[35]J. A. Dearman, *Property Rights in the Eighth Century Prophets*, SBLDS 106 (Atlanta: Scholars Press, 1988), pp. 117-26; A. F. Rainey, "Aspects of Life in Ancient Israel," in *Life and Culture in the Ancient Near East*, ed. Averbeck, Chavalas and Weisberg, pp. 253-67.

[36]G. C. Chirichigno, *Debt-Slavery in Israel and the Ancient Near East*, JSOTSup 141 (Sheffield, U.K.: JSOT Press, 1993); G. H. Haas, "Slave, Slavery," in *Dictionary of the Old Testament: Pentateuch*, ed. David W. Baker and T. Desmond Alexander (Downers Grove, Ill.: InterVarsity Press, 2002), pp. 778-83.

[37]M. L. Chaney, "Systemic Study of the Israelite Monarchy," *Sem* 37 (1986): 53-76; D. N. Prem-

for export and consumption by the well to do (1 Kings 4:22-23) also reconfigured land use and impacted the livelihood of the peasantry.

The precariousness of existence is the background to much Old Testament legislation. The institution of the Jubilee (Lev 25), for example, offered farming families the chance for a new start by the periodic cancellation of debt and return of property.[38] It envisions problems of debt in the countryside (Lev 25:25-28) and in the cities (Lev 25:29-34), again interconnecting urban and rural realities. Everyone would have had to trust God for provision during the Jubilee and the following year (Lev 25:18-22).

The conscription of people from farms for royal construction projects most likely had repercussions on sowing and harvesting, too. The problem would not have been limited to the removal of able-bodied men from the fields. One wonders if at these work sites some would have been injured, become sick or even died. If this were the case, there would have been lasting detrimental consequences for the extended family and clan farms.

The prophets proclaim that these transgressions brought defeat and exile. But exploitation of the poor did not end with those judgments; it continued after the return to the land. Nehemiah denounces the powerful for exploiting those in the countryside (Neh 5), and prophets censure anew the injustice of the community (Zech 7:9-10; Mal 3:5). This concern for the poor, of course, is also an important New Testament theme. The fledgling church put into place mechanisms to care for the vulnerable (Acts 6:1-7; 2 Cor 8–9; 1 Tim 5:3-16; cf. James).[39]

In addition to the environmental impact related to systemic injustice, the prophetic literature correlates unethical behavior with natural catastrophes (for example, Jer 9:7-11; 14:2-12; Joel 1). The land of promise lacks rain; crops fall victim to blight and do not yield good

---

nath, *Eighth Century Prophets: A Social Analysis* (St. Louis: Chalice, 2003), pp. 56-70.

[38]Wright, "Sabbath, Sabbatical Year, Jubilee," *Dictionary of the Old Testament: Pentateuch*, pp. 695-706; M. D. Carroll R., "Wealth and Poverty," *Dictionary of the Old Testament: Pentateuch*, pp. 881-87; cf. R. Kinsler and G. Kinsler, *The Biblical Jubilee and the Struggle for Life: An Invitation to Personal, Ecclesial, and Social Transformation* (Maryknoll, N.Y.: Orbis, 1999).

[39]S. Ely Wheeler, *Wealth as Peril and Obligation: The New Testament on Possessions* (Grand Rapids: Eerdmans, 1995); C. L. Blomberg, *Neither Poverty nor Riches: A Biblical Theology of Possessions*, NSBT 7 (Downers Grove, Ill.: InterVarsity Press, 1999).

harvests; fields are stripped bare by locusts, and earthquakes bring terrible destruction. Some of these misfortunes are an unavoidable part of rural existence in that part of the world, but the biblical text argues that they can come from God because of socio-economic and political transgressions. The three doxology passages in Amos underline that the God who judges is the Creator (Amos 4:13; 5:8-9; 9:5-6), who has devastated and will smite the countryside (Amos 1:1-2; 4:6-10; 7:1-6; 8:7-9). Jesus announces that famine, pestilence and earthquakes will accompany the fall of the city of Jerusalem (Mt 24:7; Lk 21:11). The most expansive expression of judgment and its impact on the environment occurs in the book of Revelation (Rev 6:12-14; 8:7–9:19; 11:13; 16).

Metaphorical descriptions of ruin. Another manner in which the biblical text correlates sin and its effects on the environment is through multiple metaphors. I mention two.

The first is that sinful land and its defeated cities will be overrun by creatures outside the controlled boundaries of an ordered existence. They will be overwhelmed by wild animals (Lev 26:22; Deut 32:24; Is 13:20-22; Jer 9:11; 49:33; 51:37; Lam 5:18; Ezek 14:15, 21),[40] infested with thorns (Is 7:23-25; 34:13; Hos 9:6) and invaded by insects (Is 7:18-19); the bodies of the dead will be devoured by predators and birds of prey (Deut 28:26; Jer 7:33; 16:4; 19:7-8; 34:20; Ezek 32:4). These word pictures communicate a picture of chaos; life among the ruins is precarious. The cities that once ruled nations and were the pride of their peoples have been transformed into a hostile wilderness.

The second metaphor is that the land mourns because of the judgment of God.[41] Like someone in a mourning ritual, the land has torn off its clothes and shaved itself bare; its plants are withered (cf. Job 1:20; Is 15:2-

---

[40]Cf. J. Galambush, "God's Land and Mine: Creation as Property in the Book of Ezekiel," in *Ezekiel's Hierarchical World: Wrestling with a Tiered Reality*, ed. S. L. Cook and C. L. Patton, SBLSS 31 (Atlanta: Society of Biblical Literature, 2005), pp. 91-108; A. Labahn, "Wild Animals and Chasing Shadows: Animal Metaphors in Lamentations as Indicators for Individual Threat," in *Metaphor in the Hebrew Bible*, ed. P. van Hecke, Bibliotheca Ephemeridum Theologicarum Lovaniensium 187 (Leuven: University Press, 2005), pp. 67-97.

[41]The Hebrew verbal root is *'bl* (*HALOT* 6-7). Arguing for the meaning "mourn" instead of "dry up" are D. J. A. Clines, "Was There an *'BL* II 'Be Dry' in Classical Hebrew?" *VT* 42, no. 1 (1992): 1-10; K. M. Haynes, *"The Earth Mourns": Prophetic Metaphor and the Oral Aesthetic*, SBLAB 8 (Atlanta: Society of Biblical Literature, 2002), pp. 9-18; cf. *DCH* 1:107-8.

3; Mic 1:8, 16). The ground, along with the animals that depend on it for sustenance, suffers as a result of the punishment for human transgression. It laments its condition and cannot produce its fruit (Is 33:9; Jer 12:4; 23:10; Hos 4:3; Joel 1:10, 18). This mourning also can be its response to the condemning voice of God or coming judgment (Is 24:7; Jer 4:28; 12:11; Amos 1:2).[42] The impact of sin engulfs creation itself.

The impact of growth. A final point to consider is the ecological effect of items intrinsic to city life and growth. The impact on natural resources calls for constant attention, then and now, so that the interrelationship between urban life and the environment might not be a destructive one. A few examples from the ancient world illustrate this.

The construction of aqueducts, irrigation canals and water catchment systems for urban areas and farms required redirecting water sources.[43] The use of stones and the development of quarries for the construction of homes, royal precincts and fortifications would have altered the landscape. The felling of trees for firewood (for example, Deut 29:11; Jer 7:18; Lam 5:13), building and international trade (1 Kings 5:6-10, 14, 18), to fire industry (for example, pottery making and metallurgy), and clearing land for habitation and farming (Josh 17:17-18) reduced forests that once covered Palestine. Terracing for cultivation reshaped hills, and the domestication of animals and developments in farm technology expanded the reach of agriculture and diversified crops and flora. The potential for contamination of food and water sources related to the disposal of human waste and inadequate hygiene was a constant danger (Is 36:12; Ezek 4:12; cf. Deut 23:12-13 [Hebrew vv. 13-14]). In the New Testament, Jerusalem's dump in the Hinnom Valley, with its smoldering refuse, became a metaphor for the fires of

---

[42]N. Habel accuses the biblical text of not valuing the earth, since it portrays the earth as suffering through no fault of its own. Idem, "The Silence of the Lands: The Ecojustice Implications of Ezekiel's Judgment Oracles," in *Ezekiel's Hierarchical World*, ed. Cook and Patton, pp. 127-40. These texts actually underscore the importance of the land and the far-reaching impact of human sin.

[43]For this paragraph, see, for example, Bowrowski, *Agriculture in Iron Age Israel;* J. D. Currid, "The Deforestation of the Foothills of Palestine," *PEQ* 116 (1984): 1-11; P. J. King and L. E. Stager, *Life in Biblical Israel*, Library of Ancient Israel (Louisville, Ky.: Westminster John Knox, 2002), pp. 68-84.

hell (Mt 5:22, 29-30; Mk 9:43-48; Lk 12:5; Jas 3:6).[44]

These issues (construction, industry, food, waste and garbage) inevitably surface in discussions of the city. Although the biblical text does not engage them theologically in terms of the environment, they must be factored into a theology of the city and the created order. They take on moral import in light of the preceding discussion concerning the effects of sin on the natural surroundings of communities. The Bible is realistic, with a rich repertoire of imagery, in its depictions of these negative consequences of sin. Is there no positive word, no alternative for the city and its environs?

THE NEW JERUSALEM AND THE NEW EARTH: FUTURE HOPE BEYOND THE FAILURES

Although the original creation was tainted by human transgression (Gen 1–3) and the first city was conceived in sin (Gen 4), in the future lies a holy city wonderfully engaged with creation (Rev 21–22). In the present, nature groans in anticipation of that redemption (Rom 8:19-25). One day, however, there will be harmony between the city and the natural environment.

Predictions of a radically changed sociopolitical situation and of agricultural plenty beyond the judgments of God fill the prophetic books (for example, Is 11:1-9; 32:1-4, 14-20; 60–66; Jer 33; Ezek 36; 40–48; Amos 9:11-15). This hope centers on the exaltation of Zion, the cessation of war, and the joys of abundant harvests, children and long life. All nations will participate in this future era, which is related to the coming of Messiah. These passages present largely agrarian scenes—an outlook befitting the world of ancient Israel. Yet, a city stands at the center of these expectations. Two passages deserve special mention.

Isaiah 65:17-25 speaks of a "new heavens and a new earth" (v. 17; cf. Is 66:22). What the text describes is not a wholly different earth, however, but a renewed one. People are born and die, and the land is tilled and harvested. Jerusalem, too, will be rebuilt, and it will be a delight to God (vv. 18-19). There will be no more infant mortalities or premature

---

[44]In the Old Testament this valley is associated with human sacrifice (2 Kings 16:3; 23:10; Jer 7:30-33; 19:1-13).

deaths (v. 20), no more danger of invaders taking over their homes and fields, and the people of God will enjoy their families, what they have built and sown (vv. 21-23) and intimacy with God (v. 24).

This is a description of the capital city with its adjoining countryside filled with functioning and successful farms. To this glorious city and surrounding rural areas is added a picture of tranquility in nature (Is 65:25). These words echo an earlier passage connected to the prediction of a Spirit-filled, royal Messiah (Is 11:1-9). The important point to grasp is the conjunction between the chief urban center in the Bible (Jerusalem) and a bountiful and peaceful creation (cf. Mic 4:1-4). This hope of wedding human habitations to the marvels of creation is the goal to which God is sovereignly moving history. Harmony between humankind and the created order finally will be restored.[45] Nevertheless, this is not a return to the Eden, to a pristine garden without the footprints of civilization. This is another kind of paradise, one with both cities and farms.

Ezekiel 40–48 presents enlarged boundaries of the Promised Land (47:13–48:29), at whose center is a "city" with a temple in which the glory of God dwells. The temple is at the core of this city, Jerusalem. From that temple flows a river of water, which brings life to the trees on its banks; even the Dead Sea will have fresh water and teem with creatures! The river is reminiscent of the river in Genesis 2:10-14, but again the echo does not signal reverting to a simpler time. This body of water is grander and is connected to this special urban area. This city nurtures the land; it does not exploit it. Like Isaiah 65, this is a vision of a city in a mutually beneficial relationship with the environment.

These and other passages are reapplied to describe the new heavens, new earth and new Jerusalem of Revelation 21–22.[46] Christians debate the meaning of these two chapters (which in turn affects their interpretation of Is 65:17-25 and Ezek 40–48). Some argue that what is in view is our planet renewed; others contend that a different

---

[45]Wright, *Old Testament Ethics*, pp. 140-44; Fretheim, *God and the World*, pp. 189-98.
[46]D. Mathewson, *A New Heaven and a New Earth: The Meaning and Function of the Old Testament in Revelation 21.1–22.5*, JSNTSup 238 (London: Sheffield Academic Press, 2003).

world replaces this one cursed since the Fall, which will be annihilated by God.[47]

Despite differences in interpretation,[48] it is enough to emphasize that the Bible's closing involves a sanctified urban setting at peace with creation. The Old Testament longs for this hope, and the New Testament reveals that it will be a reality. The depiction of this divinely constructed city stands in contrast to Babylon of the earlier chapters.[49] The people of God are told to leave that sinful city, whose sin triggers catastrophic judgment upon planet earth (Rev 18:4). This Babylon is the descendent of that ancient city. There can be no good future for the metropolises of humanity or creational renewal until that old and ever-new urban site of transgression is removed.

In light of this future hope, it is not realistic to champion some sort of an idealized past golden era of a simple life with no urban areas. That stage of human history was left behind thousands of years ago. Instead the Bible offers a future, when urban areas will be coordinated in healthy ways with the environment. The last word for the city and nature is not one of despair.

CONCLUSION

The Bible has much to say about the city and its relationship with the created order. There is an awareness of the impact of sin on the environ-

---

[47]Note the essay in chapter 1 of this volume by Douglas J. Moo. Sources favoring the renewal view not mentioned by Moo or Mathewson include G. C. Berkouwer, *The Return of Christ*, Studies in Dogmatics (Grand Rapids: Eerdmans, 1972), pp. 210-34; A. A. Hoekema, *The Bible and the Future* (Grand Rapids: Eerdmans, 1979), pp. 274-87; Wright, *Old Testament Ethics*, pp. 184-86. A less common view is that this is a vision of the church (for example, R. H. Mounce, *The Book of Revelation*, rev. ed., NICNT [Grand Rapids: Eerdmans, 1998], pp. 380-82).

[48]There are also debates about how literal is the description vis-à-vis Old Testament promises. Each position is connected to a belief in, or denial of, a millennium as a stage preceding the eternal state. For those who argue for a physical millennial reign of Christ, many of those predictions find initial fulfillment at that time yet point to a greater fulfillment afterward. For different perspectives, see, for example, D. L. Turner, "The New Jerusalem in Revelation 21.1–22.5: Consummation of a Biblical Continuum," in *Dispensationalism, Israel, and the Church: The Search for Definition* (Grand Rapids: Zondervan, 1992), pp. 264-92; D. I. Block, *Book of Ezekiel, Chapters 25–48*, NICOT (Grand Rapids: Eerdmans, 1998), pp. 494-511; Beale, *Temple and the Church's Mission*.

[49]Bauckham, *Theology of the Book of Revelation*, pp. 131-32; cf. B. R. Rossing, *The Choice Between Two Cities: Whore, Bride, and Empire in the Apocalypse*, HTS 48 (Harrisburg, Penn.: Trinity Press International, 1999).

ment, from the curse of the Fall to pictures of war, the hardships brought on by poverty, and the difficulties of farming and city life in that region of the world. It is clear that the character and behavior of human communities is interconnected with the health of the environment.

This realism allows the biblical text to interface with today's pressing urban-ecological problems. It is truly a valuable resource to which one can turn to comprehend better the role of human sin in shaping the city and its negative influences on nature. On the other hand, the Bible indicates that it does not have to be this way; in the future the destructive cycle will be broken.

Can the Scriptures point us in a constructive direction within the present, even as we look to a better time? One word of advice can be gleaned from a letter the prophet Jeremiah wrote to his compatriots exiled in Babylon (Jer 29). To counteract false voices that had tried to convince the people that their stay in that foreign land would be brief he counseled that they invest themselves in their new context, to build houses and plant their gardens. If they lived righteously and influenced society positively, everyone would prosper (Jer 29:4-7).

A couple of phrases in Jeremiah 29:7 are especially relevant. One is "seek the welfare of the city." The English word "welfare" translates the Hebrew term šālôm. The word suggests inner as well as social well-being in every dimension of life.[50] This exhortation can encourage us today to get involved in our communities to promote the common good, including the health of the environment. Another phase to be highlighted is "in its welfare you will find your welfare" (literally, "in its šālôm will be šālôm for you"). In other words, such commitment to the multiple aspects of the context rebounds to one's own benefit.

A second way in which the Scripture can have an impact is through its visions of the future. Hope can lead to action. The prophetic literature and the book of Revelation are laced with exhortations to respond on the basis of what is shown of the future.[51] The conviction that the

---

[50]*TDOT* 15:13-49; *NIDOTTE* 4:130-35.

[51]Walter Brueggemann, *The Prophetic Imagination*, 2nd ed. (Minneapolis: Fortress, 2001). For Revelation, see the commentaries on its paraenesis and Rossing, *Choice Between Two Cities*; cf. P. Richard, *Apocalypse: A People's Commentary on the Book of Revelation*, trans. P. Berryman, The Bible & Liberation Series (Maryknoll, N.Y.: Orbis, 1995), pp. 159-73.

hand of God will change this ecological mess we have created should motivate those of faith to participate in positive ways to reshape the status quo. The biblical hope then is relevant and not an escapist dream. It can be a compass for the way forward. May we respond to the challenge.[52]

[52]I would like to thank my graduate assistant, Jacki Soister, for her help in the research for this essay.

PART THREE

THE DIVERSITY OF LIFE

4

THE DIVERSITY OF LIFE

Its Loss and Conservation

Fred Van Dyke

WHAT IS BIODIVERSITY?

Biodiversity is a new word. According to conservation biologist Stuart Pimm, it first appeared in a relatively obscure government report authored by Elliot Norse in 1980.[1] It did not attain common use until after 1986, following the work of the American National Forum on Biodiversity.[2] The word itself is really a contraction of two words, "biological diversity," and its definition is difficult because the concept it attempts to encompass is so vast. Biodiversity refers to variety of life, or, as The Nature Conservancy puts it, "the full array of life on Earth" and thus collectively to variation at all levels of biological organization. The 1992 Convention on Biological Diversity (CBD), the world's normative international document for pursuing biodiversity conservation, defines biodiversity as "the variability among living organisms, including, *inter alia* [among other things], terrestrial, marine, and other aquatic ecosystems, and the ecological complexities of which they are a part; this includes diversity within species, between species, and of ecosystems." The CBD definition, as broad as it is, omits an important dimension of

---

[1]Stuart Pimm, *The World According to Pimm: A Scientist Audits the Earth* (New York: McGraw-Hill, 2001), quoted in J. Kaiser, "Taking a Stand: Ecologists on a Mission to Save the World," *Science* 287, no. 5456 (February 2000): 1188-92.

[2]R. Thomson and B. M. Starzomski, "What Does Biodiversity Actually Do? A Review for Managers and Policy Makers," *Biodiversity and Conservation* 16 (2006): 1359-78.

biodiversity, which is diversity of life at the genetic level. Thus, the units of biodiversity in a given context may be genes, species, landscapes or entire ecosystems.

This chapter, concerned as it is with the diversity of life, will focus on understanding biodiversity as a biological element of communities and ecosystems.

SPECIES—THE FUNDAMENTAL UNITS OF BIODIVERSITY

Although we can define biodiversity in terms of genes, habitats, landscapes or ecosystems, the most commonly used entity in biodiversity description and measurement is that of *species*. In some ways, this only exacerbates our problem of definition, because if the definition of *biodiversity* if problematic, the definition of *species* is more so. Traditionally, the *biological concept* of species based the definition on reproductive isolation: species are groups of individuals that breed together to produce viable offspring that resemble the parents and do not breed with other such groups. This definition has been useful because of its operational test: if a male and female can breed together to produce viable offspring, they are the same species. If not, they are different species. Unfortunately, many species, particularly in the realm of fungi, bacteria and protozoans, are asexual, so the definition becomes meaningless. And in plants, unlike animals, two species with very different physical appearance can often produce hybrid offspring that are healthy and viable. As our skill and technology to investigate and understand living genomes has grown, genetic differences and similarities have increasingly been invoked to define and describe a species, but this approach brings its own unique set of conundrums to the question. Despite such problems, genetic approaches are gaining prominence in biology today, so that now the most widely used concept is that of the *phylogenetic species concept*. This view asserts that a species is defined by its genetic similarities and differences between and among groups which reflect a common past lineage of individuals within the group. But this definition, despite its growing acceptance, only accentuates the problem of conserving biodiversity, because now it is not just a population of "lookalike" individuals that must be saved, but the distinct genetic lineages that such a group contains. And the number of lineages to be saved is invariably more than the number of physically unique species to be saved. But regardless of how species are defined, the questions for biodiversity conservation are: How many species are there? Where are they found?

How many species are there? Science puts itself in a difficult position when it must respond to its most foundational and important question with the very unsatisfactory answer of "we don't know," but that is where things begin in the study of biodiversity. Currently there are (depending on the sources consulted) 1.5 to 1.8 million named species in the world, but no reputable scientist supposes that this is the actual number of species on Earth. It is likely that we have named and described most of the fishes, amphibians, reptiles, birds and mammals. However, our understanding of invertebrates and plants still remains sketchy with respect to a knowledge of total species numbers, with many new species being added with every new investigation. When we move to less studied groups like bacteria, fungi and protozoans, our ignorance is vastly multiplied. Based on the rate at which new species are being discovered, an oft-quoted estimate of the total species on Earth is 13.5 million, but the confidence interval on this estimate ranges from 3.5 to 111.5 million species.[3] (With a range of this size, the estimate might be better described as a "lack of confidence" interval.) The total number of species poses a major challenge to the work of biodiversity. Much good work remains for scientists to find, describe, and name new species, especially in groups that have been historically under-studied.

Where are these species found? In addition to naming and describing species, it would be helpful to know where exactly to find them. Here again is another difficult problem of biodiversity conservation. The distribution of species on Earth is not equitable. It is disproportionately concentrated in relatively small areas. More species live at low (tropical and subtropical) latitudes than at high latitudes. More species live at lower elevations than at higher elevations at a given latitude. More spe-

---

[3]Kevin J. Gaston and John I. Spicer, *Biodiversity: An Introduction*, 2nd ed. (Malden, Mass.: Blackwell Science, 2004), p. 39.

cies per unit area live on a coral reef than in any other part of the ocean, and more species live in an acre of tropical moist forest than in an acre of Arctic tundra. Similarly, the distribution of species is not politically proportional. Among the 192 member states of the United Nations, The United Nations Environmental Program (UNEP) has identified just 17 "megadiverse countries," each of which, on a per area basis, holds a disproportionate number of the world's species of plants and vertebrates. Collectively, the megadiverse countries harbor 66 to 75 percent of all known species on Earth. They are, in order of species numbers, Brazil, Indonesia, Colombia, Mexico, Australia, Madagascar, China, Philippines, India, Peru, Papua New Guinea, Ecuador, U.S.A., Venezuela, Malaysia, South Africa and Democratic Republic of Congo.[4] Even a casual glance at such a list raises questions and cause for concern. Most megadiverse countries are tropical or subtropical, developing rather than developed, poor rather rich, have high human population growth rather than low growth or stasis, have low rather than high capacities for government enforcement of environmental protection, suffer high rates of habitat and landscape degradation and destruction, and are often politically unstable. It is not unfair to say that most of the world's biodiversity is being held, politically, in unsteady and often inattentive hands.

SAVING BIODIVERSITY: WHAT MAKES "ENDANGERED SPECIES" ENDANGERED?

The work of naming new species and describing geographic locations of biodiversity is important, but the question of the moment goes beyond it. The critical question today is: what is the status of the species we already have described? Put another way, how many of the known species on Earth have secure populations that can be expected to persist for the foreseeable future? Here again, an honest answer is "we are not sure." But we can make reliable estimates. Current extinction rates are estimated to be 100 to 1,000 times higher than historical extinction rates that can be determined from the fossil record. This means there is cause for concern. The World Conservation Union is now monitoring

---

[4]Ibid., p. 63.

the status of 41,415 species of conservation concern. Of these, 16,306 were considered to be threatened with extinction in 2008, or one in four species of mammals, one in eight species of birds, one in three species of amphibians, and seven in ten species of all assessed plants.

The endangered species of the Earth are threatened by multiple factors, but the most important are (1) habitat loss and degradation, (2) pollution and climate change, (3) introduced species, (4) disease, and (5) overexploitation. All of these factors are anthropogenic. Threatened species are threatened because of what humans do.

Habitat destruction. The largest and most complex category of endangerment factors is that of *habitat loss and degradation.* Direct human behaviors that cause such loss and degradation are many and varied. The most important are residential and commercial development, agriculture and aquaculture, energy production and mining, development of transportation and service corridors (mainly and especially road building), direct human intrusions and disturbance, and the modification of natural systems (such as building a dam across a formerly free flowing stream or river). One of the reasons that habitat loss and degradation pose such a pervasive threat to biodiversity can be understood by using a simple mathematical relationship called the species-area curve, expressed in the mathematical formula $S = cA^z$, where S represents the number of species, A represents the area under consideration, c is a constant for a particular species group (for example, the relationship is different in reptiles than it is in birds), and z is the slope of the line that relates species to area, the so-called "extinction coefficient" that integrates a species extinction rate to changes in the amount of area available. In a "typical" species relationship such as that shown in figure 4.1, derived from data on grassland bird communities in Iowa (U.S.A.),[5] a 90 percent reduction in available area (habitat) from 20 hectares to 2 hectares along the 1998 curve results in a reduction of total species present from 12 species to 6 species, a loss of 50 percent of

---

[5]Fred Van Dyke, Jamie D. Schmeling, Shawn Starkenburg, Sung Heun Yoo and Peter W. Stewart, "Responses of Plant and Bird Communities to Prescribed Burning in Tallgrass Prairies," *Biodiversity and Conservation* 16 (2007): 827-39; Fred Van Dyke, S. E. Kley, C. E. Page and J. G. Van Beek, "Restoration Efforts for Plant and Bird Communities in Tallgrass Prairies Using Prescribed Burning and Mowing," *Restoration Ecology* 12 (2004): 574-84.

the species that live in that habitat. As habitat is destroyed or degraded, species lose resources needed to complete their life cycles. As their populations become smaller, they become more vulnerable to random

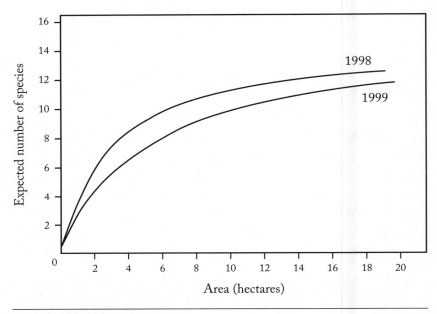

Figure 4.1. A species-area curve

This curve depicts the relationship between area and the number of species likely to be encountered in it. As the area of acceptable habitat declines, the number of species in the area also declines, but not at a constant rate. In these data derived from grassland bird communities at the DeSoto National Wildlife Refuge in Iowa (in the United States), note that for the curve reflecting the year 1998, a 90 percent reduction in habitat area from 20 hectares to 2 hectares results in a 50 percent reduction in the expected number of bird species, from 12 to 6.

events (we could say "catastrophes") such as extreme weather, changes in climate or disturbances (like fire, flood and famine) that, while not posing a threat to large populations, can exterminate small ones.

   Pollution and climate change. Pollution and climate change are another category of significant direct and indirect threats to global biodiversity. Although pollution can pose a form of habitat loss, as when acid precipitation kills trees in a forest, pollutants also can kill organisms directly. When the same acidic precipitation that kills forest trees falls into a lake, it can render the lake's water more acidic. In more acidic water, metallic ions like aluminum, lead or cadmium that formerly were dissolved in the water as solutes now form solid precipitates that can be deadly to aquatic species. Aluminum is especially dangerous because under acidic conditions, it not only precipitates but binds to the gills of fishes, hindering their breathing and often killing them.

Extinction events associated with climate change are more difficult to document because they require long-term record keeping of climatic data, concurrent with careful surveillance of populations that might be affected by climate. Nevertheless, we are seeing increasing signs of stress in many species caused by changes in seasonal temperatures, and outright extinctions in others. The Monte Verde Golden Toad (figure 4.2) was an inhabitant of the "cloud forests" of Costa Rica, high altitude tropical moist forests characterized by frequent rains and relatively constant high humidity. Beginning in the 1980s, biologists studying the Golden Toad began noticing an increasing number of "dry day" periods (five or more consecutive days without measurable precipita-

Figure 4.2. Monte Verde Golden Toad

This toad is a species unique to tropical cloud forests and their environments of high humidity. Under increasingly dry conditions in these forests, the Golden Toad has disappeared from the wild. Photo is taken and copyrighted by Michael and Patricia Fogden. Used by permission.

tion) that had formerly been extremely rare. Alan Pounds, a conservation biologist who has long studied tropical amphibians noted, "Whereas mist free periods in the 1970s rarely exceeded two days, they have recently lasted up to three weeks."[6] Massive declines of populations of many species of frogs and toads had become apparent by the 1990s, and after a particularly long dry period in 1987 (figure 4.3), the golden toad disappeared. It has not been seen again in the wild.

The effects of climate change are already here, but its projected

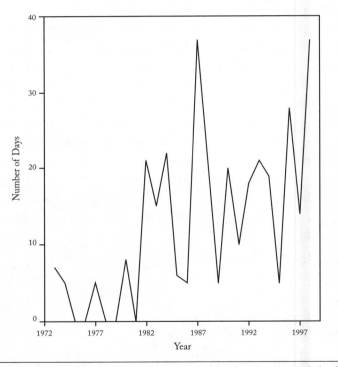

Figure 4.3. Trends and fluctuations in the number of dry days in a tropical cloud forest in Costa Rica's Monte Verde Cloud Forest

The values on the y-axis show the number of dry days (days with no measurable precipitation) that formed periods of five or more consecutive dry days during the dry season. Note the trend over time toward more and more dry day periods. The Monte Verde Golden Toad (figure 4.2) disappeared after the peak of dry days in 1987. (J. A. Pounds, M. P. L. Fogden and K. L. Masters, ©2005 by Yale University Press. Used by permission.)

---

[6]J. A. Pounds, M. P. L. Fogden and K. L. Masters, "Responses of Natural Communities to Climate Change in a Highland Tropical Forest," in *Climate Change and Biodiversity*, ed. T. E. Lovejoy and L. Hannah. (New Haven, Conn.: Yale University Press, 2006), p. 71 [70-74].

future effects force new considerations for biodiversity conservation that have never been required before. Climate change has the power to render existing strategies for habitat conservation planning, and the species such habitats protect, obsolete, because changing climate will change the location, arrangement and dispersion of habitats that species require. Conservation biologists have now been forced to develop so-called Climate Change-Integrated Conservation Strategies (CCCS) that mitigate the projected effects of climate change. In a CCCS, habitat preserves now must be treated as a moving target. Strategies to protect habitat and habitat-dependent species must consider not only what land to protect now, but whether additional areas can be acquired in the future in the face of climatic shift. Further, as habitat distribution shifts with climate change, habitat-dependent species must shift with it or perish. Therefore the CCCS must be able to calculate a species' bioclimate envelope (the range of habitat and climates it can occupy), estimate the species' capacity for migration, and determine if effective routes exist or can be acquired that can permit species movement to new areas as habitat distribution shifts. These adjustments in biodiversity conservation strategy are now necessary, but they are not easy. CCCS approaches place greater demands for information on the already scarce resources available for conservation research, and increase the level of uncertainty associated with species preservation in what is already an inexact science. Climate change has the potential to become the most deadly threat to world biodiversity ever known, for it has the power to overwhelm any local or regional conservation action, however well executed, by changing the environment itself.

Introduced species. Introduced species have become one of the most significant threats to world biodiversity over the last thirty years, with the introductions invariably facilitated by humans, sometimes intentionally and sometimes by ignorance and inattention. The introduction of the brown tree snake to the Pacific Island of Guam led to the extermination (by the snake) of all native species of birds on that island, including species that were found nowhere else in the world. In this case, the introduced species caused extinction directly through *predation*. In other cases, effects can be more subtle. In U.S. waters, the introduced European carp pollutes freshwater habitats in lakes and rivers through its habit of "rooting" in bottom sediments for food, often destroying native aquatic vegetation in the process. Introduced species also can be a factor in exterminating other species through *disease*, another major threat to global biodiversity. The red swamp crayfish, native to North America, has been a factor in exterminating populations of Europe's native white-clawed crayfish in Spain because it carries a fungal disease. Like Typhoid Mary, the red swamp crayfish is resistant to the disease it transmits, but spreads it to non-resistant species like the white-clawed crayfish. In southeastern Spain, the only streams that now retain white-clawed crayfish are those that had some sort of physical or ecological barrier separating them from streams that contained red-swamp crayfish.[7]

Overexploitation. In most developed industrial nations, the threat of overexploitation has become relatively rare, at least in terrestrial species, because governments have scientifically informed and well-enforced hunting, fishing and trapping regulations. This is not the case in most developing countries. There are sometimes few or no laws against killing or capturing native species, and laws that do exist often are not applied. Estimates of exploitation in developing countries are sometimes imprecise and not always current, but Western observers in 1995 estimated that the amount of bushmeat (meat from wild animals) arriving in Yaoundé, the capital of Cameroon, was about 2.3 tons *per day*.[8] In Indonesia, the endangered Bornean orangutan and Sumatran orangutan (figure 4.4) are threatened primarily by habitat loss that occurs as tropical forests are cut for timber, mining exploration or conversion to agriculture. But orangutan populations also are threatened by exploitation, not for food, but for the pet trade. It is a common practice among local village hunters to search out a female orangutan in the forest with a nursing infant. The hunter shoots the mother, and the infant, now easily captured, is sold at the market for a pet, where it can bring a high price. Although officially illegal,

---

[7]J. M. Gil-Sánchez and J. Alba-Tercedor, "The Decline of Native Populations of the Native Freshwater Crayfish *(Austropotamobius pallipes)* in Southern Spain: It Is Possible to Avoid Extinction," *Hydrobiologia* 559 (2006): 113-22.

[8]Fondo Sikod, Estherine Lisinge, John Mope-Simo and Steve Gartlan, "Cameroon: Bushmeat and Wildlife Trade," in *The Root Causes of Biodiversity Loss*, ed. Alexander Wood, Pamela Stedman-Edwards and Johanna Mang (London: Earthscan, 2000), p. 127 [126-52].

this practice remains common because the law is not consistently enforced. Even if the hunter is fined or jailed, the infant orangutan has no hope of survival in the forest without its mother. The problem has become so severe that a number of conservation organizations are now working together to provide "orangutan orphanages" in which such orphans are taught forest survival skills with the hope of their eventual return to the wild.[9] The number of such orphans is currently estimated at about two thousand, a significant number given that the total population of wild orangutans is probably only between fifty thousand and seventy-five thousand.

Figure 4.4. A Bornean orangutan

This species is endangered both by the habitat destruction of its forest home and by overexploitation for the pet trade. Photo is copyrighted by Jo-lan van Leeuwen (BOS Nyaru Menteng). Used by permission.

I have, in these few stories, not even scratched the surface of the extent of human-caused events that threaten the world's biodiversity. Ultimately, the study of biodiversity assumes that the loss of any species is a preventable event, or at least one that can be significantly delayed. How can biodiversity be preserved?

STRATEGIES FOR BIODIVERSITY PRESERVATION

The actual work and strategies associated with biodiversity conservation are complex, but all of them, regardless of complexity and detail, address one of five things that can be done to conserve biodiversity. These are (1) purchasing or gaining operational control of land of conservation value, (2) regulating the use of land and water for conservation purposes, (3) influencing land and water use through non-regula-

---

[9]For one example of an exemplary effort to address the problem of orphaned orangutans, see the website of the Nyaru-Menteng Orangutan Rehabilitation Project at <www.orangutan .net/projects/nyaru-menteng>.

tory means, (4) regulating the use of wild plants and animals, or (5) directly managing or manipulating wild or captive populations in ways that reduce or eliminate extinction threats. The first three strategies tie species conservation directly to land (habitat) conservation, and the fourth and fifth usually require some access to land and some knowledge of which lands are the best targets for regulation, management or re-introduction. Thus, in examining strategies for biodiversity conservation we begin with an array of measures that are collectively referred to as "geographically based approaches."

Global hotspots and biodiversity conservation. Recall that of the 192 member states of the United Nations, 66-75 percent of all world biodiversity is contained in only 17 of them. A more careful and critical analysis reveals that the distribution of biodiversity is even more disproportionate than that. The global conservation community today recognizes 34 biodiversity "hotspots," relatively small areas within these and other countries that, although covering only 1.4 percent of the Earth's land surface area, contain 44 percent of the world's terrestrial plant species and 35 percent of all its vertebrate species.[10]

Like the megadiverse countries discussed earlier, biodiversity hotspots tend to be concentrated in tropical and subtropical latitudes and developing countries. Biodiversity hotspots are often associated with expanding and typically poor human populations in areas experiencing accelerating habitat loss and degradation. Although hotspots offer an attractive "biggest bang for the buck" approach to the conservation of biodiversity, they are fraught with problems. In many hotspots, most of the original habitats have been lost, so conservation must be highly site-specific. Some hotspots, although containing a high level of species richness, hold relatively low numbers of rare and threatened species, which, ideally, should be the primary targets of conservation. And some hotspots, as noted earlier, are located in politically unstable regions where governments have little or no capacity to enact or enforce conservation laws. For a moment, let us step back from the hot spot approach and consider the more general strategy of land preservation for conservation.

---

[10]Conservation International, "Resources: Maps and GIS Data," <www.biodiversityhotspots .org/xp/hotspots/resources/Pages/maps.aspx>.

Protected lands for biodiversity. In the United States, The Nature Conservancy estimates that 80 percent of imperiled species could be protected on about 3 percent of the total U.S. landmass. To encompass the remaining 20 percent, the land area needed would have to be doubled to 6 percent. This goal is not unrealistic in terms of size, but, as in all real estate transactions, the issue is location, location, location. The Convention on Biological Diversity sets a goal for biodiversity conservation, called Target 4, that "at least 10% of the world's ecological regions [are to be] effectively conserved."[11] If the devil is in the details, it is the modifying words in this sentence that provide the best clues of where the devil may be lurking. What does it mean for an ecological region to be "effectively conserved?" In the United States, such ecological preservation began with the establishment of Yellowstone National Park in 1872, the first of what would become an entire system of parks spanning the nation. This approach, which has become known throughout the world as the "Yellowstone Model," has been the subject of lavish praise and severe criticism. The U.S. historian and environmental novelist Wallace Stegner called the U.S. national park concept "the best idea we ever had."[12] The ideal of a system of national parks, accessible to every citizen (and, for that matter, every *person* who comes to the parks, citizen or not) without regard for financial status, social rank or political affiliation, is indeed both a genuinely noble and democratic vision, uniquely American in its applications of equity and accessibility. Unfortunately, the U.S. national park system was developed at a time when the concept of "biodiversity" did not exist. The actual congressional charge given to the U.S. National Park Service was not to preserve biodiversity, but to "conserve the scenery and the natural and historic objects and the wild life therein and to provide for the enjoyment of the same in such manner and by such means as will leave them unimpaired for the enjoyment of future generations."[13] Conservation

---

[11]United Nations Environmental Program, *Convention on Biological Diversity* (The Hague, Netherlands: United Nations, 2002), p. 7.

[12]Wallace E. Stegner, *Marking the Sparrow's Fall: The Making of the American West* (New York: Henry Holt, 1998), p. 137.

[13]*U. S. National Park Service Organic Act of 1916*, 64th Congress, 16 U.S.C. Section 1 (1916) (39 Stat. 535).

biologists Mark Shaffer and Bruce Stein of The Nature Conservancy recently noted that the National Park Service, faithfully following this congressional mandate, has "done a much better job preserving scenic landscapes than biodiversity."[14]

But failure to preserve native biodiversity successfully is not the only problem. People in developing countries have been critical of the Yellowstone Model on the basis of its cultural insensitivity and political injustice, noting that the Native Americans in Yellowstone, and in many other U.S. national parks, were dispossessed without consideration, negotiation or compensation when their land was "reserved for nature." When the Yellowstone Model has been applied in other countries, such as African nations, such displacements were not only unjust but sometimes catastrophic. As the environmental historian Ramachandra Guha noted regarding the establishment of game reserves and national parks in the Republic of South Africa, "Where did the African fit into all this? To be precise, nowhere. . . . In game reserves Africans were barred from hunting, while in national parks they were excluded altogether, forcibly disposed of their land if it fell within the boundaries of the designated sanctuary."[15]

The man and biosphere reserve. International organizations, such as the United Nations, and their member nation-states of developing countries, have been anxious to avoid the perceived injustices of the Yellowstone Model by crafting plans for preserves that permit some measure of extractive industry and sustainable development to take place within and around the reserve, thus maintaining the residence, culture and economy of indigenous people. This goal is the foundation for the United Nations Man and Biosphere Reserve model that has been used throughout the world to designate and administer strategic biosphere reserves, primarily to conserve national and regional biodiversity. Unlike the Yellowstone Model, where the entire reserve is declared off limits to permanent human residence or resource extraction, the Man and Biosphere Model creates reserves with three "zones" that

---

[14]Mark L. Shaffer and Bruce A. Stein, "Safeguarding Our Precious Heritage," in *Precious Heritage: The Status of Biodiversity in the United States*, ed. Bruce A. Smith, Lynn S. Kutner and Jonathan S. Adams (Oxford: Oxford University Press, 2000), p. 305 [301-21].
[15]Ramachandra Guha, *Environmentalism: A Global History* (New York: Longman, 2000), pp. 46-47.

differ in degree of protection and human residence and use. A central reserve "core" is managed intensively, often exclusively, for biodiversity conservation. Permanent human residence is usually, although not always, excluded, and human activities are limited to those that benefit such biodiversity, although sometimes this criterion does permit some resource use or extraction if it improves habitat or food resources for wildlife. Surrounding the "core" is the "buffer" zone, where human habitation and activity are permitted, but (supposedly) regulated to mitigate their effects on the core reserve and its biodiversity. Surrounding the "buffer" zone is the "transition" zone, an area of relatively minimal modification and restriction on human activity and development, which is intended to "transition" the reserve into fully-impacted human landscapes beyond the zonal boundary.[16]

Admirable in concept, the biosphere reserve model often has proven dysfunctional in practice. Part of the problem is that, in most cases, only the core area requires and receives legal protection and status as a reserve, and thus only the core area is managed and "owned" by the national government. The buffer and transition zones usually remain under the control of regional or local governments or private citizens or companies. China's Yancheng Biosphere Reserve, for example, contains 35-65 percent of the world's migratory population of the red-crowned cranes, an endangered species native to Russia, China, Korea and Japan, in a given year. When this reserve was established in 1983, none of its core, 15 percent of the buffer zone, and 34 percent of the transition zone had been developed. Over the next eleven years the core remained undeveloped, but the buffer and transition zones suffered annual habitat losses from development of 1.5 percent and 0.6 percent, respectively. During the same period, cranes increasingly shifted their habitat use and reproductive activities to the core zone, so that now the density of cranes in the core is 10 times that of the buffer zone and 100 times that of the transition zone. To accommodate this dramatic increase in crane numbers within the core, managers of Yancheng have resorted to the construction of artificial wetlands in the core, but these

---

[16]Fred Van Dyke, *Conservation Biology: Foundations, Concepts, Applications*, 2nd ed. (Dordrecht, The Netherlands: Springer, 2008), pp. 21-22.

retain only some of the characteristics, and much less biodiversity, of natural wetlands. The cranes concentrated in the core area are now more vulnerable to a site-specific catastrophe or disease that could decimate a small, crowded population. Most crane habitat, and its associated biodiversity in the buffer and transition zones, is being lost.[17] This is not the way biodiversity conservation is supposed to work.

Figure 4.5. A captive female okapi, Sophie

She is part of the okapi population at the Antwerp Zoo in Belgium. Wild okapi populations are found only in the Democratic Republic of Congo, where human population growth, habitat destruction and political instability threaten the okapi's protection in established nature reserves. Photo by Patrick Immens and is used by permission.

The problems with protected areas. Today the global network of protected areas for nature and biodiversity conservation covers 12 percent of the world's land surface, or nearly one acre in eight. One might think this would be enough, but, by every current indicator, it is not even close. Part of the problem is that, in some countries, lands designated as "reserves" or "protected areas" receive no real protection, much less active conservation management, to guard the species within them. The Democratic Republic of Congo (DRC) holds all of the world's remaining populations of the okapi, a large forest-dwelling herbivore considered to be the closest living relative of the giraffe (figure 4.5). Although several large reserves were established in the DRC to preserve populations of okapi and other indigenous wild-life, enforcement of reserve boundaries and protection of species within the reserves was never secure. The situation grew worse due to high levels of human population growth and immigration of refugees into reserves and surrounding areas. Okapi populations declined as a result of slash-and-burn cultivation and subsequent forest succession associated with such human population growth that occurred around and within the reserve. To make matters worse, the government of the DRC was destabilized by civil war and the incursions of neighboring countries, which backed rebel forces. For several years during the 1990s, rebels controlled most of the eastern portion of DRC, where the reserves are located. During this period the headquarters of three of the four most important reserves were looted, technical equipment and vehicles were stolen, and park guards were killed. In the face of such instability, conservation funding from Western organizations declined, crippling the budgets that supported these reserves and their conservation efforts.[18] DRC enjoyed some relative stability from 2003 to 2007, but in October 2008 more unrest and civil war erupted. No nature preserves are secure in DRC at this time.

GLOBAL LAND ACQUISITION STRATEGIES FOR BIODIVERSITY CONSERVATION

Lack of government stability and enforcement capacity are not the only problems plaguing the current global reserve system. A second constellation of problems centers around the conflict of conservation objectives and strategies used by major conservation organizations and international organizations in selecting which areas to conserve. We can place most global biodiversity conservation strategies in one of three categories. One group of strategies, such as the Biodiversity Hotspot approach employed by organizations like Conservation International, target regions of high biodiversity and high vulnerability to human development. This strategy tends to maximize the number of species protected per given unit of area, but does not necessarily protect those

---

[18]A variety of published sources have provided an overall picture of what happened to nature preserves in DRC. These are summarized in Van Dyke, *Conservation Biology*, p. 196.

species that are most at risk of extinction, which sometimes occurs in areas of lower biodiversity.

A second kind of strategy focuses on what could be called "irreplaceable regions." Although a Hotspot approach incorporates some elements of this strategy, it is more explicit in examples like the Global 200 Ecoregions approach employed by the World Wildlife Fund.[19] The aim of Global 200 Ecoregions is to ensure that the world's full range of ecosystems is represented in the global reserve system. Here the criterion for site selection is not species diversity, but ecosystem uniqueness and overall representation, with the assumption that, if all major world ecosystems are protected in a global preserve system, all of the Earth's species will be too. A more species-specific version of this strategy is the "Endemic Bird Areas" approach employed by BirdLife International.[20] BirdLife targets its conservation dollars on protecting areas that contain large numbers of bird species unique to the protected area (endemic species). This strategy ensures that areas with the most "unique" bird species will be preserved, but endemic species and endangered species are not always the same things. Species endemism and endangerment do not always correlate with the endemic species and endangered species of other plant or animal groups. In an analysis on rare and endangered species of high conservation priority, Conservation scientist Richard Grenyer of the Royal Botanic Gardens at Kew (U.K.) and his colleagues studied the relationship between distributions of species in birds, mammals and amphibians and found that, although there was correlation in species richness patterns, the relationship was much weaker for rare and threatened species, especially for the very rarest species.[21]

A third group of strategies places emphasis on areas of low vulnerability to human impact (a sort of "last best places" approach). Here the strategy, exemplified in an approach like the "Last of the Wild" program of the Wildlife Conservation Society (WCS), places conservation priority on protecting the largest and least degraded (wilderness) areas

---

[19]WWF, "List of Ecoregions," <www.panda.org/about_our_earth/ecoregions/ecoregion_list/>.
[20]BirdLife International, "Endemic Bird Areas," <www.birdlife.org/action/science/endemic_bird_areas/index.html>.
[21]Richard Grenyer et.al., "Global Distribution and Conservation of Rare and Endangered Vertebrates," *Nature 444* (2006): 93-96.

on Earth.[22] This strategy has the advantage, when successful, of preserving areas that retain most or all of their functional ecosystem characteristics and functions with minimal degradation. As a result, species within such areas are unlikely to be at risk from the kind of ecosystem degradation that affects areas experiencing higher human impact. The drawback is that remaining wilderness areas, especially in the northern hemisphere, often have low levels of species diversity compared to even more highly impacted areas in tropical regions.

Without descending into cynicism toward these genuine efforts at biodiversity conservation, we must face an important reality in all of these approaches. The biodiversity conservation strategies used by global conservation organizations are not solely designed to save species. They also are designed, like well-managed political campaigns, to give donors, especially large donors, clear targets for their donations. In this respect, all of these strategies are effective as donor-motivating and fund-raising tools. Unfortunately, they are not effective in producing a coherent set of goals for world biodiversity conservation. For example, strategies that prioritize the same thing, such as high vulnerability, tend to place priority of conservation effort on many of the same areas, but those that prioritize different things (for example, irreplaceability versus vulnerability) have much less overlap in their selection of priority conservation areas. As a result, 79 percent of all land on Earth ends up being prioritized in at least one of these systems.[23] To conserve all of this land would be a hopelessly unrealistic goal in a world with over 6 billion human beings. Confusion also results because different strategies require different tactics. A strategy that prioritizes wilderness areas can use landscape level management practices over large areas applied for long time periods. A strategy that prioritizes irreplaceability and threat must act quickly and effectively at specific sites. As already noted, global conservation priority strategies are good at raising money because they offer identifiable targets that attract large donors. These same strategies, however, often fail to inform or affect actual conservation management and implementation because they are, in fact, not designed to address it.

---

[22]Wildlife Conservation Society, "Where We Work," <www.wcs.org/where-we-work.aspx>.
[23]T. M. Brooks et al., "Global Biodiversity Conservation Priorities," *Science* 313 (2006): 58-61.

Financial incentives for biodiversity conservation. As we can see in the array of approaches to global conservation, most strategies to preserve biodiversity are about land use. One approach is for a government or conservation organization to purchase land outright, with all accompanying property rights, in order to maintain its natural biodiversity. But given the limits of financial resources in even the largest governments, not to mention private organizations, outright purchase will be useful only for a small number of the highest priority areas. It will never provide enough "room" to fully conserve global biodiversity. An alternative approach is to purchase or in some way appropriate certain property rights associated with such land, even while it remains under the ownership of someone or something else. By restricting some forms of land use, biodiversity can be conserved without direct land purchase. Zoning is one of the oldest and most basic forms of such property rights restrictions, and it can be an extremely effective tool in biodiversity conservation.

Zoning is an arrangement in which some of the property rights normally associated with the individual owner of a property are transferred to or held by the community in which the property is located, effectively restricting what individual property owners can do on their property because of the context in which the property is located. This tactic represents a kind of "police power" of the public to regulate "external" costs associated with the individual decisions of private landowners. Thus, if a community zones an area around its town as "open space" or "native prairie," the community is specifying a land use that will protect biodiversity that no private landowner can violate.

Conservation easements are a special kind of land use zoning, applied specifically to conservation, and have been developed to make the value of conservation on private land more explicit and more profitable to landowners. In an easement, the landowner agrees to restrict some activities or forms of development on his or her land to achieve specific conservation goals, such as habitat protection or biodiversity conservation. Such restrictions lower the assessed value of the land, generating a reduction in property taxes for the owner and a reduction in inheritance taxes for the owner's heirs. The owner, however, retains possession, residence and non-prohibited activities, and legal title to the land. Conservation easements work because they provide incentives for conservation by private citizens on their own land, and they permit management objectives that focus on the biological and community-based integrity rather than on individual species.

A more explicit collection of strategies that uses financial incentives for biodiversity conservation is the so-called *direct payment* (DP) or *payments for environmental services* (PES) schemes. PES approaches are voluntary, conditional agreements between at least one "seller" and one "buyer" with regard to a well-defined environmental service or, less directly, to a land use presumed to produce that service.[24] PES strategies usually aim at short-term results, and can often achieve them because they combine performance indicators with explicit assumptions and informed consent of all parties. For example, one category of PES schemes for biodiversity conservation is various forms of *international habitat reserve programs* (IHRPs). An IHRP is a system of institutional arrangements that facilitates conservation contracting through multiple individuals or groups that supply ecosystem services. The contracts specify that the outside agents will make periodic performance payments to local resident landowners if a targeted ecosystem remains intact or if target levels of wildlife or biodiversity are found in the ecosystem.[25]

Some of the most effective direct-payment programs can be found in countries where governments have developed high capacities for administration and enforcement of conservation programs. In Canada, the United States and much of western Europe, federal governments provide financial incentives to farmers to keep land out of agricultural production or shift it to alternative uses, thereby reducing the supply of agricultural commodities and augmenting the supply of environmental services. In Europe, 14 nations spent an estimated $11 billion from 1993-1997 to divert over 20 million hectares (ha) of land into long-term set-aside and forestry contracts. In the United States, the Conservation Reserve Program spends about $1.5 billion annually on contracts for

[24]Swen Wunder, "The Efficiency of Payments for Environmental Services in Tropical Conservation," *Conservation Biology* 21 (2007): 48-58.
[25]Ibid.

12-15 million ha, an area twice the size of all national and state wildlife refuges in the lower 48 states. Similarly, the U.S. Wetland Reserve Program (WRP) provides for direct payments of subsidies to farmers who remove cropland from production in formerly wetland areas and then return the removed area to its original wetland state.[26] Each of these programs, rightly managed and applied, can effectively conserve important elements of regional and national biodiversity.

A similar approach can work in developing countries. For example, Costa Ricans have created institutional mechanisms through which local, national and international beneficiaries of ecosystem services compensate those who protect ecosystems. Costa Rica's Forestry Law recognizes four ecosystem services: carbon fixation and sequestration, hydrological services, biodiversity protection and scenic beauty. The law gives landowners opportunity to be compensated for developing and implementing land use management plans that ensure provision of these services. Funds for the program come from the National Forestry Financial Fund, sources for which include fuel taxes and direct payments from other countries.[27]

ESTABLISHING THE FOUNDATIONAL VALUE OF BIODIVERSITY

In their landmark paper, "The Death of Environmentalism," authors Michael Shellenberger and Ted Nordhaus assert, "What the environmental movement needs more than anything else right now is to take a collective step back to re-think everything. We will never be able to turn things around as long as we understand our failures as essentially tactical and make proposals that are essentially technical."[28] Traditional "goal-rational" approaches to biodiversity conservation have emphasized technical competency and assumed that the rewards that motivate such conservation must be financial and instrumental. The problem with this approach is that it consistently fails to frame biodiversity con-

---

[26]Van Dyke, *Conservation Biology*, p. 410.
[27]Paul J. Ferraro, "Global Habitat Protection: Limitations of Development Interventions and a Role for Conservation Performance Payments," *Conservation Biology* 15 (2001): 990-1000.
[28]Michael Shellenberger and Ted Nordhaus, "The Death of Environmentalism: Global Warming Policies In a Post-Environmental World," <http://thebreakthrough.org/PDF/Death_of_Environmentalism.pdf>.

servation as a moral endeavor. Without a moral framework, even the most elaborate payment "schemes," such as those described previously, will fail to make a lasting impact. The problem of conservation's moral vacuity is increasingly attracting the attention of environmental ethicists, such as Kyle Van Houtan, who assert that "to succeed as a social cause conservation needs a hope that academic science itself cannot provide. Conservation needs a cultural legitimacy that inspires enthusiasm, allegiance, and personal sacrifice—in other words, actual changes in human behavior."[29]

To be successful in the long run, the conservation of biodiversity cannot simply be a clever combination of technical expertise and tactical strategy. For this kind of success to occur, biodiversity conservation must be embedded in a system of values that can provide warranted affirmation for the intrinsic value of the biodiversity that is conserved, one that can name the human actions needed to achieve biodiversity conservation as virtues rooted in transcendent goals and purposes, not simply enlightened self-interest. Without such moral grounding, the conservation of biodiversity will remain, for most people, an interesting but irrelevant distraction from the real business of human life. In the next chapter, Daniel Block explains the foundation of a comprehensive and transcendent basis for biodiversity valuation, the value of biodiversity within a biblical Judeo-Christian tradition.

---

[29]Kyle Van Houtan, "Conservation as Virtue: A Scientific and Social Process for Conservation Ethics," *Conservation Biology* 20 (2006): 1371 [1367-72].

5

TO SERVE AND TO KEEP

Toward a Biblical Understanding of Humanity's
Responsibility in the Face of the Biodiversity Crisis

Daniel I. Block

INTRODUCTION: BIODIVERSITY IN BIBLICAL PERSPECTIVE

The Scriptures place a high stock in non-human life in general and biological diversity in particular. The Bible contains 110 plant names.[1]
Some of these are generic expressions,[2] and some represent different
words for the same or similar plants,[3] but the rest refer to a wide variety
of specific plants. The same may be said of animals.[4] While some of the
over two hundred Old Testament terms for animals serve as generic
expressions for more than one species,[5] and several different expressions
are used for some animals,[6] the majority represent designations for dif-

---

[1]Thus Michael Zohary, *Plants of the Bible* (Cambridge: Cambridge University Press, 1982), p. 14.

[2]For example, *śîaḥ*, "wild shrub"; *ʿēśeb*, "grass"; *dešeʾ*, "green vegetation"; *ʿēṣ*, "tree."

[3]The Bible contains twenty names for thorns. For further discussion of the names for plants, see Zohary, *Plants of the Bible*, pp. 14-15.

[4]According to Peter Riede, *Im Spiegel der Tiere: Studien zum Verhältnis von Mensch und Tier im Alten Testament*, OBO 187 (Göttingen: Vandenhoeck & Ruprecht, 2002), p. 170, the Old Testament contains ca. 208 designations for animals, of which 90 are mammals, 42 are birds. Edwin Firmage, "Zoology (Animal Names in the Bible)," *ABD* 1.1151-59, lists 118 biblical Hebrew designations for animals.

[5]For example, *ḥayyâ*, "animal, wild animal," in the expression *ḥayyat haśśādeh*, "animal of the field"; *běhēmâ*, high carriage animal, especially domesticated, as opposed to wild animals; *ʿôp*, "flying creature," used of birds, insects and bats; *dāg/dāʾ ĝ*, used indiscriminately of sea creatures; *remeś*, "creeping creatures, low carriage animals."

[6]For example, lion (*ʾaryēh* / *layiš* / *lābîʾ* / *šaḥal* / *kĕpîr*), locust (*ʾarbeh* / *ṣĕlāṣal* / *ḥargōl* / *ḥāgāb* / *gāzām* / *gōbay*). Whether these expressions designate different species or different stages of development in a limited number of species is unclear. So also Firmage, "Zoology," p. 1159 n. 67.

ferent kinds of animals. And these lists of terms are obviously incomplete. Although elephants are never mentioned in the Bible, the numerous references to ivory[7] demonstrate an awareness of these creatures.

The creation account in Genesis 1 reflects a clear taxonomy of animal species divided into four categories: creatures of the sea, flying creatures of the sky, [high carriage] animals,[8] and "crawlies" that crawl on the ground (Gen 1:26, a literal rendering of the Hebrew).[9] The prohibition of the manufacture of images in Deuteronomy 4:17-18 represents the same four-fold division of the animal kingdom: (a) "any animal that is on the earth"; (b) "any bird of wing that flies in the sky"; (c) "any creeper on the ground"; (4) "any fish that is in the water" (author's translations). The categories are not based on the creatures' physical or biological characteristics, but on their spheres of existence, the vertical relationships of which are illustrated diagrammatically in figure 5.1.

Figure 5.1. **The fourfold division of animals and their spheres of existence**

The dietary instructions of Leviticus 11:2-23, 29-31 and Deuteronomy 14:4-20 provide more detailed information on ancient Israel's taxonomy of creaturely life. Although Lev 11:29-31 adds a class of low-carriage land animals that "swarm on the ground," both lists of clean and unclean animals follow the traditional taxonomy (see table 5.1).[10] Specifically Deuteronomy

---

[7]1 Kings 10:18, 22; 22:39; 2 Chron 9:17, 21; Ps 45:8; Song 5:14; 7:4; Ezek 27:6, 15; Amos 3:15; 6:4.

[8]Here *běhēmâ* represents both non-threatening high carriage animals (equids, bovines, caprovines) and wild animals (Gen 1:24; dangerous ursines, canines and felines).

[9]See also Psalm 148. For a discussion of these and other taxonomies see Richard Whitekettle, "Where the Wild Things Are: Primary Level Taxa in Israelite Zoological Thought," *JSOT* 93 (2001): 17-37; Riede, *Im Spiegel der Tiere*, pp. 216-19.

[10]Many of the names are uncertain. See Riede, *Im Spiegel der Tiere*, pp. 200-8.

Land Animals[1]				Low Carriage Land Animals	Aquatic Animals			Aerial Animals		Winged Insects	
Ruminants		**Non-ruminants**			**Finned**		**Non-finned**	**Clean**	**Unclean**	**Swarming Insects**	**Clean**
Split hooves	Non-split hooves	Split / Non-split hooves	Paws		Scaled	Non-Scaled					
ALL[2]	ALL				ALL	ALL	ALL	ALL	ALL	ALL	ALL
ox	camel	pig (Split hooves)	cat	*weasel*	fish	*dolphin*	*octopus*	*quail*	*eagle*[4]	*bees*	*locusts*
sheep	hare	*donkey*[3] (Non-split)	lion	*rat*		*seal*	*crab*	*dove*	*vulture*	*bugs*	*grasshoppers*
goat	hyrax	*horse* (Non-split)	dog	*any large lizard*		*sharks*	*lobster*	*chicken*	*black vulture*	*ants*	
deer			hyena	*gecko*		*catfish*	*eel*	*[turtledove]*	*red kite*	*flies*	
gazelle			bear	*monitor lizard*		*sturgeon*	*mussels*	Lev. 12:6	*falcon*	*moths*	
roe deer				*wall lizard*			*shrimp*		*raven*		
wild goat				*skink*					*ostrich*		
ibex				*chameleon*					*screech owl*		
antelope									*gull*		
mountain sheep									*hawk*		
									little owl		
									great owl		
									white owl		
									desert owl		
									osprey		
									cormorant		
									stork		
									heron		
									hoopoe		
									bat		

[1] Deuteronomy 14 mentions only high carriage land animals. Leviticus 11:29-31 adds the class of low carriage land animals that "swarm on the ground." Leviticus 11:10-11 refers to corresponding aquatic "swarmers."

[2] Underlined: permitted as food.

[3] Italic font: examples, not named in Leviticus 11 or Deuteronomy 14.

[4] The identity of some of these birds is uncertain.

Table 5.1. Clean and unclean animals according to Leviticus 11 and Deuteronomy 14

14:4-20 recognizes four broad categories of animals: high carriage land animals (vv. 4-8), sea creatures (vv. 9-10), birds (vv. 11-18),[11] and insects, which are divided into unclean insects (lit. "swarmers of fliers," v. 19)[12] and edible (clean) insects (v. 20).[13] The relationship between the categories in Leviticus 11 and Deuteronomy 14 and modern designations may be compared by isolating the gazelle and juxtaposing the classifications as follows in table 5.2.

Table 5.2. A Comparative Taxonomy

Category	Scientific Name	Hebrew Designation
Kingdom	Animalia	*ḥayyâ* (animal)
Phylum	Chordata	
Class	Mammalia	*bĕhēmâ* (high carriage land mammal)
Order	Artiodactyla	*mapreset parsâ wĕšōsaʿat šesaʿ pĕrāsôt* (divided and cleft of hoof)
Family	Bovidae	*maʿălat gērâ* (chews the cud, ruminant)
Subfamily	Antilopinae	
Genus	*Gazella*	
Species	*G. arabica***	*ṣĕbî* (gazelle)

*The exact identity of *ṣĕbî* is uncertain. *G. arabica* is a good guess, but other possibilities include *G. gazella, G. dorcas,* or *G. subgutturosa.* See Oded Borowski, *Every Living Thing: Daily Use of Animals in Ancient Israel* (Walnut Creek, Calif.: AltaMira, 1998), p. 187.

Whereas hooves and ruminant stomachs provide the bases for division of high carriage animals, sea creatures are divided into groups that have fins and scales and those that do not. Apparently unclean animals would include sea mammals like dolphins and whales, as well as octopus, catfish and shrimp. Birds ("sky fliers") seem to be divided on the basis of their eating habits: carnivorous birds (whether predators or those that eat carrion) and those that eat grains. Deuteronomy 14:19

---

[11]Cf. Deut 4:17, where the expression *ṣippôr kānāp,* "bird of wing."

[12]Elsewhere *šereṣ,* "swarmer," identifies primarily swarming insects and aquatic creatures and *remeś,* "creeping thing," low carriage mammals and small reptiles. Cf. *NIDOTTE,* 3.1127-28.

[13]Hebrew *ʿôp* derives from *ʿûp,* "to fly." In Deut 28:26 and elsewhere the full expression, *ʿôp haš-šāmayim,* refers to "birds of the sky." Gen 1:21 refers to birds as *ʿôp kānāp,* "bird of wing." The general designation *šereṣ hāʿôp,* "swarmers of fliers," followed by a list of edible locusts in Lev 11:20-23 confirms that in Deut 14:20 *ʿôp* denotes flying insects rather than birds.

seems to exclude all winged insects (*šereṣ hāʿ ôp*, "swarmers that fly"),
though Leviticus 11:20-23 distinguishes winged insects with four feet[14]
from winged insects with jointed legs and that hop (crickets, locusts,
grasshoppers),[15] which are edible. Although not specified, Deuteronomy 14:20 involves the latter.

Whereas scientists today classify species according to anatomical
features, behaviors, breeding patterns and similarities in genome, biblical classifications are based on phenomenological observations. To the
ancient Israelites and their ancient Near Eastern neighbors, creaturely
spheres of existence and animals' diets were more significant than the
boundaries we recognize between cold and warm-blooded animals or
feathered and furry creatures.

If the inanimate and voiceless heavens declare the glory of God (Ps
19:1), how much more do all living things.[16] The degradation of the
environment through loss of vegetation or animal life robs the cosmic
choir of voices to praise Yahweh.[17] Perhaps this is the key to the eschatological hope of creation. As Doug Moo argues in the opening chapter
of this volume, the pervasive anthropocentric understanding of the divine program of redemption needs to be revised. The significance of
the incarnation and the cross extends beyond the reconciliation this
achieves between God and humanity to reconciliation with the rest of
the created world. If inanimate creation groans with pain because of
corruption brought on it by human rebellion against God, and awaits
liberation into the freedom of the glory of the children of God (Rom
8:18-23), how much more the living world. Surely Paul includes these
in his reference to "all things," "whether on earth or in heaven," that are
reconciled to God who has made peace through the blood of Christ's
cross (Col 1:20). Without restoring the "fullness" of creation, the fullness of the curse is not removed. The conclusion to the description of
the new heavens and new earth in Isaiah 65:17-25 focuses on the effects

---

[14]Even though all insects have six, some have two dominant pairs of legs.

[15]These general categories carry over into the New Testament (Acts 10:12; 11:6).

[16]In Luke 19:40, Jesus raises the possibility of stones crying out if the praises of people are
stifled.

[17]On the voices of living things, both vegetation and animals, giving praise to Yahweh, see
Psalms 65:12-13 [vv. 13-14 Heb.]; 96:11-12; 98:7-8; 148:7-10; 150:6.

of Yahweh's renewal of the cosmos on the creatures:

> "The wolf and the lamb shall feed together, the lion shall eat straw like
> the ox; but the serpent—its food shall be dust! They shall not hurt or
> destroy on all my holy mountain," says the LORD. (Is 65:25)

Although this declaration does not speak explicitly to the issue of
biodiversity, it paints a representative picture of reconciliation even
among the animals, with the result that wolves and lambs graze together, and serpents eat dust rather than scurrying creatures. When
Yahweh restores this harmony among the creatures, predators will cease
their predation and dangerous animals will be tamed. In so doing they,
along with the plants of the field and the trees of the forest, will join
their voices in praise to God.

John envisions a quartet of living creatures around the heavenly
throne[18] that offer ceaseless praise to God (Rev 4:6-9; 5:8-12, 14; 7:11-
12; 19:4), and serve as the Lamb's agents (Rev 6:1; 15:7) and as inter-
mediaries between the redeemed and the Lamb (Rev 14:3). The inclusion of these creatures with the twenty-four elders before the throne
and the Lamb suggests they represent redeemed creation. The four
creatures were all different, resembling an ox, a lion, an eagle and a human being, all selected for their links with royalty. While sea and neth-
erworldly creatures are not represented among the four, the four creatures represent the four corners of the earth. Whatever their function
in Revelation 5:13, John declares expressly that he heard "every creature
in heaven and on earth and under the earth and in the sea, and all that
is in them," saying, "To the one seated on the throne and to the Lamb
be blessing and honor and glory and might forever and ever!" This vision of a redeemed cosmos includes all creatures, with all their territorial and biological diversity, giving eternal praise to the Creator.

HUMANITY'S RESPONSIBILITY IN THE
FACE OF THE BIODIVERSITY CRISIS

What can this high stock in non-human life in general and biological
diversity in particular teach us about human responsibility in the face

---

[18]Rev 4:6, 8-9; 5:6, 8, 11, 14; 6:1, 6; 7:11; 14:3; 15:7; 19:4.

of the biodiversity crisis facing the world today? Many species have already disappeared and the number considered endangered or vulnerable grows daily. From a biblical perspective, this means that the voices of more and more creatures and plants are eliminated, and that the harmony in the cosmic symphony of praise to God is diminished.[19] All of these have intrinsic value,[20] based upon their origin in the creative work of God and their roles as objects of God's affection and sustaining care. However, contemporary attitudes toward ecological crises in general and the threats to life in particular are seldom based on biblical foundations. Even Christians' attitudes tend to be grounded more in utilitarian,[21] aesthetic,[22] and dominionistic[23] values than in the theistic values of Scripture. At best we are concerned about "phenomenologically significant animals,"[24] that is, "species that are large, aesthetically attractive, phylogenetically similar to human beings, and regarded as possessing the capacities for feeling, thought, and pain,"[25] and at worst

---

[19]See also Ruth Page, "The Fellowship of All Creation," in *Environmental Stewardship: Critical Perspectives—Past and Present*, ed. R. J. Berry (New York: T & T Clark, 2006), pp. 97-105.

[20]So also Andrew Linzey, *Animal Theology* (Urbana: University of Illinois Press, 1995), p. 108; Robert N. Wennberg, *God, Humans, and Animals: An Invitation to Enlarge Our Moral Universe* (Grand Rapids: Eerdmans, 2003), p. 194. See the discussion of intrinsic value in Judeo-Christian tradition, by Fred Van Dyke, *Conservation Biology: Foundations, Concepts, Applications*, 2nd ed. (Dordrecht, The Netherlands: Springer, 2008), pp. 39-44.

[21]Van Dyke defines these as "values associated with species as sources of material benefit of use," primarily for human beings. See Van Dyke, *Conservation Biology*, p. 35, for a detailed discussion of the attitudes that North Americans have toward wildlife (pp. 30-55).

[22]"Values associated with the species' possession of beauty or other perceived qualities admired by humans." Thus ibid., p. 35.

[23]"Values associated with the mastery and control of animals, typically through sport." Thus ibid.

[24]An expression coined by Paul Shepherd Jr., *Thinking Animals* (New York: Viking, 1978), p. 233. For a more recent edition of the book see idem, *Thinking Animals: Animals and the Development of Human Intelligence* (Athens: University of Georgia Press, 1998). This approach underlies Martha Nussbaum's "capabilities approach," which suggests sentient animals, which appear to communicate and experience pain and feeling, deserve greater protection than lower forms. See Martha Nussbaum, "Animal Rights: The Need for a Theoretical Basis," in a review of *Rattling the Cage: Toward Legal Rights for Animals* (Cambridge, Mass.: Perseus Books, 2000) in *Harvard Law Review* 114 (2001): 1506. Wennberg, *God, Humans, and Animals*, pp. 54-57, rejects the sentient approach and advocates a "doctrine of gradations in intrinsic value" as basis for a living thing's claim to moral consideration and concern.

[25]Thus Stephen R. Kellert, "Social and Perceptual Factors in Endangered Species Management," *The Journal of Wildlife Management* 49 (1985): 533; also available in "Social and Perceptual Factors in the Preservation of Animal Species," in *The Preservation of Species: The Value of Biological Diversity*, ed. B. G. Norton (Princeton, N.J.: Princeton University Press, 1986), pp. 50-73.

we are accomplices in self-interested destructive exploitation of the earth's natural resources.[26] Of course, Christians are not alone in their anthropocentrism. Rabbi Bunam, the Hasidic teacher, said, "A man should carry two stones in his pocket. On one should be inscribed, 'I am but dust and ashes.' On the other, 'For my sake was the world created.' And he should use each stone as he needs it."[27]

But how does one develop a thoroughly biblical disposition toward the matter, especially in the face of the apparent silence of the Scriptures on the ecological crises we face today? Even if the Scriptures do not speak directly to these issues, they provide a perspective with which to examine and evaluate them. We will respond to the issue with three basic propositions.

Proposition 1: The primary cosmic relationships involve God, the world and all life on the earth. The picture we have painted above involves a triangular relationship that may be portrayed diagrammatically in figure 5.2.

From the beginning God intended a trialogical symbiotic relationship in which each of the members responds to the other two in a dynamic covenantal relationship.[28] In

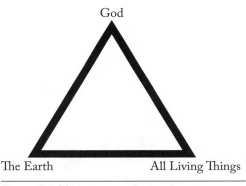

Figure 5.2. The covenantal triangle

[26]An accusation leveled at Christianity in Lynn White's famous article, "The Historical Roots of Our Ecological Crisis," *Science* 155 (1967): 1203-7. Thomas B. Dozeman rightly observes that to the extent that White's thesis holds, its truth lies in the history of interpretation rather than in the biblical texts themselves. See Thomas B. Dozeman, "Creation and Environment in the Character Development of Moses," in *Character Ethics and the Old Testament: Moral Dimensions of Scripture*, ed. M. D. Carroll R. and J. E. Lapsley (Louisville, Ky.: Westminster John Knox, 2007), p. 33.

[27]As cited by Robert Gordis, *The Book of God and Man* (Chicago: University of Chicago Press, 1965), p. 131.

[28]My perspective differs slightly from that of Christopher Wright, who has God, humanity and the earth at the apexes of the triangle. See Christopher J. H. Wright, *Old Testament Ethics for the People of God* (Downers Grove, Ill.: InterVarsity Press, 2004), pp. 182-86. Terence E. Fretheim, *God and World in the Old Testament: A Relational Theology of Creation* (Nashville: Abingdon, 2005), pp. 13-22, tends to underplay both the covenantal nature of the relationship and

this relationship God's sovereignty over the whole is clearly expressed in several ways: (1) He is the creator of the earth and its inhabitants.[29] (2) He is the acknowledged owner of the earth[30] and its fullness, that is, all living things.[31] (3) He determines how the other two function within this relationship. He relates to the left apex by watering the earth so plants may grow and nourish the animals,[32] or cursing the ground[33] and turning off the rains.[34] He relates to the right apex by feeding the creatures,[35] or by withholding food and withdrawing his animating breath.[36] Indeed, within the creation narrative itself, God blesses the earth, energizing it with his performative word to produce all kinds of vegetation (Gen 1:11-12). He also energizes the waters to swarm with living creatures, the sky to come alive with birds (Gen 1:20-21), and the earth to produce all kinds of land creatures (Gen 1:24-25). In the end he blesses the creatures themselves and charges them to multiply and fill the earth (Gen 1:22).

Although the word "covenant" *(běrît)* is lacking in Genesis 1, the relationship between God and his created world appears covenantal. In this environment, God, the divine Suzerain, creates the vassals specially to participate in this covenant relationship.[37] Blessings and curses, which were fundamental elements in ancient Near Eastern suzerainty treaties, are evident in Genesis 1:11-12, 20-21, 24, which speak implicitly of the blessing of earth, and in Genesis 1:22, where God blesses the creatures explicitly, adding the covenantal stipulation that the creatures multiply and fill the earth. Neither Genesis 1 nor 2 alludes to a curse should the earth or the life that fills it fail to fulfill their obligations.

God's absolute sovereignty within this relationship, but his work offers a helpful corrective to anthropocentric and docetic perceptions of the cosmos, common especially in evangelicalism.

[29]Gen 1:1–2:4; Ex 20:11; Neh 9:6; etc.

[30]Ex 9:29; 19:5; Deut 10:14; Ps 24:1; 89:11 [v. 12 Heb.]; 1 Cor 10:26.

[31]Deut 10:14; Job 41:11; Ps 24:1; 50:12; 104:24.

[32]Lev 26:4; Deut 11:14; 28:12; Job 37:1-13; Ps 65:9-13 [vv. 10-14 Heb.]; 104:10-17; Ezek 34:26-27; Heb 6:7.

[33]Gen 3:17-19; 5:29.

[34]Lev 26:19-20; Deut 11:17; 28:23-24; Heb 6:8.

[35]Job 38:39-41; Ps 104:27-30; 136:25; 145:14-16.

[36]Job 12:10; 34:14-15; Ps 104:29.

[37]Contra Paul R. Williamson, "Covenant," in *Dictionary of the Old Testament: Pentateuch*, ed. David W. Baker and T. Desmond Alexander (Downers Grove, Ill.: InterVarsity Press, 2003), pp. 141-43. The language of suzerain and vassal is derived from ancient Near Eastern diplomatic texts.

However, by the end of Genesis 3, we have clearly arrived in a cursed world. The curse upon the serpent (Gen 3:14-15) suggests that the creatures were to be satisfied with their created form and sphere of existence, and that they were not to operate contrary to their vassal status. In twisting the significance of the Tree of the Knowledge of Good and Evil and promising the woman god-likeness, the serpent overstepped its divinely established boundaries, for which it was demoted from the status of the most clever among all the animals[38] to the most cursed among the creatures, both domestic and wild.[39] Although God did not expressly curse the man and the woman, because of their actions, he cursed the earth itself. Whereas earlier the earth had spontaneously yielded all kinds of plants pleasing to the eye and good for food, as a consequence of human rebellion, the earth would produce plants that would actively resist human efforts to cultivate the soil by producing thorns and thistles and yield its food unwillingly (Gen 3:17-19).

In the narrative describing the aftermath of the Great Flood in Genesis 8:20–9:17 the covenantal relationship between God and his creation becomes explicit. First Yahweh promises never again to curse the ground or to destroy every living thing because of human sin, and he guarantees the cosmic order in perpetuity (Gen 8:21-22; cf. Gen 9:11).[40] Second, he protects creatures from human beings by instilling in animals innate fear toward them (Gen 9:2). Third, while formally authorizing human consumption of animal flesh, he declares the sanctity of all animal life (Gen 9:3-4). Fourth, he calls on creatures to recognize humankind's status as his image, and prohibits them from taking the lives of human beings (Gen 9:5-6). Having made this declaration, God announces the establishment[41] of his cosmic covenant not only with

---

[38]In the wisdom writings the term *ʿārûm*, "crafty, shrewd, prudent" represents a virtue to be cultivated by the wise (Prov 12:16; 13:16).

[39]The Hebrew statement rendered, "You are cursed more than all the livestock and than all the wild animals," assumes a curse upon all land creatures. Cf. Rom 8:19-22.

[40]See Ronald A. Simkins, *Creator & Creation: Nature in the Worldview of Ancient Israel* (Peabody, Mass.: Hendrickson, 1994), pp. 152-54, following L. Dequeker, "Noah and Israel: The Everlasting Divine Covenant with Mankind," in *Questions disputées d'Ancien Testament: Méthode et Théologie*, ed. C. Brekelmans, BETL 33 (Leuven: Leuven University Press, 1974), pp. 115-29, in arguing for the implicit covenant in Gen 8:20-22.

[41]The use of *hāqîm běrît*, "to establish a covenant," rather than *kārat běrît*, "to cut/make a covenant," in Gen 9:9, 11, 17 (cf. also Gen 6:18) suggests the confirmation of a pre-existent cov-

Noah and his descendants, but also with every living creature of "all flesh that is on the earth" (Gen 9:17; cf. Gen 9:11, 15). God's relationship with the world and all that lives on it is primary.

Proposition 2: Human beings were created to serve the primary relationship, that is, God's covenant relationship with the cosmos. The narratives of Genesis 1–2 emphasize that human beings are earthlings: (1) They are one with land animals, which were also created on day six (Gen 1:24-31). (2) They share the divine blessing and the mandate to multiply and fill the earth (Gen 1:22, 28). (3) They share vegetation as food with the animals (Gen 1:29-30). (4) The appellation for the human species, 'ādām, "humankind," derives from the same root as 'ădāmâ, the Hebrew word for "ground/land" (Gen 1:25; 2:5, 6). (5) Since they are made of "dust from the ground" (Gen 2:5-7), like the animals (cf. Gen 1:24; 2:19) human beings originate in the earth itself (Gen 2:7). (6) They share with animals the breath of life and the generic classification as a *nepeš ḥayyâ,* "living creature" (Gen 2:7; cf. Gen 1:20, 21, 24). As earthlings, human beings participate in the covenant that God made with the earth and its living things.

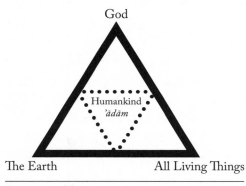

Figure 5.3. The place of humankind within the covenantal triangle

However, it also is clear from the narratives that humankind is not simply one among equals. Their special status role within creation may be illustrated in figure 5.3.

Although humans *('ādām)* are earthlings along with the rest of the creatures, the creation narratives demonstrate that their arrival represented the climax of the creation week: (1) 'ādām was created last. (2) 'ādām was the product of divine deliberation. (3) The description of the

---

enant rather than the creation of a new arrangement. So also William J. Dumbrell, *Covenant and Creation: A Theology of the Old Testament Covenants* (Carlisle, U.K.: Paternoster, 1997), pp. 22-26.

creation of *'ādām* is more intensive and extensive than any other element of creation. (4) The verb used to describe the creation of *'ādām*, *bārā'*, always involves a special creative act of God (cf. Gen 1:1, 27 [3x]). (5) Once *'ādām* was on the scene Yahweh pronounced the created world extremely good (v. 31). (6) *'ādām* was expressly created as *ṣelem 'ĕlōhîm*, "the image of God" (Gen 1:26-28). But what does this special status mean for human beings and for the world?

In the past, theologians have tended to interpret humankind's status as *imago Dei* in ontological terms, that is, in terms of qualities we possess enabling us to relate to God or that make us like God (for example, spirituality, rationality, triunity).[42] However, based on the use of images outside Israel and the demands of the context of Genesis 1:26-31, "imageness" should be understood in more functional terms. Imageness has less to do with being representations of God (which concentrates on qualities) than with representing him (which concentrates on role). Although humans share many features with other creatures, as the images of God they are assigned a special role in the administration of the cosmic scheme.[43]

There is obvious overlap in the two expressions used in Genesis 1:26-27, "likeness" *(dĕmût)* and "image" *(ṣelem),* and many treat them as synonyms.[44] Based on biblical and extra-biblical evidence, Randall Garr suggests these expressions reflect the bi-fold nature of human relationships. As the "likeness" of God, humans stand before him dependent and petitionary, while before the world they function as theophanies, imitating God in perpetuity and registering "his everlasting presence in the world."[45] As the "image" of God, humans stand before

---

[42]For the history of interpretation see David J. A. Clines, "Humanity as the Image of God," *On the Way to the Postmodern: Old Testament Essays 1967-1998*, vol. 2, JSOTSup, 292 (Sheffield, U.K.: Sheffield Academic Press, 1998), pp. 447-56; Henri Blocher, *In the Beginning: The Opening Chapters of Genesis*, trans. D. G. Preston (Downers Grove, Ill.: InterVarsity Press, 1984), pp. 79-83.

[43]Clines, "Humanity as the Image of God," develops this position in detail.

[44]Nahum Sarna, *Genesis: The Traditional Text with the New JPS Translation*, JPS Torah Commentary (Philadelphia: Jewish Publication Society, 1989), p. 12, asserts the terms are used "indiscriminately and interchangeably."

[45]See W. Randall Garr, *In His Own Image and Likeness: Humanity, Divinity, and Monotheism*, CHANE 15 (Leiden: Brill, 2003), pp. 118-32. Earlier, Garr had argued that from the perspective of creation the notion of humankind as "image" connotes a majestic, absolute and

God as his vice regents, through whom he administers divine lordship and justice in the world.[46] As his images, God authorizes human beings to serve as his deputies and his representatives, commissioning them to care for the world as he would were he physically present. Although Psalm 8 is framed by enthusiastic praise to Yahweh, whose name is majestic in all the earth (i.e., who is the ultimate Sovereign over all), between these refrains the psalmist celebrates our status before God and before the world.[47] Yahweh has authorized human beings to rule over the rest of creation ("the works of your hands") and empowered them by crowning them with glory and majesty—qualities that characterize God himself.

As the image of God, humankind is charged to subdue and exercise dominion over all creation. The words *kābaš*, "to subdue," and *rādâ*, "to exercise dominion," are admittedly strong words, calling for an aggressive style of royal leadership.[48] To ensure that creation would respond to humanity's rule after the entrance of sin, Yahweh instilled a disposition of fear toward human beings in all the creatures (Gen 9:2). Although these expressions suggest control and occupation of the natural world, contrary to those who insist that Christianity is responsible for the current ecological crisis,[49] they do not justify autocratic, utilitarian and exploitative rule. Admittedly, in a fallen world authorization to lead often degenerates into exploitation, as if those who are led exist for the sake of the leaders.[50] This is how Hebrew narratives often portray leaders, whether they are kings like Rehoboam (1 Kings 12:6-15) or David (2 Sam 12:1-9), or the heads of households like Abraham (Gen 12:10-20; 20:1-7). However, this is a far cry from the biblical ideal, which insists that leaders exist for the sake of those led, rather than vice

---

commemorative figure, whereas from the perspective of divinity as "likeness" the posture is petitionary and directed at deity. See W. R. Garr, "'Image' and 'Likeness' in the Inscription from Tell Fakhariyeh," *IEJ* 50 (2000): 227-34.

[46]Garr, *In His Own Image and Likeness*, pp. 132-65.

[47]The structure of the psalm itself reflects the three-tiered administrative structure of the universe: the realm of God (Ps 8:1-3); the realm of humans (Ps 8:4-6); the realm of creatures (Ps 8:7-8).

[48]Garr, *In His Own Image and Likeness*, pp. 156-58, 172.

[49]See White, "Ecological Crisis."

[50]This is anticipated in the "curse" of the man and woman in Gen 3:16. After Genesis 3, responsible collaborative headship degenerates into exploitative and autocratic rule.

versa.[51] As images of God, human beings are to pattern their style of governing the world according to the model of the divine Shepherd in Psalm 23 (cf. 1 Pet 5:1-7), who provides for the sheep what they need (nourishment and rest), who stands by them in times of distress, who delights in their company, and whose agenda concerning them is expressed in the words "goodness, well-being" *(tôb)* and "faithful covenant commitment" *(hesed)*.[52] Psalm 72 portrays the ideal king as accountable to God, responsible for maintaining the covenant relationship between his subjects and God, and committed to establishing justice and protecting the weak.[53] And according to Deuteronomy 17:14-20 the primary role of the king in Israel was to embody and model covenant righteousness among the people.[54]

In charging humans to be fruitful and multiply and fill the earth (Gen 1:27), God arranges for human occupation to be co-extensive with the territories occupied by the animals. Whereas the animals would populate the far reaches of the earth with all their richness and diversity of species, God's design was for a single species of *Homo sapiens* to go where the animals go, thereby ensuring the operation of God's covenant with them worldwide.

Genesis 2 elaborates on humankind's status as image of God by assigning to humanity the role of royal gardener in the Garden of Eden.[55] After God had placed the man *(hā'ādām)* in the Garden of Eden, which was sufficient for the needs of every animal and human (Gen

---

[51]For further discussion, see Daniel I. Block, "Leader, Leadership, Old Testament," *The New Interpreter's Dictionary of the Bible*, ed. Katherine Doob Sakenfeld (Nashville: Abingdon, 2008), 3:620-26.

[52]The supreme example is Jesus Christ, the good Shepherd who gives his life for the sheep, in stark contrast to self-serving false shepherds (Jn 10:1-10; cf. Ezek 34:1-6). For similar interpretations of *kābaš* and *rādā* see James Barr, "Man and Nature—The Ecological Controversy and the Old Testament," *BJRL* 55 (1972): 9-32; Rodd, *Glimpses of a Strange Land*, p. 236; Wright, *Old Testament Ethics*, pp. 120-21; Fretheim, *God and World*, pp. 48-53.

[53]See further Walter Houston, "'And let them have dominion . . .' Biblical Views of Man in Relation to the Environmental Crisis," *Studia Biblica* 1 (1978): 161-84.

[54]See further Daniel I. Block, "The Burden of Leadership: The Mosaic Paradigm of Kingship (Deut. 17:14-20)," *BSac* 162 (2005): 259-78.

[55]On Adam as a royal gardener, see Manfred Hutter, "Adam als Gärtner und König (Gen 2,8.15)," *Biblische Zeitschrift* 30 (1986): 258-62. William P. Brown, *The Ethos of the Cosmos: The Genesis of Moral Imagination in the Bible* (Grand Rapids: Eerdmans, 1999), p. 269, observes that "the gardeners are the covenant keepers."

2:9), he charged him to serve and preserve the garden (Gen 2:15). Many have observed that elsewhere the verbs ʿābad, "to serve," and šāmar, "to keep, guard," speak of the service Levites render in the tabernacle.[56] Just as priests and Levites maintained the covenant relationship between Israel and God through their service in the tabernacle/temple, a microcosm of the world so the man was charged to serve and guard the garden, thereby ensuring the operation of Yahweh's covenant with the world in general and living things in the garden in particular.

However, the verb ʿābad demands further comment. Although many translations render the word as "till" or "cultivate," when used of cultivation, the object of the verb is usually "the ground" (hāʾădāmâ).[57] But a garden (gan) is more than soil. This garden consists of vegetation of all kinds (Gen 2:9), rivers (Gen 2:10-14), precious metals and gemstones (Gen 2:12), and all kinds of land and sky creatures (Gen 2:19-20). All these were within the purview of the charge to serve and preserve the garden. Strictly speaking the verb "to serve" assumes the subordination of the subject to the object.[58] Indeed, both verbs, "to serve" and "to keep, guard," demand that the subjects expend their efforts in the interests of and for the well-being of the object.[59] While the garden satisfied human aesthetic and utilitarian interests, the man was not placed there merely to indulge himself with its resources. On the contrary, the purpose clause of Genesis 2:15 reverses the roles; he was put into the garden to serve it and to guard it, presumably to protect it from inside and outside threats.[60]

The creation of the woman as a counterpart to the man also had the

---

[56]Num 3:7-8; 8:26; 18:5-6. See Wenham, *Genesis 1-15*, p. 67; G. K. Beale, *The Temple and the Church's Mission: A Biblical Theology of the Dwelling Place of God*, NSBT 17 (Downers Grove, Ill.: InterVarsity Press, 2004), pp. 66-70; John H. Walton, *Genesis*, NIVAC (Grand Rapids: Zondervan, 2001), pp. 192-93.

[57]Gen 2:5; 3:23; 4:2, 12; 2 Sam 9:10; Zech 13:5; Prov 12:11; 28:19. The closest analogue to the present construction occurs in Deut 28:39, where *kerem*, "vineyard," is the object of this verb.

[58]Similarly Fretheim, *God and World*, p. 53.

[59]Rightly recognized by Steven Bouma-Prediger, *For the Beauty of the Earth: A Christian Vision for Creation Care* (Grand Rapids: Baker, 2001), pp. 74, 154.

[60]Some argue that the world outside the garden was not a perfect paradise, but was characterized by predation and death (Wright, *Old Testament Ethics*, pp. 130-31), in which case the man's function was to protect the garden from the encroachment of the violence outside. Ironically, after Genesis 3, human beings constitute the greatest threat to the well-being of the cosmos. Cf. Gen 6:1-8.

interests of the garden in mind (Gen 2:18-25). Contextually, when God said, "It is not good for the man to be alone," and determined to provide him with a counterpart to serve as his assistant, he had in mind primarily the charge to serve and guard Eden. Assuming an ever expanding garden to accommodate the increasing numbers of animals and apparently eventually to envelop the entire world, the task of maintaining the covenant relationship between the earth, the creatures and God would be impossible for a single man. Besides the work overwhelming him, he could not be everywhere at the same time. Genesis 2 is silent on reproduction, but to accomplish that goal required an expanding human population, which necessitated a female counterpart for him. As the image of God, 'ādām is male and female (Gen 1:27).

In naming the animals the man exercised responsible leadership as the image of God. The procession of animals before him served several purposes: (1) the social function of proving that Adam was actually alone, lacking a counterpart among all the creatures; (2) an administrative function: through naming the creatures he exercised authority over them (cf. 2 Kings 23:34; 24:17; Dan 1:7); (3) an intellectual function, calling on Adam to examine each animal carefully, and then ascribe a name based on the characteristics of the creature; and (4) an aesthetic function—just as the plants of the garden provided pleasure for his eyes (Gen 2:9), so the procession of animals invited Adam to delight in the richness and biological diversity of the creaturely world.

Although the entrance of sin into the cosmos seriously diminished humans' ability and willingness to function as responsible governors of the created order, Genesis 5:1-5 and Genesis 9:6 demonstrate that after the fall, humankind's fundamental status as the images of God was not withdrawn. In later texts this status provides a foundation for the ethical treatment of fellow human beings (Gen 9:6-7; Prov 14:31; 17:5; Jas 3:7-11), and for human's disposition to the world over which they had been appointed governors (Ps 8).

Finally, in Noah's construction of the ark and his care for the animals during the Great Flood we witness a dramatic illustration of what it means for humankind to serve and guard the living creatures that occupied not only the Garden of Eden but also the rest of the world after the entrance of sin.[61] The purpose of the ark was to keep alive[62] a male and female representative of each category of land and sky creature by protecting them from the destructive force of the deluge and providing them with food during the flood (Gen 6:19-22). In so doing Noah would serve not only the animals but also God's covenant with them. "My covenant with you" in Genesis 6:18 is sometimes interpreted as a reference to a pre-existent covenant with Noah, analogous to God's covenant with Abraham and Israel.[63] However, it is preferable to interpret the preposition adverbially, that is, with Noah, Yahweh would establish/confirm his covenant with the cosmos. Noah and his descendants would be heirs to Adam and his descendants, whose role was to govern the world on God's behalf and thereby maintain his covenant with the cosmos. Genesis 9 reinforces this interpretation. While Genesis 9:1-7 reaffirms Noah's status as the new Adam (despite the degeneracy of the human heart, Gen 9:21), the concluding declaration ("This is the sign of the covenant that I have established between me and all flesh that is on the earth," Gen 9:17) reminds readers of the primary focus. As the image of God, Noah was deputized to represent the cosmos in God's covenant confirmation process, but throughout he functions primarily in the interests of the creatures, rather than having them serve him. As the fountainhead of humanity, Noah's actions are paradigmatic for all his successors who encounter threats to the environment. Based on very specific divine instructions, Noah built the ark to preserve animal life in the plurality of species and its rich biological diversity.

Proposition 3: In governing the world as God's deputies and representatives, human beings must recognize that all life is sacred. Genesis 9:1-7 emphasizes that as images of God, the lives of human beings are sacrosanct, and the willful elimination of any individual by another agent, whether human or non-human, is a capital crime. To take the life of a

---

[61]William P. Brown, "The Moral Cosmologies of Creation," in *Character Ethics and the Old Testament*, pp. 13-14, credits Noah with being the first to implement an "endangered species project."

[62]"To keep alive" *(lĕhaḥăyōt)* in Gen 6:19 involves the same word that Joseph uses of God's design in sending him to Egypt to prepare a place where the chosen family could find refuge during a devastating seven-year famine (Gen 45:7).

[63]Thus Wenham, *Genesis 1-15*, p. 175, who sees in Noah a parallel with Israel.

human being is the highest form of treason, robbing God of a deputy and representative of himself. This standard is not applied to animals. Although we have no record of the official authorization of animal flesh for human consumption until after the flood (Gen 9:3-4), several features of the narrative indicate that animals were being slaughtered for sacrifice: (1) God killed an animal to provide Adam and Eve with more substantial garments to replace the covering of fig leaves (Gen 3:21); (2) Abel brought the best of his flock to Yahweh as a tribute offering (Gen 4:4); (3) Along with a male and female of each species of animal, Noah took into the ark seven clean animals and birds (Gen 7:1-9), a category that makes sense only in the context of sacrifice or food. (4) Although the previous narratives had been silent on the matter, Noah responded spontaneously to the survival of all on the ark by sacrificing the clean animals as a soothing aroma to Yahweh (Gen 8:20-21). This act preceded Yahweh's promise never again to destroy the earth and its creatures and his confirmation of the covenant (Gen 8:21; 9:8-17). Given the link between "clean" sacrificial animals and "clean" food for human consumption in later texts,[64] it is reasonable to imagine that sheep, for example, were raised for their meat prior to this. Furthermore, it is doubtful animals would have been domesticated primarily for their value as offerings to deity, or for the contributions they make to human culture apart from their meat. Whatever the case, Noah's sacrifice of the animals led to the first recorded divine authorization for humans to consume the flesh of animals, along with plants, the consumption of which had been authorized earlier (Gen 1:29-30).

The permission to eat the flesh of animals comes with a paradoxical proviso: Humans were permitted to eat any and every kind of meat, but they were prohibited from consuming the flesh with its life, that is, its blood (Gen 9:4). Issued to Noah, at the beginning of history, this ordinance supersedes in importance all the food laws of Israel, for this law was absolute and its scope was universal.[65] Although this taboo is reiterated for Israelites no fewer than six times in the constitutional

---

[64]Cf. Leviticus 11; Deuteronomy 14.

[65]Hence the extension of the law to the *gēr* in Lev 17:10-16 and the affirmation of this ordinance for Gentile converts by the Jerusalem Council in Acts 15:19-21.

literature,[66] Leviticus 17:10-16 provides the most detailed version of the prohibition:

> If anyone of the house of Israel or of the aliens who reside among them eats any blood, I will set my face against that person who eats blood, and will cut that person off from the people. For the life of the flesh is in the blood; and I have given it to you for making atonement for your lives on the altar; for, as life, it is the blood that makes atonement. Therefore I have said to the people of Israel: No person among you shall eat blood, nor shall any alien who resides among you eat blood. And anyone of the people of Israel, or of the aliens who reside among them, who hunts down an animal or bird that may be eaten shall pour out its blood and cover it with earth. For the life of every creature—its blood is its life; therefore I have said to the people of Israel: You shall not eat the blood of any creature, for the life of every creature is its blood; whoever eats it shall be cut off. All persons, citizens or aliens, who eat what dies of itself or what has been torn by wild animals, shall wash their clothes, and bathe themselves in water, and be unclean until the evening; then they shall be clean. But if they do not wash themselves or bathe their body, they shall bear their guilt.

This text concerns the slaughter of animals in two different circumstances. When animals would be slain as sacrifices, the blood was to be returned to God either by being poured out (Deut 12:27) or splattered on the altar (Lev 17:1-7). When animals would be slaughtered for human consumption, the blood was to be returned to God by pouring it out on the ground like water (Deut 12:16, 24; 15:23) and covering it with earth (Lev 17:13). Deuteronomy 12:23 provides the rationale for the taboo on blood: "for the blood is the life." Even while authorizing the consumption of meat, God retained ultimate authority over the lives of the creatures.

This identification of the blood with life[67] derives from the common observance of the life of an animal or person ebbing away with the loss

---

[66]Lev 3:17; 7:26; 17:10-16; 19:26; Deut 12:15-24; 15:23. See also 1 Sam 14:32-34; Ezek 33:23-26; and the shocking caricature of the fellowship meal in Ezek 39:17-21.

[67]Whereas in Deut 12:15 and 20-21 *nepeš* had referred to the seat of desire, in verses 23-25 the word denotes "life," "the vital self." Cf. *DCH*, 5.728.

of blood.[68] Because blood is identified with life, consuming blood was viewed as consuming life itself, which explains Moses' added comment in Deuteronomy 12:23, "You may not eat the life with the meat." Since all slaughter is sacrificial and substitutionary—a life for life—the slaughter of animals may be profane (dissociated from the cult), but it is never secular.[69] The taboo on consuming blood provides a perpetual reminder that even animal life is sacred, and that life itself is a gift of God. In Acts 15:20 the Council of Jerusalem bound Gentile Christians to this ordinance, thereby testifying both to its permanence and its supra-Israelite validity. The principle of the sanctity of all life transcends the Torah of Moses.[70]

The ethical sensitivity of this ordinance is profound. The slaughter for meat could easily degenerate into savagery and a ruthless disregard for the life of the animal. However, the ritual of draining the blood reminded the persons who slaughtered the animal and those who ate its meat, that even the life of the creature is sacred. If the meat was eaten with its blood, the blood would cry out to God and the offender would become the target of divine fury. While the flesh is sanctioned for human consumption, life itself is inviolable. God remains the guarantor of the sanctity of the life of the animal.[71] However, another aspect of the ordinance is seldom noted. It is easy to imagine hunters being calloused toward the life of their victims, especially when the animals are killed from a distance with a projectile (arrow, spear) or in a trap. This ordinance forces hunters to identify with the creatures by touching them and personally bearing responsibility for their deaths. This ordinance enhances humans' appreciation for life and forces them to grieve over the loss, even as they take advantage of the benefit the animal offers them.

---

[68]Cf. Homer's reference to "life running out." *Iliad* 14.518.

[69]Contra Moshe Weinfeld, *Deuteronomy and the Deuteronomic School* (Winona Lake, Ind.: Eisenbrauns, 1992), p. 214, who argues that "pouring the blood out like water" means "the blood has no more a sacral value than water has." But the comparison with water relates to its liquid constitution rather than its religious significance.

[70]Whereas Lev 17:10 and Lev 17:14 had sought to motivate compliance by warning that God would cut off the offender, Deut 12:25 provides positive motivation: "that it may go well with you and your descendants after you, for you will be doing what is right in Yahweh's eyes" (author's translation).

[71]For detailed discussion of these passages in Leviticus, see Milgrom, *Leviticus 1-16*, pp. 704-13 and *Leviticus 17-22*, pp. 1469-84.

Conclusion

Those who argue that the authors of biblical texts never had in mind the ecological degradation that we witness today are correct. Theirs was a pre-scientific and pre-industrial world, where the struggle for existence itself consumed people's energy. But the view that the Scriptures do not speak to the contemporary crisis is mistaken. First, the sage declared expressly that the treatment of animals was a matter of righteousness and wickedness: "The righteous know the needs[72] of their animals, but the mercy of the wicked is cruel" (Prov 12:10). Second, the Scriptures explicitly rein in the temptation to abuse creatures with a variety of ordinances: (1) Like the rest of the household, draft animals are to be given a weekly day of rest (Ex 20:10; 23:12; Deut 5:14). (2) Lost animals are to be returned to their owners (Ex 23:4; Deut 22:1-3). (3) Overburdened pack animals are to be helped by those who pass by (Ex 23:5; Deut 22:4). (4) Oxen used to thresh grain are not to be muzzled (Deut 25:4).[73] And wild animals are to be treated in ways that ensure the species' survival (Deut 22:6-7).[74] Third, the Scriptures lay the theological and anthropological foundations from which contemporary issues may be addressed and debated. Above all, they present a picture of a universe created by God to declare his praise and to provide him with endless delight.

Today that world is in jeopardy. The ecological crises resulting from global warming and humankind's exploitation of the earth's resources in ruthless self interest threaten to stifle many voices of praise to God. At best many evangelicals have taken a back seat in the environmental agenda, leaving the heavy lifting to people and groups that lack theological perspective and eschatological vision. At worst they have sat in the bleachers and cynically thrown refuse onto the playing field, hampering the efforts of those whose eyes have been opened to

---

[72]For the range of meanings of *nepeš*, literally "gullet, throat," see Riede, *Im Spiegel der Tiere*, p. 64.

[73]On the relationship between humans and domestic animals see Riede, "Der Gerechte kennt die Bedürfnisse seiner Tiere: Der Mensch und die Haustiere in der Sicht des Alten Testaments," in *Im Spiegel der Tiere*, pp. 57-64.

[74]See Daniel I. Block, "All Creatures Great and Small: Recovering a Deuteronomic Theology of Animals," in *The Old Testament in the Life of God's People: Essays in Honor of Elmer A. Martens*, ed. J. Isaak (Winona Lake, Ind.: Eisenbrauns, 2009), pp. 283-305.

the issues. Even as we spend billions of dollars annually to feed our pets,[75] we are oblivious to the fate of hundreds of other species of animals whose voice is not heard by those whom God has placed in charge of his universe. All life is sacred, and all living things play significant roles in ensuring the vitality of the world. Evangelical responses must begin with a rediscovery of the world as God sees it, and a rediscovery of humanity's divinely ordained role in it. The restoration of a robust global environment depends upon the recovery of an "ethos of creation," that views the world as a dwelling place produced by the interplay between the environment and human moral actions.[76] Those moral actions involve compliance with the divine will in seeking his glory and in seeking the well-being of the world over which we have been put in charge.

But is this realistic in a world characterized by human sin and rebellion? When the prophets considered the sorry state of the environment they tended not to attribute this to the direct mismanagement of the land or its creatures by the Israelites. Instead, the world languished because of the rebellion of the "caretakers" against Yahweh. The eighth-century B.C. prophet Hosea gives classic expression to this perspective:

> Hear the word of the LORD, O people of Israel;
> for the LORD has an indictment against the inhabitants of the land.
> > There is no faithfulness or loyalty,
> > and no knowledge of God in the land.
> > Swearing, lying, and murder, and stealing and adultery break out;
> > bloodshed follows bloodshed.
> Therefore the land mourns,
> and all who live in it languish;
> together with the wild animals and the birds of the air,
> even the fish of the sea are perishing. (Hos 4:1-3)

In Israel the cosmic covenant was in jeopardy; the triangular rela-

---

[75]According to Mindbranch, an industry market research company, in 2005 national advertising for pet food was estimated at $300 million, and sales of pet food at $14.5 billion. See <www .mindbranch.com/Pet-Food-Riding-R567-532/>.

[76]Cf. Brown, *Ethos of the Cosmos*, pp. 10-33.

tionship involving God, the land and the creatures, had unraveled. Because of the moral failures of those in charge of the environment, the land itself mourned and the inhabitants languished. Significantly, although the length of the exile in Babylon was set by the number of Sabbatical years missed (2 Chron 36:21; cf. Lev 26:34), the prophets do not respond with direct appeals to take better care of the land or its creatures. Instead, building on Leviticus 26:40-45 and Deuteronomy 30, they speak of a gracious God calling his people back to himself and to the land, installing over them a Davidic messiah, and implanting in them a new heart and mind. These are all divine actions, but they will be accompanied by Israel's repentance, and her renewed covenant commitment, demonstrated by walking in his ways, which in turn will be accompanied by environmental renewal (Ezek 34:23-29; 36:22-38). Accordingly, Israel's own exile and the devastation of the land could not be the end of the story. Hosea himself had previously spoken about the restoration of Israel, which would be accompanied by the restoration of God's covenant with the natural world:

> I will make for you a covenant on that day with the wild animals,
>   the birds of the air, and the creeping things of the ground;
> and I will abolish the bow, the sword, and war from the land;
> and I will make you lie down in safety.
> And I will take you for my wife forever . . .
>   On that day I will answer, says the LORD,
>   I will answer the heavens and they shall answer the earth;
>   and the earth shall answer the grain, the wine, and the oil,
>   and they shall answer Jezreel;
>   and I will sow him for myself in the land. (Hos 2:18-23)

The references to the three classes of creatures and three classes of produce yielded by the earth speak eloquently to the issue of biodiversity. In the restored world the covenantal triangle is fully functional.

Isaiah's vision of Israel's future exhibits similar features. Because of the people's sin, as agents of divine judgment, enemies would lay the land waste and empty it of life (Is 2:12-17; 6:11-12; 32:14). However, this devastation would only be temporary,

until a spirit from on high is poured out on us,
 and the wilderness becomes a fruitful field,
 and the fruitful field is deemed a forest.
Then justice will dwell in the wilderness,
 and righteousness abide in the fruitful field.
The effect of righteousness will be peace,
 and the result of righteousness, quietness and trust forever.
My people will abide in a peaceful habitation,
 in secure dwellings, and in quiet resting places. (Is 32:15-18)

If this oracle focuses on the renewal of the vegetation, another oracle, messianic in nature, balances out the picture by focusing on the creatures:

The wolf shall live with the lamb,
 the leopard shall lie down with the kid,
the calf and the lion and the fatling together,
 and a little child shall lead them.
The cow and the bear shall graze,
 their young shall lie down together;
 and the lion shall eat straw like the ox.
The nursing child shall play over the hole of the asp,
 and the weaned child shall put its hand on the adder's den.
They will not hurt or destroy
 on all my holy mountain;
for the earth will be full of the knowledge of the LORD
 as the waters cover the sea. (Is 11:6-9)

This text speaks less about the profusion of species than about their inner transformation. In that day not only will Yahweh be in covenant relationship with the earth and its living things, but the creatures will enjoy the blessing of covenant relationship with God, each other and the human population. In this new creation the violence of humans against creation, and of the creatures against each other and against humans will be eliminated. True *šalôm* will reign over all. This is the eschatological ideal for which all creation longs. And this is the vision that should inspire Christians in particular, for as the redeemed of the Lord, they have one foot in this world and another in the next. As redeemed images of God, we seek to relate to our environment as he would, were he physically present. Because the world and its fullness are important to him, they should also be important to us.[77]

[77]I am grateful to my colleagues Noah J. Toly, Richard Schultz, Fred Van Dyke and Kristen Page, and my graduate assistants Rahel Schafer and Jason R. Gile for their helpful counsel in matters of substance and style in preparing this essay. Of course, any infelicities in content or presentation are my own responsibility.

PART FOUR

WATER RESOURCES

6

WATER FOR LIFE

Global Freshwater Resources

Michael Guebert

INTRODUCTION: WATER FOR LIFE

Water, one of our most important global resources, is absolutely essential to the proper function of many natural processes—including life itself—and is worthy of particular care and protection. Water nourishes crops and ecosystems while regulating our climate. Humans make extensive use of this indispensable resource and often endow it with powerful religious value.

Access to adequate clean freshwater resources is essential to human health and development, improving the economic status and potential of women who no longer must devote large portions of each day to fetching water. Children's education and health improve as they spend proportionally less time retrieving water. Conflict decreases as water becomes accessible to all. Water is necessary for personal and public health, as well as for household uses such as food preparation, laundry and cleaning. Water is also essential to global food production. Eighty-five percent of all water consumed is used for agriculture.[1] And irrigated land, comprising only 20 percent of the world's cropland, produces 40 percent of the world's food supply and 60 percent of its cereals.[2]

---

[1]Peter Gleick, "Water for Food: How Much Will Be Needed?" in *The World's Water 2000-2001, The Biennial Report on Freshwater Resources* (Washington, D.C.: Island Press, 2000), pp. 63-92.

[2]UN Water, *Water for Life Decade 2005-2015*, United Nations Department of Public Information, 2005 <www.un.org/waterforlifedecade/factsheet.html>.

Access to water has at least partially determined patterns of human settlement throughout history. Ancient civilizations arose along fertile river valleys, facilitating water supply and transportation. And many of today's largest cities are situated close to water for some of the same reasons. Earth, often called the "Blue Planet," has abundant water resources. Yet billions of people around the world struggle daily to meet their basic need for water and sanitation. How can this be?

Three-fourths of the world is covered by oceans, which implies that our water supply ought to exceed our demand. However, of the global water supply, only a minute portion is available as fresh water; about 97 percent of the world's water supply is salt water while 2 percent is frozen in ice caps and glaciers. The remaining 1 percent is fresh water, found in lakes, streams and underground aquifers. Some of the freshwater supply is simply inaccessible—dammed or too far beneath the earth's surface to extract. In the final tally, only 0.02 percent of the global water supply is readily available to us as surface water or shallow groundwater.[3]

As a result of an increasing human population, higher-than-ever per capita resource demands, and widespread improper use of freshwater resources, humans have induced a global water crisis. People and institutions—including governments and markets—are guilty of overallocating water resources for unworthy tasks, polluting water supplies from our lake and stream ecosystems, and overpumping and depleting groundwater resources. Political ineptitude, social barriers and other global failures have prevented us from devoting sufficient freshwater resources to human needs. Our planet is facing a freshwater crisis, and it is of our own doing.

This chapter addresses these challenges, reviewing the nature and functions of the water cycle and the impacts of human exploitation upon it. It will also discuss the increasing challenges of meeting human demands for clean water, sanitation and development.

WATER IN THE ENVIRONMENT: IN THE AIR, ON THE SURFACE AND UNDER THE GROUND

Earth systems refine water by the evaporation and precipitation pro-

---

[3]G. Tyler Miller, *Sustaining the Earth,* 8th ed. (Belmont, Calif.: Thomson Brooks/Cole, 2007), p. 44.

cess, purifying it as it flows across the landscape in lakes, streams and wetlands, and filtering it as groundwater percolates through geologic layers. In the air, on the surface and underground, the proper functioning of the water cycle is critically important for life.

Water in the air. Cycling through the atmosphere, evaporation leaves behind impurities and transports water into the atmosphere, where it is stored, even if only briefly. Evaporation and condensation processes are critical to the transfer of heat energy from the equator to the poles, creating the climates of the world and moderating temperatures, making the planet habitable. Were it not for this great conveyor of atmospheric energy, most of the earth would be intolerably hot or cold. Human existence would be possible only in a narrow, mid-latitudinal range, instead of at all latitudes from the equator nearly to the poles.

Water on the surface. Water in the atmosphere condenses and falls to the ground, becoming the ultimate source of the fresh water upon which life on Earth depends. Whether from centuries-old rainfall slowly released from melting glaciers or from this week's storms, the water running across our landscape and percolating into the ground is vital, providing habitats for a diverse range of life and sustenance for humans. The value of these services is immense. Through erosion and sediment transport, rivers deliver silt to build deltas and maintain fertile floodplains and functional wetlands. In their varied flows and patterns, they provide a delicate habitat for plants and animals in complicated food webs. As rivers convey water and sediment from the mountains, across the plains and to the sea, they deliver nutrients critical to the integrity of river habitats and coastal ecosystems.[4] When a river basin—the area of land drained by a river and its tributaries—retains functional wetlands and connected floodplains, the negative effects of flood and drought are mitigated by absorption of rainwater and river flows, slowed runoff, and increased groundwater recharge.[5]

---

[4]Sandra Postel and Brian Richter, *Rivers for Life: Managing Water for People and Nature* (Washington, D.C.: Island Press, 2003), pp. 1-13.

[5]B. G. Colby, "The economic value of instream flows—Can instream values compete in the market for water rights?" in *Instream Flow Protection in the West*, ed. L. J. MacDonnell, T. A. Rice and S. J. Shupe (Boulder, Colo.: Natural Resources Law Center, University of Colorado, 1989), pp. 87-102; and D. Moore and A. Willey, "Water in the American West: Institutional

Water under the ground. Ground water is derived from rainfall and stream flow percolating into the layers of hidden strata beneath the soil-mantled landscape. In some cases, shallow ground water may return relatively quickly to the surface in nearby streams, sustaining river flow for weeks and months after any significant rainfall. In other cases, water percolates further downward into deep aquifers for long-term equilibrium storage. It is estimated that one quarter of the world's population receives its water supply from groundwater, including over 90 percent of people in rural or non-industrialized areas,[6] where it is especially important for irrigation.

When compared to surface water, groundwater is more accessible, more economical and of higher quality. Surface water is extracted from rivers and reservoirs vulnerable to surface contamination sources and often must be transported great distances to the user in open conveyance channels prone to evaporation losses. In addition, surface water supplies fluctuate with short-term climate changes such as drought. On the other hand, ground water is accessible almost everywhere, if wells are drilled deeply enough, and is naturally filtered as it passes through the aquifer. Therefore, groundwater is often less expensive to extract and transport than most surface water, yields no evaporation losses during conveyance, and is a long-term renewable resource if not over-pumped.[7] More abundant and available than surface water, ground water will play a very important role in meeting the increasing demands for water in the future, especially in the production of food for a growing population.

WATER RESOURCE CHALLENGES

A number of developments put pressure on the quantity and quality of water available for human uses and for the welfare of non-human nature. These challenges have human origins, and their impacts are disproportionately distributed across space and time. That is, degra-

---

Evolution and Environmental Restoration in the 21st Century," *University of Colorado Law Review* 62, (1991): 775-825. Recreational water uses, such as fishing, shoreline recreation and open water recreation, are also extremely valuable for these purposes.

[6]G. Tyler Miller, *Sustaining the Earth*, p. 180.

[7]Ibid., p. 181.

dation of water resources impacts distant populations as well as future generations.

Increasing demand. On a global scale, rivers, lakes and aquifers supply fresh water for a variety of human uses such as agriculture (irrigation and animal), industry (hydropower and manufacturing) and household uses (drinking, washing, cooking and sanitation). Since 1950, the global population has doubled while withdrawals from the aquatic environment have more than tripled.[8] By 2025, water withdrawals will increase by another 50 percent, continuing to outpace population growth. This will place a strain on irrigation water withdrawals, and in turn constrain food production.[9]

Albeit more productive than rain-fed agriculture, intensification of irrigation has placed a greater strain on water resources, altering the natural timing and variation of flows, affecting rivers, wetlands and groundwater recharge.[10]

The amount of irrigated land has increased nearly fivefold in the last century, boosting crop yields and stabilizing food production,[11] but depleting valuable ground water resources. For example, due to over-pumping, India and northern China have seen water table declines of two to four meters per year.[12] As pressures for irrigation continue to increase, meeting future demands will require a combination of new water sources, greater water efficiency, less food waste and a reduced demand for water-intensive foods.[13]

Efficiency of water use for irrigation depends on climate, technology, agricultural practices and crop type. In the driest climates, where irrigation is most necessary, *less than half of the water applied to a field is taken up by the crop*—the rest is lost by evaporation and transpiration.

---

[8]I. A Shiklomanov, "World Freshwater Resources," in *Water in Crises: A Guide to the World's Freshwater Resources* (New York: Oxford University Press, 1993), pp. 13-24.

[9]Mark W. Rosegrant, Ximing Cai and Sarah A. Cline, *Global Water Outlook to 2025, Averting an Impending Crises* (Washington, D.C.: International Food Policy Research Institute, 2002), p. 2.

[10]M. Falkenmark and V. Galaz, *Agriculture, Water and Ecosystems*, Swedish Water House Policy Brief No. 6 (Stockholm: Swedish International Water Institute, 2007), pp. 1-15.

[11]Rosegrant, Cai and Cline, *Global Water Outlook to 2025*, p. 2.

[12]Gleick, "Water for Food," p. 87.

[13]Ibid., p. 83.

Evaporation loss can be reduced by implementing more efficient irrigation technologies (such as changing from flooding and furrow irrigation to sprinkler and drip irrigation) and by irrigation policies (such as timing controls). In some Indian fields, shifting from conventional surface irrigation to drip irrigation has halved water use while doubling productivity.[14]

Water can be managed better through new agricultural practices appropriate for the climate and landscape, such as check dams to capture and retain flood flow, terracing to reduce runoff, and percolation ponds to maximize groundwater recharge during the rainy season.[15] Tilling before planting and after a heavy rain can break up soil crusts, improve water absorption and reduce evaporation. Transpiration losses can be minimized by controlling weeds and selecting more water-efficient crop types with shorter life cycles, deeper root systems, and tissues and leaf structures that retain water more effectively.[16]

Adjusting the global demand for water-intensive food products can also achieve greater agricultural water efficiency. It takes approximately 70,000 kg of water to produce one kg of beef, which is approximately thirty-five times more than the 1800 to 2000 kg of water needed to produce one kg of potato, wheat, alfalfa, corn, sorghum or soybean.[17] Largely due to high levels of meat consumption, the diets of people in industrialized regions of the world demand as much as two to three times more water than do diets in non-industrialized or industrializing regions.[18] Over the next few decades, it is expected that food demand will double and shift toward more water-intensive products, increasing the demand for irrigation.[19]

Developing new techniques in agriculture and irrigation is necessary, but insufficient for achieving more sustainable irrigation and global food production. Any solution will require policies that create

[14]Ibid., p. 84.
[15]Ibid.
[16]Randy Creswell and Franklin W. Martin. *Dryland Farming: Crops and Techniques for Arid Regions*, ECHO Technical Notes (North Fort Myers, Fla., 1993), pp. 8-21.
[17]Gleick, "Water for Food," pp. 78-79.
[18]Ibid., p. 67.
[19]Falkenmark, *Agriculture, Water and Ecosystems*, p. 5.

incentives for sustainable practices while also stimulating regional economies. And water governance must allow users at all levels a stake in decisions regarding water management. Individual farmers and the private sector should be supported by public investments in the development of effective agriculture.

As the global population increases and people consume more food and materials, the demand for freshwater resources will continue to grow, severely limiting the amount of water available for irrigation. This means that more food will be produced with a smaller percentage of the water supply, leading to more intensive use of fertilizers and pesticides, and consequently to a greater potential for water pollution from these chemicals.[20]

Water pollution. Pollution is contributing to a rapid decline in the quality of water resources—both on the surface of the earth and underground. As human populations grow, changes in land use—such as deforestation, urbanization and intensive agriculture—cause increases in the rate and volume of runoff into streams. In agricultural river basins, runoff often contains high levels of pesticides, nutrients from fertilizers such as nitrogen and phosphorus, and especially sediment from the exposed and eroding landscape. As a result, these non-point sources of pollution have set aquatic ecosystems out of balance. Rivers that once flowed cool and clean now run choked with high amounts of silt and algae or are drying up, impacting ecosystems and threatening the health and livelihoods of people who depend on them for drinking, irrigation and industry.

The decline in water quality, especially of our rivers, has increased the rate of freshwater fish extinction and biodiversity loss.[21] For example, where rivers flow into oceans, large areas of coastal waters are being severely degraded by seasonal *eutrophication*, or overenrichment of nutrients resulting in algal blooms. Eventually, dead organic matter sinking to the bottom of coastal waters decomposes and consumes

---

[20]U. Aswathanarayana, "Use of Water in Agriculture," in *Water Resources Management and the Environment* (Rotterdam: A. A. Balkema Publishers, 2001), pp. 187-228.

[21]UNEP World Conservation Monitoring Center (WCMC), 1998; and International Union for Conservation of Nature and Natural Resources (IUCN), 2000, as referenced in UN Water, *Water for Life Decade 2005-2015.*

available oxygen, forcing fish to leave the area while killing bottom-dwelling organisms. While we lack complete information regarding the global extent of eutrophication and the sources of nutrients, scientists estimate that over 400 coastal areas around the world experience some form of eutrophication. Of such areas, 169 are hypoxic (depleted of oxygen), while only 13 are considered in recovery.[22]

The extent of groundwater contamination is affected by characteristics of the contaminant and the aquifer media, and the distance from the contaminant source to the well.[23] Common sources of contamination include agricultural pesticides and fertilizers from fields or pathogens from animal feeding lots, underground storage tanks, landfills, and failing septic systems for household waste. Shallow, unconfined aquifers lacking overlying protective strata are especially vulnerable to contamination from surface activities. In many parts of the world, especially among the rural poor that depend upon ground water, shallow household and community wells are contaminated. Many of these rural households have both a latrine and a well—often located in close proximity to one another and to the home. In this situation, shallow, open, hand-dug wells are readily contaminated from surface runoff and from leakage from the nearby latrine, leading to high incidence of waterborne diseases, especially among children.

Water, sanitation and health. Access to adequate, clean water is essential to human health—as important as access to water. Unfortunately, proper sanitation receives less attention even though it is a considerably more complicated problem. Without basic sanitation, the benefits of access to clean water are greatly diminished.[24]

As a result of inadequate water and sanitation, water-related diseases are common throughout the world. According to the World Health Organization (WHO), lack of clean water, adequate sanitation and

---

[22]Mindy Selman et al., *Eutrophication and Hypoxia in Coastal Areas: A Global Assessment of the State of Knowledge*, Water Policy Note 1 (Washington, D.C.: World Resources Institute, March 2008).

[23]Ralph C. Heath, "Basic Ground-Water Hydrology," U.S. Geological Survey Water Supply Paper 2220 (1989): 66-67.

[24]Water Supply and Sanitation Collaborative Council, *A Guide to Investigating One of the Biggest Scandals of the Last 50 Years* (Geneva: International Environment House, 2008) <http://esa.un.org/iys/docs/san_lib_docs/WASH_media_guide_en%5B1%5D.pdf>.

proper hygiene are the leading causes of preventable diseases such as schistosomiasis, trachoma, intestinal parasites, encephalitis and hepatitis A.[25] Close to 250 million cases of such diseases are reported each year, resulting in 5 to 10 million deaths worldwide, 98 percent of these in non-industrialized countries.[26] Specifically, diarrheal disease is a leading cause of death from infectious diseases related to water, sanitation and hygiene.[27] Every year, 1.8 million people—most of them children under five years of age—die from diarrheal diseases such as cholera. Eighty-eight percent of these deaths are attributed to unsafe water, inadequate sanitation and hygiene, and they could be prevented through relatively low-cost improvements. Diarrheal morbidity can be dramatically reduced by taking measures to improve water supply, point-of-use water treatment, and hygienic interventions, including education and the promotion of hand washing.[28] Proper sanitation breaks fecal-oral transmission pathways, improving health at family and community levels. Even simple advances in sanitation access can lead to great improvements in health. As Dr. Lee Jon-wook, former director-general of the WHO states, "once we can secure access to clean water and to adequate sanitation facilities for all people, irrespective of the differences in their living conditions, a huge battle against all kinds of diseases will be won."[29]

Clean water, proper sanitation and personal hygiene are the three foundations underlying any strategy for enhancing public health.[30] Therefore, the highest priority for improving public health should be to provide basic access to water for those who lack it. Among those who have basic access, the next priorities should be to protect water sources

---

[25]World Health Organzation (WHO), *Water, Sanitation and Hygiene Links to Health*, November 2004 <www.who.int/water_sanitation_health/publications/facts2004/en/index.html>.

[26]Peter H. Gleick, *Water: Threats and Opportunities—Recommendations for the Next President*, (Oakland, Calif.: The Pacific Institute, 2008), p. 1-3; Annette Pruss-Ustun, Robert Bos, Fiona Gore, and Jamie Bartram, *Safer Water, Better Health: Costs, Benefits and Sustainability of Interventions to Protect and Promote Health* (Geneva: World Health Organization, 2008), pp. 7-15.

[27]Pruss-Ustun et al., *Safer Water, Better Health*.

[28]WHO, *Water, Sanitation and Hygiene Links to Health*.

[29]Ibid.

[30]United Nations, *Human Development Report, 2006* (New York: United Nations, 2006) <http://hdr.undp.org/en/reports/global/hdr2006/>.

and to promote good water handling practices, household water treatment, sanitation and personal hygiene.[31]

Conflict. Historically, water has been both a source and an instrument of conflict—locally, regionally and internationally.[32] However, while disputes have arisen over water availability, access and quality, water is rarely the only source of conflict. Attacks on water supplies and systems occur as the result of disputes over other issues such as religion, national borders, ideology and economics. But because water is rarely the sole source of conflict, many international security experts all too often ignore the presence and complexity of water security and conflict.[33] Nevertheless, the Pacific Institute has chronicled the history of water conflicts over the past five thousand years. The Institute's most recent report identifies six categories for the role of water in conflict:[34]

1. conflict over control of water resources

2. use of water as a military tool

3. use of water as a political tool

4. water as the target of terrorism

5. water as a military target

6. water as a source of conflict-related development disputes

Only the "control of water" and "development disputes" represent conflicts stemming from water-access disputes; the remaining four categories represent water as an instrument in conflict for other means, such as the pursuit of military, political or terroristic goals.[35] While

---

[31]Guy Howard and Jamie Bartram, *Domestic Water Quantity, Service Level and Health* (Geneva: World Health Organization, 2003), pp. 1-28.

[32]For readings on environmental conflict and resource wars, see Michael Klare, *Resource Wars: The New Landscape of Global Conflict* (New York: Holt, 2002); Thomas F. Homer-Dixon, *Environment, Scarcity, and Violence* (Princeton: Princeton University Press, 2001).

[33]Peter Gleick, "How Much Water Is There and Whose Is It? The Stocks and Flows of Water and International River Basins" in *The World's Water 2000-2001, The Biennial Report on Freshwater Resources,* Center for Resource Economics (Washington, D.C.: Island Press, 2000).

[34]Peter Gleick, "Environment and Security: Water Conflict Chronology Version 2004-2005," Water Brief 4 in *The World's Water 2004-2005, The Biennial Report on Freshwater Resources* (Washington, D.C.: Island Press, 2004), pp. 234-35.

[35]See, for example, Stephen Graham, "Urban Metabolism as Target: Contemporary War as Forced Demodernization," in *In the Nature of Cities: Urban Political Ecology and the Politics of Urban Metabolism,* ed. Nik Heynen, Maria Kaika and Erik Swyngedouw (New York: Routledge 2006), pp. 245-65.

many of the disputes fall into multiple categories, the use of water as a means to military and political ends is present in over 70 percent of the disputes analyzed.[36]

Mark Zeitoun, a water engineer with extensive experience in conflict zones, identifies a condition he refers to as "hydro-hegemony," in which one dominant nation in a shared river basin maintains a position by which it receives more than its equitable share of the basin's water. The dominant position seems to be less related to proximity to the water than to the relative economic and political power in the basin. Basin hegemons tend to dominate governance and "hijack" public discourse to suit their interests. Israel is the Jordan River Basin hegemon; in the Nile River Basin, Egypt is the "hydro-hegemon."[37]

In addition to this conflict, the population growth of the Middle Eastern and Northern African regions represents the most serious threat to water adequacy; larger populations require more water. The World Bank has projected the combined population of these regions to increase from 311 million people to 430 million people by 2025. By then, as many as twenty-five African countries will experience water stress (defined as the equivalent of 1500 cubic meters less available water per year, per capita), causing about 230 million people (16 percent of the continent's population) to suffer from water shortages.[38]

As the global population grows, water supplies become scarcer, cropland is degraded and depleted, and as increased stress is placed on water for irrigation, the potential for conflict over water will increase exponentially. In light of the impending scarcity of water, improved water management is essential. Transitions to best practices in water management should begin with conservation and efficiency in agriculture.

---

[36]Gleick, "Environment and Security," pp. 234-35.

[37]See Mark Zeitoun, *Power and Water in the Middle East: The Hidden Politics of the Palestinian-Israeli Water Conflict* (New York: Macmillian, 2008). For more information on water and conflict in this and other regions, see Michael Klare, "Water Conflict in the Nile Basin" and "Water Conflict in the Jordan, Tigris-Euphrates, and Indus River Basins," in *Resource Wars*, pp. 138-89.

[38]M. El-Fadel, Y. El-Sayegh, K. El-Fadl and D. Khorbotly, "The Nile River Basin: A Case Study in Surface Water Conflict Resolution," *Journal of Natural Resource Life Science Education* 32 (Madison, Wis.: American Society of Agronomy, 2003): 107-17, <www.jnrlse.org/view/2003/e02-15.pdf>.

Climate change. Added to the current problems of water pollution, conflict and scarcity are the projected effects of climate change on our freshwater resources resulting from increases in air temperature and water temperature, and from precipitation variability.[39] While some regions of the world may experience increased average precipitation and surface water resources, the negative effects of increased variability in precipitation and seasonal runoff upon water quantity and quality will offset these benefits.[40]

The negative impact of fluctuations in water supply and climate change will be most significant in arid and semi-arid regions. Reduced surface water and groundwater recharge will be exacerbated by increases in demand accompanying population growth, greater affluence and attendant higher levels of consumption, and increased need for irrigation. In addition, existing water resources will become more vulnerable to contamination from land use change and urbanization with direct effects on ecosystems and human health.[41] Mega delta regions in Asia and Africa are among the most vulnerable areas in the world to the projected impacts of climate change. They contribute little to the problem and are poorly positioned to adapt to the consequences, with few economic resources at their disposal.[42]

Given the impending impacts of climate change and the disruptions already sustained, it is more important than ever to understand the atmospheric aspect of the water cycle. We must take a precautionary approach to solving our climate crisis, as it directly affects global water resources. See chapter 9 of this book for a more thorough expla-

---

[39]Z. W. Kundzewicz, L. J. Mata, N. W. Arnell, P. Doll, P. Kabat, B. Jimenez, K. A. Miller, T. Oki, Z. Sen and I. A. Shiklomonov, "Freshwater resources and their management," in *Climate Change 2007: Impacts, Adaptation and Vulnerability. Contribution of Working Group II to the Fourth Assessment Report of the Intergovernmental Panel on Climate Change*, ed. M. L. Parry, O. F. Canziani, J. P. Palutikof, P. J. van der Linden and C. E. Hanson (Cambridge: Cambridge University Press, 2007), pp. 173-210.

[40]For a discussion of climate change and water management and global adaptation strategies, see Heather Cooley, "Water Management in a Changing Climate," in *The World's Water 2008-2009: The Biennial Report on Freshwater Resources* (Washington, D.C.: Island Press, 2009), pp. 39-56.

[41]Kundzewicz et al., "Freshwater resources," p. 175.

[42]United Nations, *Millennium Development Goals Report, 2008* (New York: United Nations, 2008), p. 37.

nation of the ways in which climate change affects the water cycle, increasing the intensity of evaporation, precipitation, floods, droughts and severe weather.

WATER RESOURCES IN SOCIAL CONTEXT: HUMAN RIGHTS, ENVIRONMENTAL JUSTICE AND DEVELOPMENT

One of the most serious global infractions of human rights and environmental justice is the failure to meet basic water and sanitation needs for all. Even though almost all countries have sufficient natural water resources to meet their need, not all people have equal access to water, and billions remain without adequate water and sanitation.[43] Almost 1 billion of the 6.7 billion people in the world (15 percent of the global population) do not have access to safe drinking water; nearly two-thirds

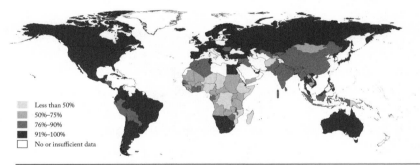

Less than 50%
50%–75%
76%–90%
91%–100%
No or insufficient data

Figure 6.1. Global water coverage, 2006 (UNICEF/WHO, "Progress on Drinking Water and Sanitation: Special Focus on Sanitation," 2008, used with permission)

of them live in Asia. In Sub-Saharan Africa, 42 percent of the population is without improved water [44] (figure 6.1). Currently, 2.5 billion people worldwide (nearly 40 percent of the global population) lack sanitation facilities, including 1.2 billion people who have no sanitation facilities at all.[45] Over half of those without improved sanitation live in

---

[43]Meena Palaniappan, Emily Lee and Andrea Samulon, "Environmental Justice and Water," in *The World's Water 2006-2007: The Biennial Report on Freshwater Resources,* ed. Peter L. Gleick (Washington, D.C.: Island Press, 2006), p. 124.

[44]UN, *The Millennium Development Goals Report, 2008,* p. 42.

[45]UNICEF/WHO, *Progress on Drinking Water and Sanitation: Special Focus on Sanitation* (New York: UNICEF; Geneva: WHO, 2008), p. 2.

China and India (figure 6.2). Rural inhabitants in developing countries are in greatest need. Only 31 percent of the rural poor have access to sanitation, compared to 73 percent of urban dwellers.[46] The problem is

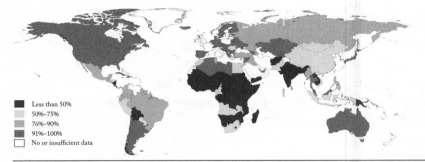

Less than 50%
50%–75%
76%–90%
91%–100%
No or insufficient data

Figure 6.2. Global sanitation coverage, 2006 (UNICEF/WHO, "Progress on Drinking Water and Sanitation: Special Focus on Sanitation," 2008, used with permission)

not so much total available water, but issues of human rights associated with political and economic power; it seems that water flows to those who have power.[47]

Human rights. The United Nations (UN) implicitly recognized the human right to water in the 1948 Universal Declaration of Human Rights.[48] The human right to water was later explicitly affirmed by the UN in 1977,[49] 1986[50] and 2002.[51] According to the UN, "The human right to water entitles everyone to sufficient, safe, acceptable, physically

---

[46]WHO, *Water, sanitation and hygiene links to health.*

[47]Palaniappan, Lee and Samulon, "Environmental Justice and Water," p. 117.

[48]United Nations, *The Universal Declaration of Human Rights,* General Assembly resolution 217 A (III), December 10, 1948, General Assembly of the United Nations, <www.un.org/en/documents/udhr/>.

[49]United Nations, *Report of the United Nations Water Conference, Mar del Plata,* No. E.77.II.A.12, March 14-25, 1977 (New York: United Nations, 1977), p. 1 <www.ielrc.org/content/e7701.pdf>.

[50]United Nations, *Declaration on the Right to Development,* adopted by General Assembly resolution 41/128, December 4, 1986 (New York: United Nations, 1986) <www.un.org/documents/ga/res/41/a41r128.htm>.

[51]United Nations Economic and Social Council - Committee on Economic, Social, and Cultural Rights. "Substantive Issues Arising in the Implementation of the International Covenant on Economic, Social and Cultural Rights," *General Comment No.15. The right to water (Articles 11 and 12 of the International Covenant on Economic, Social, and Cultural Rights* (New York: United Nations, 2002) <www2.ohchr.org/english/law/cescr.htm>.

accessible and affordable water for personal and domestic uses. An adequate amount of safe water is necessary to prevent death from dehydration, reduce the risk of water-related disease and provide for consumption, cooking, personal and domestic hygienic requirements."[52] This right is based on the inherent dignity and the equal and inalienable rights of all members of the human family. It is fundamental for life and health and a prerequisite for the realization of other human rights.

Water and equity. Recognizing the right to water is only the first step; the right must be secured through development of legislative, economic, management and organizational strategies.[53] Such a task is difficult, as the majority of people who lack adequate access to water and sanitation have "multiple marginal identities"—that is, they are either indigenous people or people of color, and they are poor—and their voice is not heard.[54] About one-third of the people lacking access to improved water live on less than $1 per day, and more than two-thirds live on less than $2 a day.[55] In Africa, per capita daily domestic water use is 44 liters (10 gal) and ranges from 13 liters (3 gal) in Mozambique to 180 liters (44 gal) in South Africa. By contrast, in the United States, where per capita consumption is 775 liters (176 gal) per day, a person taking a 5-minute shower uses more water than the typical person living in a slum in a developing country uses in a whole day.[56] The lack of access to water among the poor exacerbates poverty, as those without access are forced to invest more time, energy and resources in water collection, thus reducing their capacity to work and earn income.[57]

The problem is especially acute among urban slum dwellers and rural poor.[58] In urban settings, the cheapest and most reliable source of water is often the municipal water utility. However, impoverished households are less likely to be connected (due to the relatively high

---

[52]Ibid.
[53]For a summary of human rights to water, see Peter H. Gleick, "The Human Right to Water," in *The Worlds' Water 2000-2001: The Biennial Report on Freshwater Resources* (Washington, D.C.: Island Press, 2000), pp. 1-17.
[54]Ibid.
[55]UN, *Human Development Report, 2006*.
[56]Ibid.
[57]Gleick, "The Human Right to Water."
[58]Ibid.

cost of connection) and more likely to obtain their water from unimproved sources, a public source, or from intermediate vendors. The vast majority of the poor purchase their water from private markets that deliver water of variable quality and at high prices. Poor people living in urban slums often pay five to ten times more for their water than the wealthy people of the same city.[59]

In rural settings, often located beyond infrastructural water networks, individual homes and communities must manage their own sources and systems. Although some government agencies assist in water service provision, they often design inappropriate systems in inappropriate locations, apart from partnership with the local community.

Formal water development networks also often ignore the special circumstances of women and children.[60] Women and girls have a greater need for private, safe water and sanitation facilities and are typically responsible for collecting water for drinking, cooking, cleaning, hygiene and sanitation. Because of limited water supplies, the small amount they are able to collect is often allocated to cooking and drinking, leaving little for the proper washing of hands and food.[61]

In communities that lack sufficient water, women and children often carry water long distances, making multiple trips every day to meet the needs of the family. Women, and especially children, can become weary from the arduous task of carrying water, thus reducing their energy for other responsibilities and their resistance to disease, while increasing their risk of chronic back and neck ailments. When children devote hours to retrieving water, they become vulnerable to accidents and assault and are prevented from participation in education, not to mention rest and recreation.[62]

Because of such responsibilities, women often know the most about the location, reliability and quality of their water. They are more moti-

---

[59]UN, *Human Development Report, 2006.*
[60]For an excellent summary of another gendered resource nexus, see Margaret Skutsch and Joy Clancy, "Unraveling Relationships in the Energy-Poverty-Gender Nexus," in *Transforming Power: Energy, Environment, and Society in Conflict*, ed. John Byrne, Noah J. Toly and Leigh Glover (New Brunswick, N.J.: Transaction, 2006), pp. 61-154.
[61]UN Water, *Water for Life Decade 2005-2015.*
[62]Lifewater International "Water and Women" < http://lifewater.org/water-women.aspx> and and "Water and Children" <http://lifewater.org/water-children.aspx>.

vated to invest time and energy in providing water access, sanitation and storage. However, despite their role as important stakeholders, women are often prevented from participating in the governance of water resources and rarely benefit from governance arrangements.[63]

Water and governance. When water and sanitation projects are designed and developed with the participation of women, the projects are more sustainable and effective.[64] Therefore, the process of water resource development must focus on educating women about, and involving women in, the water management process.[65] By approaching water supply and sanitation management from a gender perspective, improvements in access to safe water and sanitation will also lead to reduction in poverty, improved educational opportunities for girls, and reduced child illness and mortality.[66]

The greatest inhibitors to improved health are the lack of technical understanding and the social stigmas regarding sanitation among political leaders and the general population. Political leaders exhibit an overwhelming tendency to treat sanitation issues as a problem to be hidden from view. While they may face criticism for lack of satisfactory water services, politicians rarely lose their position because of poor sanitation programs, especially since the people who need it the most have the least political influence.

The institutional frameworks are also notoriously ineffective; fragmenting responsibilities into many government departments, ignoring the voice of the most needy, and neglecting the role the private sector can play. More focus is given to short-term facility improvements than to long-term behavioral change through community education, capacity building and hygiene promotion.[67]

Approaches to solving sanitation issues have often been inappropri-

---

[63]P. H. Gleick and H. Cooley, *The World's Water 2006-2007: The Biennial Report on Freshwater Resources* (Washington, D.C.: Island Press, 2006).

[64]UN Water, *Gender, Water and Sanitation: A Policy Brief* (2006), p. 2 <www.genderandwater.org/page/5111>.

[65]N. Singh et al., "Women and Water: A Policy Assessment." *Water Policy* 5, no. 3 (2003): 289-304.

[66]UN Water, *Water for Life Decade 2005-2015.*

[67]Mayling Simpson-Hebert and Sarea Wood, *Sanitation Promotion* (Geneva: World Health Organization, 1998), pp. 99-140.

ate. Sanitation technologies are sometimes presented as "one size fits all," an approach that fails to recognize the diversity of needs. The needs and expectations of urban dwellers are often different from those in rural settings; the type of sanitation facilities designed must be appropriate to the cultural, economic and environmental setting. Sanitation and health promoters often lack knowledge about the performance characteristics concerning sanitation options, try to promote facilities people do not want or cannot afford, and are unaware of effective promotional techniques. The result is that sanitation promoters continue with a "top-down" approach that denies the voice, desires and involvement of the "target populations."[68]

For example, in many settings, even in developed countries, taboos regarding excreta prevent the safe recovery and profitable use of human waste for agricultural purposes. An effective approach to sanitation, requiring significant educational intervention, would promote an understanding of the essential nutrient role that human waste can play in the life cycle of plants when handled properly, as well as the potentially damaging impact on human health and the environment when handled improperly.[69]

Only a century ago, London, New York and Paris were all centers of infectious disease with death rates similar to some areas of Sub-Saharan Africa today.[70] But powerful reforms in water and sanitation thrust each city forward in human progress by improving public health. Today billions of people in the undeveloped world still lack access to water and sanitation, which may be the greatest failure of human development in the twentieth century.

Water and development in the new millennium. To resolve the global water crises, we must address problems of poverty, inequality and government failure. Such a large-scale and complex problem will require an equally large scale and integrated approach from many nations united in purpose and with shared goals.

---

[68]Ibid.
[69]Ibid.
[70]United Nations Development Programme, *Beyond Scarcity: Power, Poverty and the Global Water Crisis*, Summary Human Development Report 2006 (New York: United Nations Development Programme, 2006), p. 5.

The Millennium Development Goals (MDGs) are the world's targets for addressing extreme poverty and extending human freedom. The MDGs were developed in response to the Millennium Declaration adopted by 189 nations during the United Nations' Millennium Summit in 2000. More than simple benchmarks, the goals for the target date of 2015 represent a broad vision of shared development priorities. They are rooted in the idea that extreme poverty is not an inescapable reality but a curable affliction that diminishes us all and threatens our collective security and prosperity.[71]

The eight Millennium Development Goals are (1) eradicate extreme poverty and hunger, (2) achieve universal primary education, (3) promote gender equality and empower women, (4) reduce child mortality, (5) improve maternal health, (6) combat HIV/AIDS, malaria and other diseases, (7) ensure environmental sustainability, and (8) develop a global partnership for development.[72] The goals consist of eighteen quantifiable targets assigned to five "dimensions": poverty, gender, health, education and environment.

The eighteen targets and five dimensions are strongly linked by water and sanitation. As already noted, lack of clean water and improved sanitation is a major cause of poverty and malnutrition. Adequate water supply is vital to the world's small farmers who account for half of the world's poorest (Goal 1). The collection of water and its transportation over long distances, water-related illnesses, and limited access to water and sanitation in schools keeps millions of girls out of school (Goal 2). Women hold the responsibility of water collection and care for children ill from inadequate water (Goal 3). Diarrhea caused by poor water and sanitation accounts for the majority of child illness and mortality each year, while clean water and sanitation could potentially halve the risk (Goal 4). [73]

Millennium Development Goal 7 (ensure environmental sustainability) addresses water and sanitation most directly. Target 10 specifically aims "to halve the number of people without sustainable access to

---

[71]UN, *Human Development Report, 2006*, p. 35.
[72]United Nations, *About the MDGs: Basics* <www.undp.org/mdg/basics.shtml>.
[73]UNDP, *Beyond Scarcity*.

safe drinking water and basic sanitation." The world is currently on track to meet the drinking water target, as 87 percent of the global population has access to improved drinking water sources, compared to 77 percent in 1990. All regions of the world are now above 85 percent, except for Oceania (50 percent) and Sub-Saharan Africa (58 percent), where more than one-third of those using unimproved sources reside. Neither region is on track to meet the goal by 2015, when the global total is expected to surpass 90 percent.[74]

Progress in meeting sanitation goals, however, is less promising. Currently, only 62 percent of the world uses improved sanitation facilities, and half the developing world remains without basic sanitation. Between 1990 and 2006, the proportion of people lacking improved sanitation decreased by 8 percent. The areas of greatest need are Southern Asia (33 percent have improved sanitation) and Sub-Saharan Africa (31 percent),[75] where the number of people without access to sanitation actually increased from 335 million in 1990 to 400 million in 2004.[76] If sanitation development continues in the next decade as it has since 1990, the world will not achieve even half of the MDG goal (77 percent). In this situation, the total number of people without sanitation will decrease only slightly from 1990 levels, thus still missing the target by over 700 million people.[77]

Because of the slow progress toward meeting the water and sanitation MDG targets, and in recognition of the urgent need for greater political awareness and action, the UN General Assembly declared 2005 through 2015 as the Water for Life Decade and specified 2008 as the International Year of Sanitation. The purpose of these declarations is to raise awareness of, and improve progress toward, the MDG water and sanitation targets. To achieve these goals, the UN recommends several key governmental actions, including the following: Governments should employ practical measures that translate MDG commitments into action. Governments should treat water as a precious re-

---

[74]WHO, *Progress on Drinking Water and Sanitation—Special Focus on Sanitation.*
[75]Ibid.
[76]United Nations, *Millennium Development Goals Report, 2007* (New York: United Nations, 2007).
[77]WHO, *Progress on Drinking Water and Sanitation—Special Focus on Sanitation.*

source rather than an expendable commodity. Nations should strengthen their commitments to reduce carbon emissions and develop strategies to mitigate climate change. They should take more accurate account of the real economic losses associated with depletion of water resources. They should use integrated water resource management policies that include environmental sustainability factors. Finally, they should create incentives for conservation and eliminate subsidies and price structures that encourage waste.[78]

Specifically, to hasten the pace toward achieving water and sanitation goals, governments must work to reduce the disparity in water and sanitation coverage between the richest and poorest people, and empower regulators to hold service providers accountable for services affordable to the poor.[79] Indeed, some argue that equity, and not efficiency, is the most important consideration in water policy.[80] Others have suggested "life-line" policies, by which a certain minimum amount of water, enough to meet basic household needs, is provided freely or affordably to every family.[81]

Because the Millennium Development Goals are closely interrelated, slow progress in water supply and sanitation will stunt advances in other goal and target areas while generating growing ecological debt to future generations. Without accelerated progress toward solving the water and sanitation crises and establishing greater equity, many countries will not achieve the goals, thus consigning millions to lives of poverty, poor health and diminished opportunities.[82] Fortunately, this urgent call from the UN is being answered with purpose and vigor by many organizations, large and small, international and national, governmental, private and faith-based.[83] With the increasing, collective

[78]UN, *Human Development Report, 2006*, p. 37.
[79]Ibid.
[80]See, for example, John M. Whiteley, Helen Ingram and Richard Warren Perry, eds., *Water, Place, and Equity* (Cambridge, Mass.: MIT Press, 2008).
[81]For reference to such policies in both water and energy (electricity and heat), see Joan Martinez-Alier, "Energy, Economy, and Poverty: The Past and Present Debate," in *Transforming Power*, ed. Byrne et al., pp. 35-60.
[82]UN, *Human Development Report, 2006*, p 37.
[83]International organizations are making progress in global water and sanitation development. These include the United Nations, UNICEF and World Health Organization. Notable nongovernmental organizations include: The Centre for Affordable Water and Sanitation Tech-

and synergistic efforts of these organizations, we may achieve the Millennium Development Goals.

CONCLUSION: IT WILL TAKE MORE THAN WATER

Water is essential to life on Earth. In the air, on the surface and under the ground, the natural processes of the water cycle provide a global climate and ecosystems rich in biodiversity and habitable by humans. However, the world faces serious crises in freshwater resources. With a growing population and dwindling water resources, clean water is becoming scarcer for populations around the globe. Even as dependence upon vital water services increases, humans are degrading water resources by overuse and pollution, and we are complicating access to them by conflict and injustice. One billion people are without access to adequate supplies of potable water and 2.4 billion people lack adequate sanitation; most of these people are located in the poorest regions of the world. Apart from significant efforts to change our trajectory, our water supply and all of its ecological services and functions will be in peril. Not least among the impacts will be a decline in human health, dignity and freedom.[84]

As Christians, we must thoughtfully consider our calls to care for God's creation and to love our neighbor. Both tasks require particular care and protection of our global water resources, and both are integrated through science and faith. In the next chapter, as we turn to the Scriptures for some guidance in these matters. Dr. David Tsumura will articulate a biblical theology of water that provides us with a foundation for normative deliberation regarding the role of water in creation, and the role of humans as caretakers of this vital resource.

---

nology, Stockholm International Water Institute, Water Partners International, International Water Management Institute, Rural Water Supply Network, Wateraid, Water Supply and Sanitation Collaborative Council, the Water and Environmental Sanitation Network and the World Water Council. Some notable faith-based development organizations are World Vision, Lifewater International, Living Water International, Pure Water-Pure Life, Water for the Nations and Water Missions International.

[84]For an interesting review of local and global water issues, see the April 2010 issue of *National Geographic*, "Water: Our Thirsty World." The entire issue is devoted to water topics, including properties, global balance, spiritual values, stream quality, new technology, policy, irrigation and resource access, depletion and global crises.

7

A BIBLICAL THEOLOGY OF WATER

Plenty, Flood and Drought
in the Created Order

David Toshio Tsumura

WATER MAY BE A FORCE FOR GOOD OR FOR HARM. It can give life
or destroy it. Too little water brings thirst and desolation; too much
water causes flooding and ruin.[1] Since water is a part of God's creation,
it is necessary for Christians to include water in their concern for creation care. Management of water resources is as crucial an issue for us
modern humans[2] as it was for ancient ones.

Natural events such as cyclones, typhoons and tsunamis can cause
disastrous flooding, leading also to disease and debris flow. On the
other hand, earthquakes, wars and other events can cause sudden shortages of water and even break down entire sanitation and water provision systems.

The distribution of water resources has been a critical issue since the
earliest history of humankind, resulting at times in battles for water. Conflicts over water have often been at the root of military struggles between
two or more groups of people. Issues of water scarcity and problems of
water resource distribution were not uncommon in the Ancient Near East
(ANE). Both farmers and herdsmen required abundant water for their

---

[1]David Toshio Tsumura, "Water," in *New Dictionary of Biblical Theology*, ed. T. Desmond Alexander and Brian S. Rosner (Leicester, U.K.: Inter-Varsity Press, 2000), pp. 840-41.
[2]See Michael Guebert on water resources, in chapter 6 of this book.

products (for example, Gen 29) but water resources were sometimes scarce. In fact, a Middle Assyrian Law requires flogging as punishment for not abiding by community agreements regarding the distribution of water resources, suggesting that common pool resource management was an issue with which people of the ANE were familiar.[3]

Water, along with oil, is certainly at the center of the current global environmental crisis. Hydroelectric dams are directly related to the production of energy. Changing the courses of rivers or controlling the amount of water in the upper reaches of rivers such as the Euphrates and the Tigris represent some of the hottest issues among neighboring countries in Mesopotamia today, and Mesopotamia is not alone.[4]

In this chapter, we will concentrate on how the Bible treats water and water systems theologically. First, we will discuss the role of water as part of God's provision in the created order. Then, we will treat issues of plenty as well as problems of flooding and drought.

CREATED ORDER: GOD'S PROVISION

Water is certainly a part of the created order. In the biblical concept of creation, everything other than God himself came to exist by God's creating it. The doctrine of *creatio ex nihilo* affirms this theological truth, which is based on the Bible. The doctrine was formulated in the second century A.D. when Irenaeus refuted heretical doctrines of Gnosticism. According to the Gnostic teaching, physical matter is evil and lower than spiritual or immaterial matter. Therefore, the deity described in the Old Testament, who created material items, including

---

[3]"If there is insufficient rainwater for irrigation available, the owners of the field shall act together; each man shall perform the work in accordance with the extent of his field, and shall irrigate his field. But if there are some among them who are not amenable to an agreement, then the one among them who is amenable to an agreement shall take the tablet (with the decision) of the judges before those who are not amenable to an agreement; the mayor and five noblemen [of the city shall be present . . . (gap) . . . they shall strike] him [x blows with rods]; he shall perform [the king's service for x days]." Martha T. Roth, *Law Collections from Mesopotamia and Asia Minor*, 2nd ed., SBL Writings from the Ancient World Series 6 (Atlanta: Scholars Press, 1997), p. 181.

[4]For an analysis of contemporary issues, see Michael T. Klare, *Resource Wars: The New Landscape of Global Conflict* (New York: Henry Holt, 2001); John K. Cooley, "The War Over Water," in *Conflict After the Cold War: Arguments on Causes of War and Peace*, ed. Richard K. Betts (Boston: Allyn and Bacon, 1994), pp. 413-24.

water, was clearly inferior to the deity who is the father of Jesus Christ in the New Testament.[5] But the Christian church rejected this Gnostic teaching and accepted Irenaeus's doctrine of *creatio ex nihilo.*[6]

However, in the modern era, especially during the past one hundred years, this doctrine has been denied not only by process theologians, but also by biblical theologians and dogmaticians such as Gerhard von Rad and Karl Barth, who claimed instead that "creation out of chaos" is the biblical concept.[7] Barth's pupil Brevard S. Childs similarly holds that "the deep" and "darkness" were two elements not created by God.[8] However, the chaos theory advocated by these theologians is much influenced by Hermann Gunkel's view that since *tĕhôm,* the word for "the deep" in Genesis 1:2, is related to the name of the Babylonian sea goddess Tiamat, "the deep" in Genesis is a mythological remnant.[9] They hold that Genesis 1:2 refers to the precreation condition of waterly chaos as in the Babylonian story of "creation" in *Enuma elish.* Hence, it may be helpful to discuss the relationship between water and the biblical concept of creation, before considering specific problems of water.

Creative waters. In polytheistic myths, the water-god is just one of many important deities in the pantheon. For example, the Akkadian

---

[5]For this subject, see the present author's "The Doctrine of *creatio ex nihilo* and the Translation of *tōhû wābōhû*" in a volume for The International Workshop on the Study of the Pentateuch with Special Emphasis on Its Textual Transmission History in the Hellenistic and Roman Periods (8/28-31/07) [forthcoming from E. J. Brill].

[6]Colin E. Gunton, *The Triune Creator: A Historical and Systematic Study,* Edinburgh Studies in Constructive Theology (Edinburgh: Edinburgh University Press, 1998), pp. 73-86; cf. Gerhard May, *Creatio ex Nihilo: The Doctrine of 'Creation out of Nothing' in Early Christian Thought* (Edinburgh: T & T Clark, 1994).

[7]Ian G. Barbour, *Religion in an Age of Science,* The Gifford Lectures 1989/1991, vol. 1 (San Francisco: Harper & Row, 1990), p. 144; Sjoerd L. Bonting, "Chaos Theology: A New Approach to the Science-Theology Dialogue," *Zygon* 34 (1999): 324; Gerhard von Rad, *Old Testament Theology Vol. I: The Theology of Israel's Historical Traditions* (New York: Harper & Row, 1962 [orig. 1957]), p. 148; see also p. 144; Karl Barth, *Church Dogmatics* 3/1 (Edinburgh: T & T Clark, 1958), pp. 101-10; 3/3 (Edinburgh: T & T Clark, 1960), pp. 289-368 (§50), esp. p. 352.

[8]Brevard S. Childs, *Old Testament Theology in a Canonical Context* (London: SCM Press, 1985), pp. 223-24; also idem., *Myth and Reality in the Old Testament* (London: SCM Press, 1960), pp. 36, 42.

[9]See Hermann Gunkel, *Creation and Chaos in the Primeval Era and the Eschaton,* translated by K. William Whitney Jr. (Grand Rapids: Eerdmans, 2006 [Ger. orig. 1895]); idem., *Genesis: Translated and Interpreted,* 3rd ed. (Macon, Ga.: Mercer University Press, 1997 [orig. 1910³; 1901]). Actually, the name Tiamat is a personified form of the common Semitic word for underground waters. See David T. Tsumura, *The Earth and the Waters in Genesis 1 and 2: A Linguistic Analysis,* JSOTSupp 83 (Sheffield, U.K.: Sheffield Academic Press, 1989), pp. 56-57.

god Ea (Sumerian Enki) was the god of the underground water in Mesopotamia; he built his house on the conquered Apsu, the sweet water god. Apsu's female counterpart was Tiamat, the salt water (sea) goddess, who is symbolized as a sea dragon; from her dead body the conqueror Marduk "created" heaven and earth in the Babylonian "creation" myth, *Enuma elish.*[10] In northern Mesopotamia, the storm and rain god Baal (Adad) was thought to control not only rainwater but also subterranean water resources. But neither Ea nor Baal was the sovereign deity. Furthermore, the gods were not independent of water; on the contrary, even deities could not live without water. They needed to eat and drink like human beings; like human beings they aged and sometimes became ill and even died.[11]

Many polytheistic myths spoke of a pair of the primeval waters from which everything emanated. Even gods and goddesses were thought to come out of the pre-existent primordial waters, like Apsu and Tiamat in the Babylonian myth and Izanagi and Izanami in the Japanese myth. Thus, the world was understood to have come out of the creative waters.[12]

However, in the biblical religion, the entire universe (i.e., "the heavens and the earth" in Gen 1:1) was created and controlled by Yahweh the Creator God. Sometimes Genesis 1:1 is interpreted to mean that only "the heavens and the earth" were created, which means that the *tĕhôm*-water was not created by God. This appears to be supported by the view that originally Genesis 1:2 was the beginning of the story and verse 1 is a title that was added later. However, verse 2 begins with a *waw* ("and") + noun ("the earth"), which is very unnatural at the beginning of a Hebrew narrative.

Actually, the *tĕhôm* ("the deep")—water in Genesis 1:2—which usually refers to subterranean water in biblical Hebrew, was simply a part

---

[10]For a translation of this text see Stephanie Dalley, *Myths from Mesopotamia: Creation, the Flood, Gilgamesh and Others: A New Translation,* World's Classic (Oxford: Oxford University Press, 1991), pp. 233-74.

[11]For a useful introduction to the religions of ancient Israel and her neighboring peoples, see Richard S. Hess, *Israelite Religions: An Archaeological and Biblical Survey* (Grand Rapids: Baker Academic, 2007), chaps. 4 and 5, esp. pp. 96-104.

[12]See, for example, Samuel Noah Kramer, ed., *Mythologies of the Ancient World* (Garden City, N.Y.: Doubleday, 1962). On the themes of watery beginnings and of watery abodes of deities in the ancient Near East, see Tsumura, *Earth and the Waters,* pp. 143-54.

of the earth, i.e., an element of the created universe. It did not create anything. Water is thus a part of the created order.

Nevertheless, as noted above, it is sometimes claimed that the *tĕhôm*-water (Gen 1:2) was uncreated and, like the Babylonian goddess Tiamat, was a chaos-water out of which the cosmos came. But verse 2 has nothing to do with a watery chaos and there is no support for the view that the word *tĕhôm* was derived from the name of the goddess Tiamat, as Gunkel once advocated. The verse describes the earth simply as "not yet" normal using ordinary language. In other words, the initial situation of the earth was *tōhû wābōhû* (NRSV: "a formless void"; cf. REB: "a vast waste"), that is, it was "desolate and empty," unproductive and uninhabited, and totally covered by the water that belongs to the underground (see Gen 1:9-10).[13] According to Genesis 1, it was by God's fiats that the bare earth became full of plants on the third day (Gen 1:11-12), and of animals and human beings on the sixth day (Gen 1:24-27).

The Garden of Eden. The earth-water relationship in Genesis 2 was different from that of the intial verses of Genesis 1. Here, the underground *'ēd* ("a stream") water[14] flooded, inundating all arable land (*'ădāmâ* "ground"), which was only one part of the earth (*'ereṣ); no* rain had yet descended from heaven. Both the subterranean water and the rain were controlled by the sovereign Creator God. Although it is sometimes claimed that Genesis 2 describes a "dry chaos,"[15] the initial situation here is not a lack of water but a lack of adequate control of it. God then made a "garden" for human beings in Eden, a place with an abundant water-supply (cf. Gen 13:10).[16]

One may reasonably suggest that the role of the four rivers in the garden (Gen 2:10-14), the Pishon, the Gihon, the Tigris and the Eu-

---

[13]See David T. Tsumura, *Creation and Destruction: A Reappraisal of the* Chaoskampf *Theory in the Old Testament* (Winona Lake, Ind.: Eisenbrauns, 2005), pp. 33-35; idem., *Earth and the Waters*, pp. 41-43. See also footnote 26 (below).

[14]For this term, see Tsumura, *Earth and the Waters*, pp. 94-116; idem., *Creation and Destruction*, pp. 87-106.

[15]For example, see Werner H. Schmidt, *Die Schöpfungsgeschichte der Priesterschrift: Zur Überlieferungs- geschichte von Genesis 1:1–2:4a und 2:4b–3:24.* 2., überarbeitete und erweiterte Auflage (Neukirchen-Vluyn: Neukirchener Verlag, 1967), p. 197.

[16]For the etymology of the term *'ēden* see Tsumura, *Earth and the Waters*, pp. 123-37; idem., *Creation and Destruction, pp.* 112-25.

phrates, was to control the amount of water and spread it evenly and adequately throughout the garden. Thus, irrigation and inundation are crucial to making the land arable and fruitful in order to supply food and drink to the earthly creatures. As Michael Guebert notes in the previous chapter, even in our modern era,[17] the real problem with regard to the water supply is usually not so much an absolute lack of water as the lack of human wisdom and willingness to distribute water evenly for the benefit of others.

As long as humans kept God's command, they could stay in the garden with its abundant water supply. However, because of their rebellion (sin) against God, they were alienated from God, the source of life, became spiritually dead, and were driven from the garden, the well-watered place. The Lord's words, "cursed is the ground because of you; in toil you shall eat of it all the days of your life" (Gen 3:17), implies among else that they would suffer not only spiritually but also physically from too little or too much water.

Thus human beings became obliged to control water by making canals or using other human technology in order to get enough food from farming and raising animals.[18]

Psalm 104 describes poetically how God created the earth, especially the relationship between the earth and the water.

> You set the earth on its foundations,
>   so that it shall never be shaken.
> You cover it with the deep as with a garment;
>   the waters stood above the mountains.
> At your rebuke they flee;
>   at the sound of your thunder they take to flight.
> They rose up to the mountains,
>   ran down to the valleys
>   to the place that you appointed for them.
> You set a boundary that they may not pass,
>   so that they might not again cover the earth. (Ps 104:5-9)

---

[17]See Michael Guebert on water resources at the end of this book.

[18]For example, see Shin T. Kang, "Irrigation in Ancient Mesopotamia," *Journal of the American Water Resources Association* 8 (1972): 619-24.

God established the earth as a secure and stable place with waters properly controlled so that they might not "cover the earth" again as they did in the initial situation in Genesis 1:2, though God did allow "all the fountains of the great deep [to] burst forth" (Gen 7:11) at the time of Noah's Deluge (see below). The psalm also goes on to describe how God provides abundant water both from below (terrestrial "springs" and "streams") and from above (celestial, i.e., "from your lofty abode"), so that earthly creatures, both animals and plants, might be supplied with waters and "the earth [be] satisfied with the fruit of [God's] work" (Ps 104:13). Thus, the compassionate Creator God provided water for all creatures even after the Fall.

> You make springs gush forth in the valleys;
>> they flow between the hills,
> giving drink to every wild animal;
>> the wild asses quench their thirst.
> By the streams the birds of the air have their habitation;
>> they sing among the branches.
> From your lofty abode you water the mountains;
>> the earth is satisfied with the fruit of your work. (Ps 104:10-13)

The dependence of creatures upon God's provision contrasts with some aspects of ancient Near Eastern mythology. For example, in Canaanite mythology the sea dragon Litanu was thought to be an independent divine power of chaos against which the deity Baal had to fight in order to establish his kingly order as well as ensure the fertility of the land. This dragon is referred to in other Hebrew poetic texts such as Job 3:8, Psalm 74:14 and Isaiah 27:1, but in those texts the Canaanite divine name is depersonified and fossilized as a poetic metaphor for an enemy of Yahweh who is destined to be destroyed.[19] In the monotheistic context of Psalm 104:25-26, even the sea monster Leviathan is a creature of God, dependent upon God's provision of water.

> Yonder is the sea, great and wide,
>> creeping things innumerable are there,
>> living things both small and great.

---

[19]See Tsumura, *Creation and Destruction*, pp. 192-95.

There go the ships,
    and Leviathan that you formed to sport in it. (Ps 104:25-26)

Psalm 104 goes on to say that the Creator God planted the cedars of
Lebanon with abundant water supply.

The trees of the LORD are watered abundantly,
    the cedars of Lebanon that he planted. (Ps 104:16)

Certainly not only animals but plants as well require water. In Ezekiel 31:3-4 also, "a cedar in Lebanon, with beautiful branches and forest shade" is said to be nourished by the waters.[20]

PLENTY

The Bible, especially the Old Testament, takes material plenty as a sign
of God's blessing given by a gracious God to righteous men. For example, Psalm 112:1-3 states that wealth and riches are in the houses of
those who fear the Lord. Again, Deuteronomy 7:12-15 promises that
the Lord blesses those who observe his commandments with material
blessings and health. However, the "health and wealth gospel" can also
be a stumbling block to those who trust in God.[21] In fact, the covenant
people of Israel, as they became rich materially, forgot the Lord who
had guided them out of the house of slavery (see, for example, Deut
6:10-12; Amos 2:6-10).

The fertility theme. Fertility and the abundance of water are tightly
related. In the polytheistic Canaanite religion, fertility deities such as
Baal, Anat, Astarte and Asherah played a prominent role. The most
popular fertility god was the storm god Baal, who supposedly could give
an abundance of rain (i.e., *good*) and water, though he was unable to create or make anything.[22] On the other hand, in Hebrew religion, it is
Yahweh, the creator of universe, who graciously brings forth the produce
of the land. For example, Psalm 104:16 declares, "The trees of the LORD
are watered abundantly / the cedars of Lebanon that he planted."

---

[20]Cf. Ezek 31:8, "the cedars in the garden of God."
[21]Cf. David F. Wells, *No Place for Truth: Or Whatever Happened to Evangelical Theology?* (Grand
    Rapids: Eerdmans, 1993), p. 181.
[22]Tsumura, *Creation and Destruction*, pp. 55-56.

Like Egyptian poets,[23] Hebrew poets compared the righteous person with a tree in a garden, adding that the tree is "planted by streams of water" *(šātûl ʿal palgê māyim).*

> They are like trees planted by streams of water,
> which yield their fruit in its season,
>> and their leaves do not wither.
> In all that they do, they prosper. (Ps 1:3)

> Blessed are those who trust in the LORD,
> whose trust is the LORD.
> They shall be like a tree planted by water [*šātûl ʿal mayim*],
>> sending out its roots by the stream [*ʿal yûbal*].
> It shall not fear when heat comes,
>> and its leaves shall stay green;
> in the year of drought it is not anxious,
>> and it does not cease to bear fruit. (Jer 17:7-8)

Thus, water is often a symbol of prosperity in human life.

Dew and rain. In the land of Canaan, rain and dew are the two major sources of water from above. During the dry season, when there is no rain during daytime, dew comes down from the heaven during the night. In the Canaanite myths, among Baal's daughters are the fertility deities *Arṣay* ("land") and *Ṭallay* ("dew"). In fact, "rain" *(māṭār)* and "dew" *(ṭal)* represent a standard word pair common to Ugaritic and Hebrew languages. For example,

> You mountains of Gilboa,
>> let there be no dew or rain upon you,
>> nor bounteous fields!
> For there the shield of the mighty was defiled,
>> the shield of Saul, anointed with oil no more. (2 Sam 1:21)

Occasionally the expression "dew of heaven" occurs in parallel with "fatness of the earth." What is unique in the biblical teaching is the fact that both rain and dew are created and controlled by the creator God.

---

[23]See Miriam Lichtheim, "Instruction of Amenemope," in *The Context of Scripture, vol. 1, Canonical Compositions from the Biblical World,* ed. William W. Hallo (Leiden: Brill, 1997), p. 117. Hereafter cited as *COS*.

Job 36:27 describes him as the one who "draws up the drops of water, which distill as rain *(māṭār)* to the streams ('*ēdô*: lit. 'stream')" (author's translation).[24]

Job 37 offers the most extensive theology of rain and weather in the entire Bible. After describing God as the one who "roars" and "thunders" in Job 37:1-5, in Job 37:6-7 God is described as directly bringing the rain *(māṭār)* and snow *(šeleg)* down to the earth.

> For to the snow he says, "Fall on the earth";
>> and the shower of rain, his heavy shower of rain,
> serves as a sign on everyone's hand,
>> so that all whom he has made may know it.

Here the rain represents the link between the resources of heaven and the needs of earth, a link provided by the gracious God. Even the icy water and clouds exist to "accomplish" God's purpose "on the face of the habitable world" (Job 37:10-12). Elihu continues,

> Whether for correction, or for his land,
>> or for love, he causes it to happen. (Job 37:13)

Job is then challenged by God to consider "the wondrous works of God" (Job 37:14), the Almighty, around whom is "awesome majesty" (Job 37:22).

> The Almighty—we cannot find him;
>> he is great in power and justice,
>> and abundant righteousness he will not violate.
> Therefore mortals fear him;
>> he does not regard any who are wise in their own conceit.
>> (Job 37:23-24)

While water remains connected with the fertility of the land in the Old Testament, the Old Testament clearly portrays both water and fertility as God-given, "whether for correction . . . or for love" (Job 37:13). In fact, in the following passages the dew of heaven is described as one of the divine blessings, and the lack of it is a curse:

---

[24]For the term '*ēdo*, see Tsumura, *Creation and Destruction*, pp. 104-6.

May God give you of the dew of heaven [*ṭal haššāmayim*],
and of the fatness of the earth [*šĕmannê hāʾāreṣ*],
and plenty of grain and wine. (Gen 27:28)

Then his father Isaac answered him:

See, away from the fatness of the earth shall your home be,
and away from the dew of heaven on high. (Gen 27: 39)

The land of water. The Bible describes the promised land of Canaan
as being a land of water like the Garden of Eden (Gen 13:10). Prophets
frequently employ figures of speech involving water: "like a garden
without water [*mayim*]" (Is 1:30); "and you shall be like a watered garden [*gan rāweh*], like a spring of water [*môṣāʾ mayim*], whose waters
never fail" (Is 58:11); "their life shall become like a watered garden, and
they shall never languish again" (Jer 31:12). Ezekiel uses the image of
"Eden, the garden of God" (Ezek 28:13) and says, "This land that was
desolate has become like the garden of Eden; and the waste and desolate and ruined towns are now inhabited and fortified" (Ezek 36:35).
The image of Eden here is certainly that of a well-watered place, as
noted above, and the phrase is used by the prophet to describe the recovery of the land. Deuteronomy 8:7-8 describes the promised land in
glowing terms:

For the Lord your God is bringing you into a good land, a land with
flowing streams [*naḥălê māyim*], with springs [*ʿăyānōt*] and underground
waters [*tĕhōmōt*] welling up in valleys and hills, a land of wheat and
barley, of vines and fig trees and pomegranates, a land of olive trees and
honey.

Elsewhere the psalmist speaks of God giving fertility by the "river of
God," which is "full of water."

You visit the earth and water it,
    you greatly enrich it;
the river of God [*peleg ʾĕlōhîm*] is full of water [*māyim*]
    you provide the people with grain,
    for so you have prepared it. (Ps 65:9; 65:10 MT)

AGRICULTURE AND WATER

The Lord brought the Israelites "into a good land, a land with flowing streams, with springs and underground waters welling up in valleys and hills," (Deut 8:7). He provides rain and dew to enrich the land abundantly (Ps 65:9-10) or stops them (1 Kings 17:1).

> You *water* its furrows *abundantly* [*rawwēh*][25]
>> settling its ridges,
> softening it with showers [*rěbîbîm*],
>> and blessing its growth. (Ps 65:10; 65:11 MT, emphasis added)

Agriculturally, abundant water certainly brings rich growth to the land and its *furrows,* but the amount is always important; it must be neither too much nor too little.

Thus, the water is one of the most important natural resources of the earth and the primary element that brings plenty into the human life. However, every creature on the earth requires a suitable amount of water to live pleasantly, neither too much nor too little.

Flood. While water in a modest amount is usually a blessing to living creatures, uncontrolled water such as a flood brings disaster and can be God's way of judging the created world.

The deluge in the days of Noah brought about the destruction of almost all earth-dwelling creatures except the chosen few (Gen 7:21-23), because of the human "violence" (*hāmās*; cf. Jewish Publication Society: "lawlessness") (Gen 6:11). This deluge (or "flood"; Heb. *mabbûl;* Akk. *abûbu*) was clearly distinguished from the annual flooding "high waters" (Akk. *mîlu*), and the expression "all the fountains of the great deep [*kol maʿyĕnōt tĕhôm rabbâ*] burst forth, and the windows of the heavens were opened" (Gen 7:11) has nothing to do with what Bernhard W. Anderson claims "the near return of the earth to pre-creation chaos."[26] The phrase *tĕhôm rabbâ* simply refers to the great

---

[25]NIV reads, "You *drench* its furrows"; NJPS "*Saturating* its furrows."

[26]Bernhard W. Anderson, "Water" in *Interpreter's Dictionary of Bible* (New York: Abingdon, 1962), 4:806-10; see also idem, *Creation versus Chaos: The Reinterpretation of Mythical Symbolism in the Bible* (Philadelphia: Fortress, 1987 [orig. 1967]). Against this chaos interpretation, see P. J. Harland, *The Value of Human Life: A Study of the Story of the Flood (Genesis 6-9)*, VTSup 64 (Leiden: Brill, 1996), pp. 94-96.

mass of underground water. Genesis 6 clearly says that the reason why God sent the great Deluge against human beings was their *violence*, to which the holy God had to respond with the judgment. Hence, the Deluge itself is *not* considered as evil in this context.

> Now the earth was corrupt in God's sight, and the earth was filled with violence. And God saw that the earth was corrupt; for all flesh [*kol bāśār*] had corrupted its ways upon the earth. And God said to Noah, "I have determined to make an end of all flesh, for the earth is filled with violence because of them; now I am going to destroy them along with the earth." (Gen 6:11-13)

All flesh, not just human beings, was judged through the Deluge, due to the violence (i.e., the corruption of the earth), "for all flesh had corrupted its ways upon the earth." So, the Deluge was God's agent to make "an end of all flesh" (*qēṣ kol bāśār*) in order to judge the earth, that is, *all flesh*, including fish, bird and animals as well as human beings.[27] Using similar language, the prophet Isaiah declares in Isaiah 28:2,

> See, the Lord has one who is mighty and strong;
>　　like a storm of hail [*zerem bārād*], a destroying tempest,
> like a storm of mighty, overflowing waters [*zerem mayim kabbîrîm
>　　šōṭĕpîm*];
>　　with his hand he will hurl them down to the earth.

Because of his great mercy, God has not totally destroyed his people ever since (Neh 9:31; Ezek 20:17). God promised through Jeremiah: "The whole land shall be a desolation; yet I will not make a full end [*kālâ* "complete destruction"]" (Jer 4:27; also Jer 5:10, 18; 30:11; 46:28). However, on the day of the Lord's wrath the whole world will be destroyed, not by the Flood but by the fire of his jealousy (Zeph 1:18).

While the deluge was certainly God's agent to bring total destruction to *all flesh*, in the Bible God is often described as fighting or sub-

---

[27]This is referred to in terms of "the whole creation," that would prevent others from following in the apostate's steps, *pasa hē ktisis* in Rom 8:22. See Douglas J. Moo's article "Eschatology and Environmental Ethics: On the Importance of Biblical Theology to Creation Care" (chap. 1 of this book).

duing destructive waters such as "sea" *(yām)* and "the mighty waters" *(mayim rabbîm,* Hab 3:15), which are often personified and symbolized as Rahab (Ps 89:10; Is 51:9), Leviathan (Ps 74:14; Is 27:1), the monster (Ps 74:13), etc.[28]

In recent years, many floods have been the outworking of man's greed, which causes environmental degradation—a sort of violence toward the created order—for the sake of economic development. Cutting down large numbers of trees in mountains has often resulted in floods, as well as in destructive and deadly landslides.[29]

Drought. The dry weather of Canaan causes serious problems with a lack of water for drinking and irrigation. Hence, from ancient times, people wisely developed various methods of preserving water from rain and dew (e.g., the cisterns at Masada). In Canaan, city-states developed carefully thought-out water systems to provide enough water for its citizens. Sometimes, these involved a well on the bottom or the side of a hill for a fortified city: e.g., the Spring of Gihon, the Pool at Gibeon, the underground water system at Hazor and Megiddo as well as the Early Bronze age water tower in Jerusalem. These water systems were already established during the pre-Israelite eras.[30]

The major concern of the fertility cult in ancient Canaan was to se-

---

[28]Some scholars explain these waters as the uncreated "chaos" water, the enemy of the creator in the primordial age. But in the Bible, there is no hint of battle in the creation of the universe. It should be noted that among the ancient Near Eastern cosmogonic myths the conflict motif and the creation motif coexist only in the Babylonian creation myth *Enuma Elish.* There is no creation motif in the conflict myths of Baal and Yam, or Baal and Mot, while there is no conflict motif in the creation story in Genesis 1 as well as in Mesopotamian creation stories such as *Creation of the World by Marduk.* See Tsumura, *Creation and Destruction,* pp. 143-55; idem, "The 'Chaoskampf' Motif in Ugaritic and Hebrew Literatures ," in *Le Royaume d'Ougarit de la Crète à l'Euphrate. Nouveaux axes de Recherche,* ed. J.-M. Michaud, Proche-Orient et Littérature Ougaritique II (Sherbrooke: GGC, 2007), pp. 473-99; and also, Rebecca S. Watson, *Chaos Uncreated: A Reassessment of the Theme of "Chaos" in the Hebrew Bible,* BZAW 341 (New York: Walter de Gruyter, 2005). According to Watson, there is no intrinsic connection between *"Chaoskampf"* and creation in the extant Israelite texts. She concludes that "the term 'chaos' should be abandoned in respect of the Old Testament, since this literary collection does not seem to possess a clear expression of the idea that Yahweh engaged in combat with the sea or a sea monster in primordial times" (p. 397).
[29]As Michael Guebert notes, "deforestation, urbanization and intensive agriculture" cause a great amount of water contamination in modern life. See chapter 6.
[30]For water supply projects found at such ancient cities as Hazor, Megiddo, Gibeon, Gezer and Jerusalem, see Amihai Mazar, *Archaeology of the Land of the Bible* (New York: Doubleday, 1990), pp. 478-85.

cure food and drink for the society.[31] Myths such as the Baal-Mot conflict in Ugaritic society concerned this life-and-death issue for the ancient society. When we note that the god Mot is the god of death, infertility and drought, it is understandable that the ancients, like us, were gravely concerned with how to solve the problem of drought and the resulting famine.[32]

In the Old Testament, drought is included among divine methods by which sinners are chastised. God would usually begin with a milder form of punishment and then increase its severity, depending on the human response. Amos refers to a series of such judgments imposed on Israel in Amos 4:6-11: lack of food (v. 6); lack of rain/drought (vv. 7-8); famine (v. 9), disease (v. 10), fire (v. 11).[33] But the people did not return to the Lord. Since there was no repentance, each time a further judgment had to fall. Similarly, in the ancient Babylonian epic of Flood, the *Atra-Hasis Epic,* the divine counsel first sent a milder disaster such as famine (Tablet II), and then finally, the Flood *abubu* (Tablet III).[34]

It is well known that during the wilderness journey of the Israelites the shortage of water made the people complain to Moses and Aaron and ask for the water at Meribah in Exodus 17:1-7 and Numbers 20. These shortages were the test of whether the people of God trusted their own God for their physical needs. Certainly thirst for water is a crucial problem, especially in the desert (Ex 17:3). The Lord made water flow for the people of Israel from the rock (Is 48:21). In the days to come, the Lord will lead them "by springs of water" (*mabbûʿê mayim;* Is 49:10) and they will never again thirst (Rev 7:16; Is 49:10).

---

[31]For the Ugaritic fertility myth and ritual text of the birth of the Good Gods (UT 52/KTU 1.23), see most recently Mark S. Smith, *The Rituals and Myths of the Feast of the Goodly Gods of KTU/CAT 1.23: Royal Constructions of Opposition, Intersection, Integration, and Domination* (Atlanta: Society of Biblical Literature, 2006); David T. Tsumura, "Revisiting the 'seven' Good Gods of fertility in Ugarit: Is Albright's emendation of KTU 1.23,64 correct?" *Ugarit Forschungen* 39 (2008): 629-41.

[32]See David T. Tsumura, "Canaan, Canaanites," in *Dictionary of the Old Testament: Historical Books,* ed. Bill T. Arnold and H. G. M. Williamson (Downers Grove, Ill.: InterVarsity Press, 2005), pp. 122-32.

[33]See also the covenant curses, Lev 26:19-20; Deut 28:23-24.

[34]For the text see, *COS* 1:452; also W. G. Lambert and A. R. Millard, *Atra-Hasis: The Babylonian Story of the Flood* (Oxford: Clarendon, 1969), pp. 9-13.

PROPER CONTROL OF WATER RESOURCES

While it is impossible for human beings to control the celestial water, rain and dew, they should at least make reasonable efforts to control the terrestrial waters in rivers and lakes as well as underground. In biblical theology, human beings play a distinctive role in creation; as the images of God *(imago Dei)* they have the responsibility of having dominion over every earthly creature except other human beings. This is clearly reflected in Genesis 1:26 and Genesis 1:28 as well as in Psalm 8, which says that God had made human beings as a special creature, to whom God "[has] given them dominion over the works of [his] hands" (Ps 8:6).

WATER CONTROL AS A DIVINE CHARGE

In the biblical context of creation, the *earth* refers to every place under the *heavens*, as in Genesis 1:1, where the entire cosmos is divided into two realms by the expression *the heavens and the earth*. In fact, in Genesis 1:26 and 28, Psalm 8 and Psalm 148:7-14, which also divide the universe bipartitely, all the sea creatures, beasts and all livestock, creeping things and flying birds belong to the earth.[35]

It should be noted that *waters above the heavens* (Ps 148:4) belong to the heavens, which is the realm beyond human control.[36] As Tucker notes, the biblical worldview is more theocentric than anthropocentric.[37] That is why it speaks of creation and not nature. The Bible does not specifically talk about a theology of water; instead it presents a theology of creation. However, the relationship between nature and human beings should be clarified. Psalm 8 and Genesis 1–2, as well as other passages that deal with creation, draw clear distinctions not only between the Creator and the creatures, but also between human beings and other creatures.

While Genesis 1:26 mentions only human dominion over other creatures on the earth, which includes not only the land but also sea

---

[35]See Tsumura, *Earth and the Waters*, pp. 72-77.
[36]On the term "heavens" (*šāmayim*), see *NIDOTTE* 4:160-66.
[37]Gene Tucker, "Rain on a Land Where No One Lives: The Hebrew Bible on the Environment," *JBL* 116 (1997): 3-17.

and sky, Genesis 1:28 adds two more imperatives with regard to the earth, i.e., "fill" *(ml')* and "subdue" *(kbš)* the earth. This means that as the images of God human beings should have *dominion over (rdh)* the other creatures on the earth as God's vice regents, as the ones who reflect God's divine purpose and nature of the Creator in their dominion. Naturally, their responsibility to fill and subdue the earth should be in keeping with their royal roles as the representatives of the Creator. Hence, the idea of subduing the earth is not a negative struggle that human beings have with the earth; rather, human beings should have dominion over other creatures on the earth (that is, animals on the land, fish in the sea and birds in the sky) by ruling them properly as the royal representative of their Creator and reflecting the generosity of God.[38]

The Eden narrative portrays the proper role of human beings to their immediate environment, the garden of Eden, as *working the ground* (Gen 2:5), more specifically to *work ('bd)* and *keep (šmr)* the garden of Eden *('ēden)*, which is a part of the ground *('ădāmâ;* Gen 2:15). Here, too, human beings were entrusted by the Gardener God with the job of keeping up the garden of God.[39] So, the human beings are responsible to work and keep the environment, which includes water resources, according to the will of the Creator and Owner.

However, as the result of sin, i.e., their rebellion against God and his commandment, the relationship of human beings with the Creator was disturbed, resulting in their alienation from God, as well as from other people and from their environment. The *ground ('ădāmâ)* is hence cursed because of their sin (Gen 3:17). Human beings have lost the proper judgment and purpose in controlling other creatures as well as in living together with other human beings; they now do so in their own selfish ways and according to their sinful desires. This led to the *violence (ḥāmās)* toward their environment, toward plants and animals,

---

[38]For human beings as a royal image, see Phyllis A. Bird, "'Male and Female He Created Them': Genesis 1:27b in the Context of the Priestly Account of Creation," in *"I Studied Inscriptions from before the Flood": Ancient Near Eastern, Literary, and Linguistic Approaches to Genesis 1-11*, ed. Richard S. Hess and David T. Tsumura (Winona Lake, Ind.: Eisenbrauns, 1994), pp. 329-61.

[39]See further the discussion by Daniel I. Block in chapter 5.

as well as toward other people, resulting in severe destruction and pollution through the violence to the nature including water.

For example, history attests to the aggressive destruction of the cedars of Lebanon by the Assyrians and others. Mesopotamian records show that especially after Shalmaneser III in the ninth century B.C., the Assyrians invaded Lebanon in order to get the cedars for building materials for their magnificent palaces at Calah (i.e., Nimrud) and Nineveh. In fact, a segment of cedar wood was found at Nimrud from this period. An Assyrian relief, i.e., a sculpture that is carved out of a flat vertical surface, at King Sargon's palace depicts how Phoenicians shipped logs for the palace.[40]

According to Habakkuk, the Israelite prophet of Yahweh at the turn of the seventh century B.C., environmental violence is treated as one aspect of human greediness (Hab 2:15-17).

> For the violence done to Lebanon will overwhelm you;
>   the destruction of the animals will terrify you—
> because of human bloodshed and violence to the earth,
>   to cities and all who live in them. (Hab 2:17)

Violence toward the earth, including trees and animals, and the sacrifice of other human beings for the sake of one's own material needs, as Habakkuk describes,[41] are two basic elements of human sinfulness that we find also in modern urban life.[42]

This human sinfulness results in greed and an insatiable desire and lust for material things, expressed in the exploitative manipulation of natural resources, including water. Consequently, power and money become final means to get more and more of what they desire, and inequality increases between the weak and the strong. Thus, distribution problems have remained unsolved from generation to generation.

---

[40]See J. E. Curtis and J. E. Reade, eds., *Art and Empire: Treasures from Assyria in the British Museum* (London: British Museum, 1996), p. 108.

[41]Habakkuk 1–2 describe the Chaldaeans (i.e., Babylonians) as the archetype of sinners, whose "own might is their god" (1:11), who do "violence" (1:9) not only to Lebanon but also to animals (2:17), and who treat humans "like the fish of the sea" (1:14).

[42]See for example, Noah J. Toly, "Climate Change and Climate Change Policy as Human Sacrifice: Artifice, Idolatry, and Environment in a Technological Society," *Christian Scholar's Review* 35, no. 1 (2005): 63-78.

The distribution of water resources has become one of the most crucial issues in the modern society. In fact, international action is required to ensure that those who really need water have access to it. This matter demands *fairness*, which is the concern of Paul when he talked about the *act of grace*. Paul declares the biblical principle in 2 Corinthians 8:15, "As it is written, 'The one who had much did not have too much, / and the one who had little did not have too little.'" Here Paul is obviously quoting Exodus 16:18, "But when they measured it with an omer, those who gathered much had nothing over, and those who gathered little had no shortage; they gathered as much as each of them needed." This refers to manna, the bread from heaven, but the same principle should be applied to water also.

The ancient wisdom literature of the Old Testament often talks about the danger of having plenty:

> Two things I ask of you;
>   deny them not to me before I die:
> Remove far from me falsehood and lying;
>   give me neither poverty nor riches;
>   feed me with the food that is needful for me,
> lest I be full and deny you
>   and say, "Who is the LORD?"
> or lest I be poor and steal
>   and profane the name of my God. (Prov 30:7-9 ESV)

The desire of the sinful human beings is never satisfied; hence the tenth commandment prohibits coveting. Thus, Moses warned the people of Israel not to forget their God, who brought them out of the land of Egypt, even when they would have plenty of food and drink.

> When the LORD your God has brought you into the land that he swore to your ancestors, to Abraham, to Isaac, and to Jacob, to give you—a land with fine, large cities that you did not build, houses filled with all sorts of goods that you did not fill, hewn cisterns that you did not hew, vineyards and olive groves that you did not plant—and when you have eaten your fill, take care that you do not forget the LORD, who brought you out of the land of Egypt, out of the house of slavery. (Deut 6:10-12)

To be content with what we have is a very important principle. Paul teaches us this Christian principle in 1 Thessalonians 5:16-18:

> Rejoice always,
>   pray without ceasing,
>   give thanks in all circumstances;
> for this is the will of God [*thelēma Theou*] in Christ Jesus for you.

PART FIVE

CLIMATE CHANGE

8

THE CHANGING GLOBAL CLIMATE

Evidence, Impacts,
Adaptation and Abatement

Sir John Houghton

WHY CARE ABOUT GLOBAL CLIMATE CHANGE?

It has always been important to look after our local environment if only
so that we can pass on to our children and grandchildren an environment at least as good as the one that we have enjoyed. Today, however,
it is not just the *local* environment that is at risk but the *global* environment that is collectively in danger. Small amounts of pollution for
which each of us is responsible affect everyone in the world. Carbon
dioxide that enters the atmosphere from the burning of fossil fuels,
coal, oil and gas contributes to damaging climate change. Pressures
from rapidly increasing world population and increasing overuse of the
earth's resources exacerbate the damage both to ecosystems and human
communities. Many scientists and politicians describe it as probably
"the greatest problem the world faces" and as a "weapon of mass destruction." *Global* pollution demands *global* solutions.

To arrive at global solutions it is necessary to address human attitudes very broadly—for instance those concerned with resource use,
lifestyle, wealth and poverty. Solutions must also involve human society at all levels of aggregation: international organizations, national
and local governments, large and small industry and businesses, nongovernmental organizations (e.g., churches), and individuals. To ac-

count for the breadth of concern, a modern term used to describe such environmental care is "sustainability."

WHAT IS SUSTAINABILITY?

Imagine that you are a crewmember of a large space ship voyaging toward a distant planet. Your journey there and back will take years. An adequate, high quality source of energy is readily available in the radiation from the sun. Otherwise, resources for the journey are limited. The crew is constantly engaged in managing the resources as carefully as possible. A local biosphere is created in the spacecraft where plants are grown for food and everything is recycled. Careful accounts are kept of all resources, with especial emphasis on nonreplaceable components.

Planet Earth is enormously larger than the spaceship I have just described. The crew of Spaceship Earth at six billion and rising is also enormously larger. The principle of sustainability should be applied to Spaceship Earth as rigorously as it has to be applied to the much smaller vehicle on its interplanetary journey. In a 1966 publication, Professor Kenneth Boulding, a distinguished American economist, employed the image of Spaceship Earth. He contrasted an "open" economy (or unconstrained economy) with a "spaceship" economy in which sustainability is paramount.[1]

Sustainability is an idea that can be applied to activities and communities as well as to physical resources. Strongly linked to social sustainability and sustainable economics, *sustainable development* is a comprehensive, if ambiguous, term. There have been many definitions of sustainability. The simplest I know is "not cheating on our children"; to that may be added, "not cheating on our neighbors" and "not cheating on the rest of creation." In other words, not passing on to our children or any future generation an earth that is degraded compared to the one we inherited, and also sharing common resources with our neighbors in the rest of the world while caring properly for the non-human creation.

---

[1]Kenneth Boulding was professor of economics at the University of Colorado, and sometime President of the American Economics Association and the American Association for the Advancement of Science. His article "The Economics of the Coming Spaceship Earth" was published in *Environmental Quality in a Growing Economy,* ed. H. Jarrett (Baltimore, Md.: Johns Hopkins University Press, 1966), pp. 3-14

The human activities of an increasing world population, together with rapid industrial development, are leading to environmental degradation on a large scale. Notwithstanding, some deny that degradation is happening, others that degradation matters. The truth is that our global environment is deteriorating at an alarming rate, and unless we admit our destructive behaviors and seek more sustainable responses to global climate change, our children's children will have very little hope for a future.

Table 8.1. **Important Sustainability Issues**

Issue	Links
Global warming & climate change	Energy, transport, biodiversity, loss, deforestation, water, soil loss, agriculture, food
Land Use Change	Biodiversity loss, deforestation, water, soil loss, climate change, agriculture, food
Consumption	Biodiversity loss, deforestation, water, soil loss, climate change, agriculture, food
Waste	Consumption, agriculture, energy, food
Fish	Consumption, food

GLOBAL WARMING AND CLIMATE CHANGE: THE BASIC SCIENCE

In order to discuss the issue of global climate change, we must first define scientifically what is happening. By absorbing infra-red or heat radiation from the earth's surface, greenhouse gases present in the atmosphere as part of natural processes, such as water vapor and carbon dioxide, act as blankets over the earth's surface, keeping it on average 20 or 30°C warmer than it would otherwise be. The existence of this natural "greenhouse effect" has been known for nearly two hundred years; it is essential to the provision of our current climate to which ecosystems and humans have adapted.

A record of past climate and atmospheric composition is provided from analyses of the composition of the Antarctic or Greenland ice caps and air bubbles trapped in the ice obtained from different depths (figure 8.1). From such records we find that, since the beginning of the industrial revolution around 1750, carbon dioxide (one of the greenhouse gases) has increased by nearly 40 percent and is now at a higher concentration in the atmosphere than it has probably been for millions of years. Chemical analysis demonstrates that this increase is due largely to the combustion of fossil fuels. If no action is taken to curb these emissions, the carbon dioxide concentration will rise during the twenty-first century to two or three times pre-industrial levels.

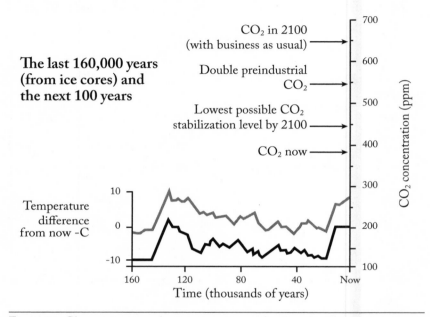

Figure 8.1. Changes in atmospheric temperature and carbon dioxide concentration in the polar atmosphere during the last ice age (as shown from the Vostok ice core drilled from Antarctica). The main triggers for ice ages have been small, regular variations in the geometry of the Earth's orbit about the sun. The next ice age is predicted to begin in about 50,000 years. (Chart based on information in D. Raynaud et al., "The Ice Record of Greenhouse Gases," *Science* 259, no. 5097 [1993]: 926-34.)

The climate record over the last thousand years shows great natural variability—including, for instance, the "medieval warm period" and the "little ice age." The rise in global average temperature (and its rate of rise) during the twentieth century (figure 8.2) is well outside the range of known natural variability. The year 1998 is the warmest year in the instrumental record. A more striking statistic is that each of the first eight months of 1998 was the warmest on record for said month. Strong evidence demonstrates that most of the warming over the last fifty years is due to the increase of greenhouse gases, especially carbon dioxide. Confirmation of this is also provided by observations of oceanic warming. The period of "global dimming" from about 1950 to 1970 is most likely due to the increase in atmospheric particles (especially sulphates) from industrial sources. These particles reflect sunlight, hence cooling the surface while masking some of the warming effect of greenhouse gases.

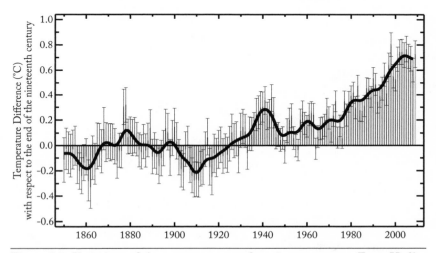

Figure 8.2. Variations of the average near-surface air temperature. From Hadley Centre, Meteorological Office, U.K. Used by permission.

The first report of the Intergovernmental Panel on Climate Change (IPCC), in 1990, projected that global average temperature would increase between 0.15 and 0.3°C per decade between 1990 and 2005. The IPCC's 2007 report provides observed temperature increase values of about 0.2°C, strengthening confidence in near-term projections. Over the twenty-first century the global average temperature is projected to rise by between 2 and 6°C (3.5 to 11°F) from its pre-industrial level; the range represents different assumptions about greenhouse gas emissions and the sensitivity of the climate model used in making the estimate (figure 8.3). For global average temperature, a rise of this amount is large. The difference between the middle of an ice age and a warm period in between is only about 5 or 6°C (9 to 11°F).[2] In the twenty-first

---

[2]See figure 8.1, noting that changes in global average temperature are about half those at the poles.

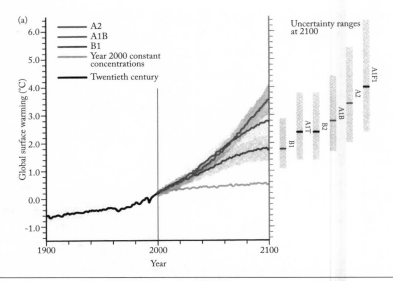

Figure 8.3. Global averages of surface warming (relative to 1980-1999) for different SRES scenarios (a set of future projections of greenhouse gas emissions organized by the IPCC, based on a range of assumptions regarding population growth, economic growth and environmental concern), shown as continuations of twentieth-century observations. Each curve is a multimodel average from a number (typically around 20) of general circulation models; shading denotes the one standard deviation range of individual model annual means. A curve is also shown for a scenario in which greenhouse gas concentrations were held constant at year 2000 values. The gray bars at the right indicate for the year 2100 the best estimate and uncertainty range for the six SRES marker scenarios, taking into account both the spread of model results and uncertainties in climate feedbacks. To obtain temperatures from preindustrial times, add 0.6 C. (From IPCC Fourth Assessment Report: Climate Change 2007 Synthesis Report [Geneva, Switzerland: IPCC, 2007], p. 46, fig. 3.2. Used with permission.)

century, we will likely see a rate of climate change equivalent to half an ice age in less than one hundred years—a larger rate of change than the earth has seen for at least ten thousand years. Adapting to this will be difficult for both humans and many ecosystems around the globe.

THE AFFECTS OF CLIMATE CHANGE

Talking in terms of global average temperature changes, however, tells us little about the impacts of global warming on human communities. Some of the most obvious impacts will result from the sea level rise that occurs when ocean water heats and expands. Furthermore, if our situa-

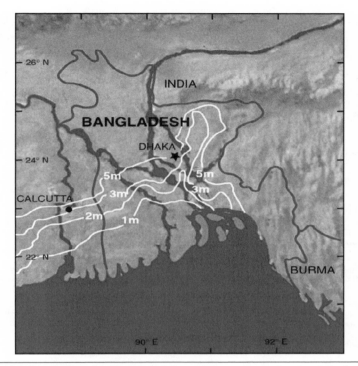

Figure 8.4. Land affected in Bangladesh by various amounts of sea level rise (adapted from J. D. Milliman, *Ambio* 261 [1989]: 48-55)

tion remains unchanged and we fail to respond to the signs of global warming, sea level will rise up to half a meter per century due to ocean warming and up to a further half metre due to melting glaciers and increasing melting of the polar ice caps. Already, between 1961 and 2003, global average sea level rose at an average rate of 1.8 mm per year, with a much faster rate from 1993 to 2003 —3.1 mm per year.[3] This will cause large problems for human communities living on coastal land and in low-lying regions. Sea defenses in many parts of the U.K., such as those in the eastern counties of England, will need costly improvements. However, many areas in other parts of the world, for instance in Bangladesh (where about 10 million live within the one meter contour;

---

[3]Intergovernmental Panel on Climate Change, "Summary for Policymakers," in *Climate Change 2007: The Physical Science Basis. Contribution of Working Group I to the Fourth Assessment Report of the Intergovernmental Panel on Climate Change*, ed. S. Solomon et al. (New York: Cambridge University Press, 2007), p. 5.

see figure 8.4), southern China, islands in the Indian and Pacific oceans, and similar places elsewhere, will be impossible to protect and many millions will be displaced.

Extreme weather will constitute a significant aspect of climate change impact. The unusually high temperatures in central Europe during the summer of 2003 (figure 8.5) led to the deaths of over twenty thousand people. Careful analysis projects that such summers are likely to be average by the middle of the twenty-first century and cool by the year 2100.

SWISS TEMPERATURE SERIES FOR JUNE–AUGUST 1864-2003

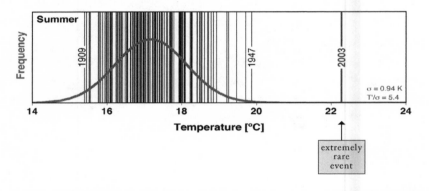

Figure 8.5. Distribution of average summer temperatures (June, July and August) in Switzerland from 1864-2003, showing a fitted Gaussian probability distribution. The 2003 value is 5.4 standard deviations from the mean, showing it is an extremely rare event far outside the normal range of climatic variability. (Graph created based on information in Christoph Schär et al., "The Role of Increasing Variability in European Summer Heat Waves," *Nature* 427 [2004]: 332-36.)

As reported in section three of this book, water is being recognized as an increasingly important resource. A warmer world will lead not only to higher sea levels, but also to more evaporation of water from the surface, more water vapor in the atmosphere, and more precipitation on average. Of further importance is that the increased condensation of water vapor in cloud formation leads to increased latent heat of condensation being released. Since this latent heat release is the largest source of energy driving the atmosphere's circulation, the hydrological cycle will intensify. This will tend toward more intense rainfall events as well as less rainfall in some semi-arid areas.

On average, floods and droughts are the most damaging of the world's disasters. Between 1975 and 2002, over 200,000 lives were lost and 2.2 billion more were affected by flooding. During the same time frame, over 500,000 lives were lost and 1.3 billion were affected by drought.[4] For floods, an increase in risk by a factor of five can be expected in many places by 2050.[5] While the most extreme droughts currently affect about 2 percent of the world's land area at any one time (twenty years ago this applied to only 1 percent of the world's land area), recent estimates suggest that by 2050 over 10 percent of the world's land area will be affected.[6] Further, extreme droughts will tend to be longer (measured in years rather than months), again leading to millions of displaced people.

There is no evidence that the number of tropical cyclones will increase with elevated greenhouse gas concentrations. However, the intensity of storms is connected to the ocean surface temperature in the region where the storms develop—not surprisingly so because the main energy source for such storms comes from the latent heat released as water vapor condenses.[7] As ocean temperatures rise at an increased rate in the future, an increase in the number of intense cyclones can be expected, although there is uncertainty about how large this increase might be. There is a high probability, however, that extratropical storm tracks will move poleward, further changing wind, precipitation and temperature patterns over the oceans and continents.[8]

---

[4]S. N. Jonkman, "Global Perspectives of Loss of Human Life Caused by Floods," *Natural Hazards* 34, no. 2 (2005): 151-75. Losses due to flooding anticipated by this analysis only include those from rainfall and not those from increased storm surge resulting from seal level rise and increased storm intensity. *Drought* here is defined according to the Palmer drought index that distinguishes between moderate, severe and extreme drought.

[5]T. N. Palmer and J. Raisanen, "Quantifying the Risk of Extreme Seasonal Precipitation Events in a Changing Climate," *Nature* 415 (2002): 512-14.

[6]E. J. Burke, S. J. Brown and N. Christidis, "Modeling the Recent Evolution of Global Drought and Projections for the Twenty-First Century with the Hadley Centre Climate Model," *Hydrometeorology* 7 (2006): 1113-25.

[7]K. Emmanuel, "Increasing Destructiveness of Tropical Cyclones over the Past 30 Years," *Nature* 436 (2005): 686-88; P. J. Webster et al., "Changes in Tropical Cyclone Number, Duration, and Intensity in a Warming Environment," *Science* 309 (2005): 1844-46.

[8]IPCC (2007), "Summary for Policymakers."

196 KEEPING GOD'S EARTH

Sea level rise, changes in water availability, and extreme events will trigger increasing numbers of environmental refugees. A careful estimate has suggested that, due to climate change, there could be more than 150 million extra refugees by 2050.[9]

In addition to the impacts summarized above are changes about which there is less certainty; however, if they occurred, these impacts would be highly damaging and possibly irreversible. For instance, dramatic changes are being observed in polar regions. With the rising temperatures over Greenland, it is estimated that the polar ice cap could begin melting down during the next few decades. Complete melt down is likely to take many centuries, but the elimination of the Greenland ice sheet alone would add 7 meters (23 feet) to sea level.

A further concern in response to global climate change regards the meridional overturning circulation (MOC), also called the thermohaline circulation (THC). The THC is a circulation that occurs throughout the deep oceans, partially sourced from water that has moved into the Gulf Stream from the tropics to the region between Greenland and Scandinavia. Because of evaporation on the way, the water is not only cold but salty, hence of higher density than the surrounding water. It therefore tends to sink, providing for a slow circulation at low levels that connects oceans together. This sinking assists in maintaining the Gulf Stream itself. In a globally warmed world, increased precipitation together with fresh water from melting ice will decrease the water's salinity, making it less likely to sink. The circulation will therefore weaken and possibly even shut down, leading to large regional changes of climate. Evidence from paleoclimate history shows that such cut-off has occurred in the past. According to the IPCC 2007 report, it is very likely that the THC of the Atlantic Ocean will slow during the twenty-first century.[10]

Climate change will also impact whole ecosystems. An estimated 20 to 30 percent of plant and animal species will potentially face extinc-

[9]N. Myers, J. Kent, *Environmental Exodus: An Emergent Crisis in the Global Arena* (Washington D.C.: Climate Institute, 1995).
[10]IPCC (2007), "Summary for Policymakers."

tion after only 1.5 to 2.5°C of warming.[11] Further major irreversible impacts on marine ecosystems are likely because of acidification of ocean water as a direct effect of rising carbon dioxide levels. Also, at lower latitudes—especially in seasonally dry and tropical regions—crop productivity may decrease dramatically with only minor increases in temperature. Global food productivity is projected to decrease if global average temperature rises above 3°C.[12]

I have thus far described adverse impacts. You will ask, "are none of the impacts positive?" Indeed, there are some positive impacts. For instance, in Siberia and other areas at high northern latitudes, winters will be less cold and growing seasons will lengthen. Also, increased concentrations of carbon dioxide have a fertilizing effect on some plants and crops which, providing there are adequate supplies of water and nutrients, will lead to increased crop yields in some places—probably most notably in northern mid-latitudes. However, careful studies dem-

Projected Impacts of Climate Change

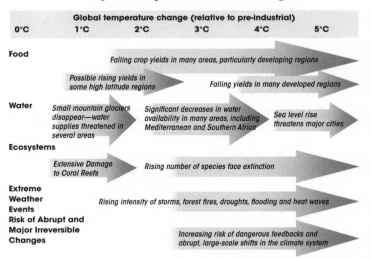

Figure 8.6. Summary of climate change in different sectors as a function of the rise in the global average temperature (from the Stern Review on the Economics of Climate Change 2006 and used with permission)

---

[11]Ibid.
[12]Ibid. See report for more complete information on particular regions.

onstrate that adverse impacts will far outweigh positive effects, especially as temperatures rise more than 1 or 2°C (2 to 3.5°F) above pre-industrial levels (figure 8.6).

A recent review of the economics of climate change by Sir Nicholas Stern estimates the likely cost of climate change impacts supposing no mitigating action is taken:

> In summary, analyses that take into account the full ranges of both impacts and possible outcomes—that is, that employ the basic economics of risk—suggest that "business-as-usual" climate change will reduce welfare by an amount equivalent to a reduction in consumption per head of between 5 and 20%. Taking account of the increasing scientific evidence of greater risks, of aversion to the possibilities of catastrophe, and of a broader approach to the consequences than implied by narrow output measures, the appropriate estimate is likely to be in the upper part of this range.[13]

These estimates in economic terms do not account for the human cost in terms of deaths, dislocation, misery and lack of security that would also accompany large-scale climate changes. Nor do they emphasize sufficiently the predominance of impacts in impoverished countries.

CAN WE BELIEVE THE EVIDENCE?

Many people ask how sure we are about the scientific story I have just recounted. Let me explain that it is based largely on the thorough work of the IPCC and its major report published in 2007.[14] I personally had the privilege of serving as either chairman or co-chairman of the Panel's scientific assessment from 1988 to 2002. Hundreds of scientists from many countries contributed to and reviewed these assessments. Our task was to distinguish honestly and objectively what is reasonably well known and understood from those areas with large uncertainty. The IPCC has produced four assessments—in 1990, 1995, 2001 and

---

[13]Nicholas Stern, "The Economics of Climate Change," *Stern Review* (Cambridge: Cambridge University Press, 2006), p. x.
[14]The IPCC was formed in 1988 jointly by two UN bodies: the World Meteorological Organization and the United Nations Environment Programme.

2007—covering science, impacts and analyses of policy options.[15] Because the IPCC is an intergovernmental body, the reports' Summaries for Policymakers were painstakingly agreed upon by meetings of governmental delegates from about one hundred countries—including all of the world's major countries. *No assessment on any other scientific topic has been so thoroughly researched and reviewed.* In June 2005, just before the G8 Summit in Scotland, the Academies of Science of the world's eleven most important countries (the G8, India, China and Brazil) issued a statement endorsing the conclusions of the IPCC and urging world governments to take urgent action to address climate change. The world's top scientists could not have spoken more strongly.[16]

ADAPTATION

In combating climate change, action has to be of two kinds: *mitigation* and *adaptation*. For example, the mitigation of greenhouse gas emissions is an absolute necessity in order to slow and eventually halt climate change. This will require us to alter our assumptions about the environment and our habits of consumption in order to produce the lasting change required. But it is also important to recognize that there is an increasing need to adapt to the climate change that is occurring. Significant climate change has already taken place and there is further change to which we are already committed—although not yet seen because of the lag introduced by the time taken for the oceans to warm. For the larger changes mentioned above in the description of impacts it is important to start preparing for adaptation now so as to minimize loss and damage.

---

[15] *Climate Change 2007*, 3 vols., *The Physical Science Basis; Impacts, Adaptation and Vulnerabilities;* and *Mitigation* (Cambridge: Cambridge University Press, 2007). All volumes of the four reports are available on the IPCC web site <www.ipcc.ch>. John Houghton, *Global Warming: The Complete Briefing*, 4th ed. (Cambridge: Cambridge University Press, 2009) is strongly based on the IPCC reports.

[16] Questions were recently raised about some emails hacked from the University of East Anglia in the UK. These questions cast no doubt on IPCC conclusions, which were also based on work with similar results from research centers in the USA. The Pew Center in the USA has studied the emails in detail and concluded that the suspect emails do not appear to reveal fraud or other scientific misconduct. See <www.pewclimate.org/docUploads/east-anglia-cru-hacked-emails-12-09-09.pdf>.

INTERNATIONAL ACTION: ABATEMENT

Because of the work of the IPCC and its first report in 1990, the 1992 Earth Summit at Rio de Janeiro addressed the climate change issue and the action that needed to be taken. The Framework Convention on Climate Change (FCCC)—agreed upon by over 160 countries, signed by President George Bush Sr. for the U.S. and subsequently ratified unanimously by the U.S. Senate—agreed that Parties to the Convention should take "precautionary measures to anticipate, prevent or minimize the causes of climate change and mitigate its adverse effects. Where there are threats of irreversible damage, lack of full scientific certainty should not be used as a reason for postponing such measures."

The FCCC recognized that developed countries have already benefited over many generations from abundant fossil fuel energy should therefore be the first to take action.[17] First, developed countries were urged to return to 1990 emissions levels by the year 2000, something achieved only by few countries. Second, in 1997, the Kyoto Protocol was agreed upon as a beginning for the process of reduction. The Protocol says that by 2012, developed countries should decrease greenhouse gas emissions by 5 percent from their 1990 benchmarks.[18] It also introduces for the first time international trading of greenhouse gas emissions so that reductions can be achieved in cost effective ways.

The objective of Article 2 in the FCCC is "to stabilize greenhouse gas concentrations in the atmosphere at a level that does not cause dangerous interference with the climate system" and that is consistent with sustainable development. Such stabilization would also eventually halt further climate change. However, because of carbon dioxide's long life in the atmosphere, the lag in the response of the climate to changes in greenhouse gases (largely because of the time taken for the ocean to warm), and the time taken for appropriate human action to be agreed upon, the achievement of such stabilization will take at least the better part of a century.

Global emissions of carbon dioxide to the atmosphere from fossil

---

[17]The terms "developed" and "developing" are used in this chapter to remain consistent with language used in IPCC reports and the UNFCCC.

[18]Although agreed to in 1997 it did not come into force until 2005. The United States and Australia failed to ratify the Kyoto Protocol.

fuel burning are currently approaching 30 billion tons of carbon dioxide per annum and rising rapidly (figure 8.8). Unless strong measures are taken, they will reach two or even three times their present levels during the twenty-first century and stabilization of greenhouse gas concentrations or of climate will be nowhere in sight. To stabilize carbon dioxide concentrations, emissions during the twenty-first century must reduce to well below their present levels by 2050 (figure 8.8) and to a small fraction of their present levels before the century's end.

Global action will be necessary to achieve substantial reductions in a timely manner. But collective action must be sensitive to the large differences between emissions from different countries. Expressed in tons of equivalent carbon dioxide[19] per capita per annum, they vary from around 25 for the U.S.A, 10 for Europe, 5 for China and 2.5 for India (see figure 8.7). Furthermore, the global average per capita, currently

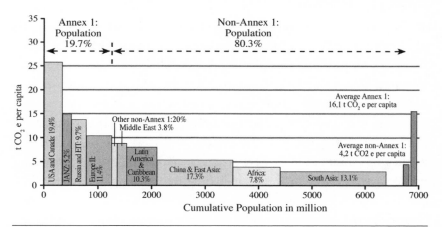

Figure 8.7. Carbon dioxide equivalent emissions in 2004 per capita for different countries and groups of countries. The percentages in the bars indicate a region's share in global greenhouse gas emissions. EIT = economies in transition; JANZ = Japan, Australia and New Zealand. To convert tons CO_2 to ton C, divide by 3.66. (From figure SPM 3a in *Climate Change 2007: Mitigation* by Working Group III to the Fourth Assessment Report of the Intergovernmental Panel on Climate Change [Cambridge: Cambridge University Press, 2007] <www1.ipcc.ch/graphics/graphics/ar4-wg3/jpg/SPM3.jpg>. Used with permission.)

---

[19]CO_2 is the most important greenhouse gas, but to allow for greenhouse gases other than CO_2, such as methane and nitrous oxide, the term *equivalent* CO_2 has been introduced which includes the effect of the other gases as if they were additional CO_2.

about 6.5 tons per annum, must fall very substantially during the twenty-first century (see figure 8.11). The challenge is to achieve reductions that are both realistic and equitable.

To meet the FCCC's objective, the first stabilization target suggested for the concentration of CO_2 was double it's preindustrial value, or about 550 ppm, which would imply a rise in global average temperature of about 3°C. Although the climate would eventually stabilize—though not for well over a hundred years—climate change impacts at such a level would be large. A steady rise in sea level will continue for centuries, heat waves would be commonplace, devastating floods and droughts would be more common in many places, and Greenland would most likely start to melt down. It is now widely recognized that a lower limit than 3°C must be the aim if such unacceptable damage is to be avoided. But is that possible?

In 1996, the European Commission proposed a limit for the rise in global average temperature from its pre-industrial value of 2°C that has since been widely studied and discussed. Chancellor Merkel of Germany reiterated the desirability of this limit before the 2007 G8 summit and many other organizations have given it wide support.[20] To achieve such a target, large emission reductions in greenhouse gases, especially CO_2, must be made. The leaders of G8 countries, meeting in Scotland in 2005, asked the International Energy Agency (IEA), the world's top international energy advisory body, to study routes for a more sustainable energy future, including the 2°C target. In their *World Energy Outlook* for 2008, they show how the 2°C target can be achieved. Figure 8.8 shows a scenario with carbon dioxide equivalent reductions that would reach this target compared with the IEA Reference Scenario, which assumes 'business-as-usual' without any particular environmental measures. Figure 8.8 (see also figure 8.11) also indicates the sort of changes in energy supply and use that would achieve these reductions and which are outlined in the next section.

To reach the 2°C target requires that carbon dioxide concentration stabilizes at about 450 ppm, which is the aim of the emissions profile of

---

[20]For example, the World Wildlife Fund, <www.wwf.org>.

figure 8.8. This means that, by 2050, global emissions must fall by at least 50 percent from their 1990 values (see figure 8.11).[21] Reference to figure 8.7 illustrates that economic development in developing countries requires some increase in developing countries' emissions, implying more drastic reductions must be made in emissions from the developed world. With this in mind, the U.K. government has taken a lead

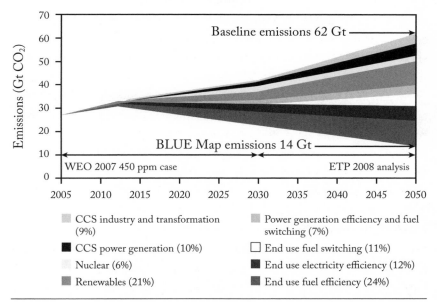

Figure 8.8. Illustrative options for contributors to emissions reductions for the IEA BLUE map Scenario 2005-2050 by sector. (This figure is 2.2 in *Energy Technology Perspectives 2008* [Paris, France: International Energy Agency, 2008]. Used with permission.)

and has recently legislated a mandatory target reduction of U.K. greenhouse gas emissions of 80 percent from its 1990 level. Governor Schwarzenegger has proposed a similar reduction target for the state of California and President Obama has indicated his intention to introduce a similar target for the United States. At the important interna-

---

[21]Note that the energy emissions in 2050 in figure 8.8 are 50 percent of 2005 emissions while in Fig 8.11 they are under 50 percent of 1990 emissions. The latter takes into account later estimates from the science of the carbon cycle of what is required to reach 450 ppm CO_2 stabilization.

tional Climate Conference at Copenhagen in December 2009 there was broad agreement on the 2°C target. But if that target is to be achieved, nations will need to face up very soon to the challenge of agreeing on the reductions in greenhouse gases necessary to achieve it.

The IEA has also addressed the additional financial investment required if the stabilization scenario of figure 8.8 is to be followed.[22] They point out that, under the Reference Scenario the global investment made by 2050, in infrastructure for energy production and in energy consuming devices (vehicles) and processes, would amount to about 6 percent of cumulative world GDP. The additional investment needed to achieve the reducing scenario shown in figure 8.8 would be about 1 percent of cumulative world GDP over the period. The IPCC and the *Stern Review*[23] have also come up with similar estimates of the cost of achieving the reductions. However, the IEA also points out that fuel savings over the period compared with the Reference Scenario amount to about 1 percent of world GDP, approximately wiping out the additional investment cost.

MITIGATION ACTION

I now address the actions that must occur if the reductions required are to be achieved. Four sorts of actions are required. First, there is the halting of deforestation especially in the tropics. About 20 percent of current anthropogenic greenhouse gas emissions result from the destruction, especially by burning, of tropical forests. Furthermore, it destroys ecosystems and habitats and is leading to much biodiversity loss. Also, since the source of much rainfall in the tropics is the evaporation of water from forests, rainfall will tend to decline as forests are lost. For instance, if more large areas of the Amazon forest are removed, some of that area is likely to become semi-desert. Finally, forests play an important role in the storage of water; their loss is already exacerbating the intensity of floods. The aim should be to halve deforestation before 2020 and halt it completely by 2030, so achieving 20 percent emissions

---

[22]Chapter 6 in *Energy Technology Perspectives 2008* (Paris, France: International Energy Agency, 2008), pp. 221-47.
[23]Stern, "Economics of Climate Change."

reduction outside the energy sector.

Second, energy efficiency in the energy sector must be addressed. Approximately one-third of energy is employed in buildings (domestic and commercial), one-third in transport, and one-third by industry. Large savings can be made in all three sectors—many with significant savings in cost. But to achieve these savings in practice will require appropriate encouragement and incentives from central and local governments and a great deal of determination from us all.

Take buildings for example. Recent projects demonstrate that "zero emissions" buildings are a practical possibility; initial costs are larger than for conventional buildings, but the operation costs are significantly less. For example, in south London is the BedZED development (ZED = Zero Emissions Development), the largest carbon neutral housing project in the U.K. This complex of eighty-two homes obtains its heat and power from the use of forestry residue and solar panels. However, most housing in Britain and the United States—built or planned—continues to be unsatisfactory in terms of an easily achievable level of energy sustainability. Why, for instance, is combined heat and power (CHP) not the norm for new housing estates? Large efficiency savings are also achievable in the transport sector, with more fuel-efficient vehicles for example. Within the industrial sector a serious drive for energy savings is becoming readily apparent. A number of the world's largest companies have already achieved energy savings of many millions of dollars.[24]

Third, a wide variety of non-fossil fuel energy sources is available for development and exploitation; for instance, biomass (including waste), solar power (both photovoltaic and thermal), hydro, wind, wave, tidal, geothermal energy and nuclear power. Fourth, there are opportunities for sequestering carbon that would otherwise enter the atmosphere either through the planting of forests or by pumping underground (for instance in spent oil and gas fields or in saline aquifers).[25] This latter is particularly important because of the many new coal-fired power sta-

---

[24]Information from Steve Howard of the Climate Group.
[25]Intergovernmental Panel on Climate Change, *Carbon Dioxide Capture and Storage* (Cambridge: Cambridge University Press, 1999).

tions being built in China, India and other countries, all of which should be equipped with Carbon Capture and Storage (CCS). The opportunities in industry for innovation, development and investment in all these areas are large (see Socolow's Wedges).

The next section will address how, for any given country or location, choices of the best technologies can be made. Figure 8.8 indicates the

Socolow's Wedges

A simple presentation of the type of reductions that are required has been created by professors Robert Socolow and Stephen Pacala of Princeton University. To counter the likely growth in global emissions of carbon dioxide from now until 2050, seven "wedges" of reduction are proposed, each wedge amounting to 1 gigaton of carbon* per year in 2050 or 25 gigatons in the period up to 2050. Some of the possible wedges he proposes are the following. They illustrate the scale of what is necessary. To provide for the total reduction of emissions required is in figure 8.8, approximately fourteen wedges would be required.

- Buildings efficiency—reduce emissions by 25 percent

- Vehicles fuel use—from 30 to 60 mpg in 2 billion vehicles

- Carbon capture and storage at 800 GW of coal plants

- Wind power from 1 million MWp windmills

- Solar power from area of 150 km^2

- Nuclear power—700 GW—2x current capacity

- Stop tropical deforestation and establish 300 Mha of new tree plantations

- Biofuel production (ethanol) from biomass on 250 Mha of land

*To convert gigatons carbon to gigatons CO_2 multiply by 3.66.

global mix of technologies that IEA describes in its *Energy Technology Perspectives* for the 450 ppm CO_2 scenario. The largest contributions are expected from efficiency improvements, carbon capture and storage, nuclear power, biofuels and solar power (PV and solar/thermal). For the transport sector it is expected that oil based fuels will be replaced by grid based electricity via batteries, hydrogen through fuel cells and biofuels.

A LONG-TERM ENERGY STRATEGY

In the last section we presented a variety of technologies and solutions, but how can they be implemented? We ask, "What are the best options?" There is no one solution and no best technology; different solutions will be appropriate in different countries or regions. Simplistic answers I have heard often are, "Leave it to the market to provide in due course," and, "The three solutions are Technology, Technology and Technology." The market and technology are essential and effective tools, but poor masters. Solutions need to be more carefully crafted than those tools provide on their own.

A long-term perspective is required. I like to think of it in terms of a sea voyage. Our boat's engine is technology, and market forces are the propeller driven by the engine (see figure 8.9). But where is the boat heading? Without a rudder and someone steering, the course will be

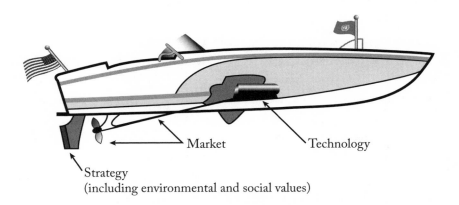

Market   Technology

Strategy
(including environmental and social values)

Figure 8.9. Where are we heading? This boat illustrates the need for an energy strategy, and it flies national and UN flags to illustrate the need for national and international strategies.

208 KEEPING GOD'S EARTH

arbitrary or even disastrous. Every voyage needs a destination and a strategy to reach it. Let me mention five components of the strategy that should direct any solutions.

First, the economy and the environment must be addressed together. It has been said that "the economy is a wholly owned subsidiary of the environment." In a speech in 2005, Gordon Brown, U.K.'s Chancellor of the Exchequer, expanded on this idea when he said:

> Environmental issues—including climate change—have traditionally been placed in a category separate from the economy and from economic policy. But this is no longer tenable. Across a range of environmental issues—from soil erosion to the depletion of marine stocks, from water scarcity to air pollution—it is clear now not just that economic activity is their cause, but that these problems in themselves threaten future economic activity and growth.[26]

Take the market. It responds overwhelmingly to price and the short term. It has been effective in reducing energy prices over the last two decades. But in its raw form it takes no account of environmental or other external factors. Although there has been general agreement among economists for many years that such factors should be internalized in the market, for instance, through carbon taxes or cap and trade arrangements, it has only been recently that such measures have begun to be introduced, for instance by the European Union in its Emissions Trading Scheme.

Second, not all potential technologies are at the same stage of development. For good choices to be made, promising technologies need to be brought to the starting gate so that they can properly compete. This implies joint programs between government and industry, the provision of adequate resources for research and development, the creation of demonstration projects, and sufficient support to see technologies through to maturity.[27] The market will provide rather little of this on its own and appropriate incentive schemes are needed.

---

[26]Gordon Brown, "Address to the Energy and Environment Ministerial Roundtable" (London, March 15, 2005).

[27]That government energy research and development in the United Kingdom is now less than 5 percent of what it was twenty years ago provides an illustration of lack of commitment or urgency on the government's part.

A third part of the strategy is to address the social and "quality of life" implications arising from the way energy is provided to a community. For instance, energy coming from large, central installations has very different social and community effects than energy from small and local energy provisions. The best urban solutions may be different from what is most appropriate in rural locations. Addressing more than one problem at once is also part of this component of the strategy.

For instance, disposal of waste and generation of energy frequently go together. It has been estimated that the potential energy value in agricultural and forestry wastes and residues could, if realized, meet at least 10 percent of the world's total energy requirement—a significant contribution.[28] Waste is just one component of biomass that is increasingly recognized as an important energy source. Biocrops (see Biomass: A Renewable Resource) can be employed either as fuel for power stations for electricity and hot water or for the production of liquid biofuels. There are also substantial advantages in local biomass energy schemes. For instance, they can easily include Combined Heat and Power (CHP), thereby achieving nearly double the efficiency of schemes providing power alone. Local biomass energy schemes also bring employment to rural areas and a feeling of ownership to local communities. Further, they are less liable to political interference.

Biomass: A Renewable Resource

Biomass is a renewable resource. The carbon dioxide that is emitted when biomass is burnt or digested is "fixed" in the next crop as it is grown. When fossil fuels are burnt, no such replacement occurs. Because biomass is bulky, transport costs can be large. Biomass is best used, therefore, to provide local energy or relatively small additional feed to large power stations (for instance, it is planned that 7 percent of the feed to the Aberthaw power station in South Wales should be from biomass).

---

[28]International Energy Agency, "Table 14.6," in *World Energy Outlook 2006* (Paris: 2006), p. 416.

An ideal energy crop should have high output and low inputs; in energy terms, gross inputs (for example, from need for fertilizer or management) have to be less than a small fraction of energy output. These characteristics tend to rule out annual grasses such as cereals, maize and sorghum, but rule in short-rotation coppice willow (from a list of woody species) and perennial grasses like Miscanthus. An urgent need is to develop commercial technologies for biofuel production from grasses such as Miscanthus.

Biomass can also be used to create biofuels. For instance, since the 1970s, large plantations of sugar cane have produced ethanol for use as a fuel mainly in transport. Other common biocrops for fuel are oil seed rape and palm oil. However, decisions about large-scale biofuel production must be guided by thorough and comprehensive assessments that address their overall efficiency and overall contribution to the reduction of carbon emissions. Also requiring careful assessment is the degree to which their use of land is competing with food crops (as in the use of maize) or adding to the deforestation of tropical forests (as, for instance, with some palm oil plantations), which contributes substantially to greenhouse gas emissions. Examples have recently come to light of adverse consequences (for instance, on world food prices) arising from a lack of adequate assessment.

There is also large potential for the development of biomass schemes—especially those using waste—in poorer countries. It is vital in impoverished nations that local energy provision to rural areas be developed to improve their quality of life and to enable small and medium sized industries to develop.

Solar energy schemes can also be highly versatile in size or application. Small solar home systems can bring electricity in home-size packages to villages virtually anywhere in the world—again with enormous benefits to local communities. Figure 8.10 is a simple illustration of the possibilities of such a system for an average home. At the other end of the size scale, developing countries with abundant sunshine but little access to freshwater are considering hybrid projects, coupling desalination with large solar thermal or PV installation.

Fourth, energy security must be part of the strategy. How safe are gas pipelines crossing continents? How safe are nuclear power stations from

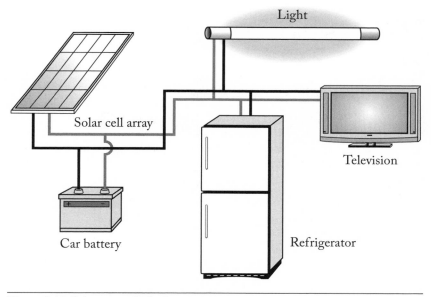

Figure 8.10. Schematic of solar home system

terrorist attack or nuclear material from proliferation to terrorist groups? It is such considerations that put into question large expansion of the contribution from nuclear energy. However, there are hundreds of tons of plutonium now in surplus from military programs that could be used in nuclear power stations (and degraded in the process)—assisting with greenhouse gas reductions in the medium term.[29] For countries such as China and India with rapidly increasing energy demands, abundant coal provides a cheap and secure energy source. A high priority is to work towards all new coal-fired power stations being substantially carbon neutral by using the latest technology, including carbon capture and storage underground.

---

[29]W. L. Wilkinson, "Management of the U.K. Plutonium Stockpile: The Economic Case for Burning as MOX in New PWRs," *Interdisciplinary Science Reviews* 26 (April 2001): 303-6.

Fifth, as the 1992 Framework Convention on Climate Change states, partnerships of many kinds are required. All nations (developed and developing) need to work together with national, international and multinational industries and corporations to craft sustainable and equitable solutions. Technology transfer from developed to developing countries is vital if energy growth in developing countries is to proceed in a sustainable manner. Through intentional, collective, preventative action, we can slow the process of global warming and even reach a stable state.

Finally, we must develop attainable goals and adopt new attitudes for thinking about our planet. Whether on the international, national, local or individual level, in order to progress towards sustainability we need goals or targets to aim at. Any commercial company understands the importance of targets for successful business. Targets are needed at *all* levels of society—international, national, local and personal. Often, there is a reluctance to agree or set targets. A common question is, "Can we not achieve what is necessary by voluntary action?" Although voluntary action has achieved a few successes, in general, it fails to bring about change on the required scale.

Not only do we need goals but also new attitudes and approaches in the drive towards sustainability at all levels of society—internationally, nationally and individually. Most significantly, we must be open to valuing sustainability as an asset and an investment, committing to measures of sustainability and developing the proper tools to apply those measures.

The issue of climate change presents a particular challenge to those of us in the rich countries of the developed world. Over the last two hundred years our wealth has largely come from cheap energy (coal, oil and gas). We did not realize until recently the damage we were doing, damage that falls disproportionately on the poor and disadvantaged in the more vulnerable areas of the world. There is therefore a very strong moral imperative to those of us who are comparatively rich to share our wealth and our skills with the poorer parts of the world. On all levels of society, we must adopt an attitude of sharing. On the individual and local levels, sharing often occurs; internationally, it occurs far less. Perhaps the most condemning of world statistics is that the rich are getting richer while the poor get poorer—the flow of wealth in the world is from the poor to the rich. This should be especially heartbreaking to Christians, when Scripture so boldly calls us to share all that we have with those in need.[30] These new attitudes are not just to provide guidance to policy makers in government or elsewhere. They need to be espoused by the public at large. If they are not, the government will not possess the confidence to act. For the public to take on this issue, the public must understand the issue of global climate change. There is a great need for the propagation of accurate and understandable information regarding all aspects of sustainability. Christian churches can—and must—play a significant role in this.

CONCLUSIONS: CAN WE WAIT AND SEE?

Unfortunately, there are strong vested interests that have spent millions of dollars to spread misinformation about climate change.[31] First they tried to deny the existence of any scientific evidence for rapid climate change due to human activities. More recently they have largely accepted the fact of anthropogenic climate change but argue that its impacts will not be great, that we can "wait and see" and in any case we can always "fix" the problem if it turns out to be substantial. The scientific evidence cannot support such arguments. In light of this evidence and the extremely damaging possibilities projected in the future, it would be irresponsible to conclude that the world should simply wait and see how global climate change turns out.

The need for action is urgent for four reasons. The first reason is *scientific*. Because oceans take time to warm, there is a lag in the response of climate to increasing greenhouse gases. Because of greenhouse gas emissions to date, a commitment to substantial change already exists, much of which will not be realized for thirty to fifty years. Further emissions add to that commitment. The second reason is *eco-*

---

[30]See, for instance, Luke 3:11 12:33; Acts 4:32; 2 Corinthians 8:13-15. Examples, of course, are not limited to these.

[31]George Monbiot, "The Denial Industry," in *Heat: How to Stop the Planet Burning* (London: Penguin Books, 2007), provides detail of this misinformation campaign.

nomic. Energy infrastructure in power stations, for instance, also lasts typically for thirty to fifty years. It is much more cost effective to begin now to phase in the required infrastructure changes rather than having to make them more rapidly later. The third reason is *political.* Countries like China and India are industrializing very rapidly. I heard a senior energy adviser to the Chinese government speak recently. He said that China by itself would not be taking the lead in reducing greenhouse gas emissions. When the big emitters in the developed nations take action, they will take action.

The International Energy Agency publishes each year a volume titled *World Energy Outlook.* The 2008 edition includes several chapters on how the world's energy systems can respond to the challenge of climate change—some of the material appears in the last section. Its executive summary begins with the following paragraphs.

> The world's energy system is at a crossroads. Current global trends in energy supply and consumption are patently unsustainable—environmentally, economically, socially. But that can—and must—be altered; *there's still time to change the road we're on.* It is not an exaggeration to claim that the future of human prosperity depends on how successfully we tackle the two central energy challenges facing us today; securing the supply of reliable and affordable energy; and effecting a rapid transformation to a low-carbon, efficient and environmentally benign system of energy supply. What is needed is nothing short of an energy revolution.
>
> Preventing catastrophic and irreversible damage to the global climate ultimately requires a major decarbonisation of the world energy sources. The 15th conference of the Parties to be held in Copenhagen in November 2009, provides a vital opportunity to negotiate a new global climate change policy regime for beyond 2012. . . . The consequences for the global climate of policy inaction are shocking. . . . The road from Copenhagen must be paved with more than good intentions.

The final reason is *spiritual*—it has to do with our responsibility as Christians within the global church. Care for the earth is an essential way that we can display the *imago Dei* within us; by caring for the earth, we reflect God's own loving care for the world. By seeking a sustainable future, we express love for people living throughout the

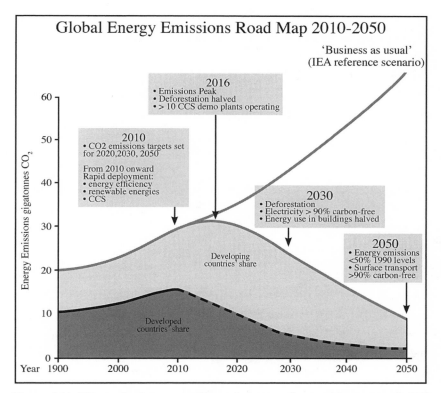

Figure 8.11. Waymarks for energy CO_2 emissions roadmap with targets of ~2°C global average temperature rise from preindustrial times and 450 ppm CO_2e stabilization (from John Houghton, *Global Warming: The Complete Briefing* [Cambridge: Cambridge University Press, 2009], figure 11.27; used with permission).

world and generations yet to come. As Rev. Dr. Christopher J. Wright expands upon in the following chapter, we have been placed in a role of servant-kingship over creation, and responsible stewardship of creation recognizes that Christ has promised to return to earth—earth redeemed and transformed.[32] As Christians, the issue of climate change goes far beyond the scientific data and projected outcomes I have described here. Environmental justice is a spiritual discipline of faithfulness that comes from the knowledge of the facts and a response of the heart.

---

[32]See N. T. Wright, *New Heavens, New Earth*, Grove Biblical Series B11 (Cambridge: Grove Books, 1999).

9

"THE EARTH IS THE LORD'S"

Biblical Foundations for Global
Ecological Ethics and Mission

Christopher J. H. Wright

THE CHALLENGE OF ANTHROPOGENIC CLIMATE CHANGE underscores both the global and ethical dimensions of contemporary environmental issues. Accidentally, incidentally and purposefully, in recent
decades, human activity has had an unprecedentedly negative impact
on the earth.[1] As Paul Crutzen and Eugene Stoermer write, "Considering . . . impacts of human activities on earth and atmosphere, and at all,
including global, scales, it seems to us more than appropriate to emphasize the central role of mankind in geology and ecology by proposing to
use the term 'anthropocene' for the current geological epoch."[2] The human dimensions, both origins and implications, of climate change and
other forms of global environmental change are both temporally and
spatially ubiquitous, requiring an ethical and practical calculus that extends both to future generations and to the ends of the earth.

Challenges of such magnitude are not merely technical matters; effectively addressing them will require reconsideration of values. For
Christians, this reconsideration must be grounded in an understanding

[1]This chapter was adapted from Christopher J. H. Wright, *The Mission of God: Unlocking the
Bible's Grand Narrative* (Downers Grove, Ill.: InterVarsity Press, 2006), pp. 397-420.
[2]Paul J. Crutzen and Eugene F. Stoermer, "The 'Anthropocene'," *Global Exchange Newsletter*,
no. 41 (2000): 17-18. See also Paul J. Crutzen, "Geology of Mankind," *Nature* 415, no. 3
(2002): 23.

of God's word. Thinking biblically about global ecological responsibility requires that we grasp two interlocking dimensions of the Bible's worldview: its teaching about the relationship between God, his Old Covenant people and the land; and its teaching about God, his New Covenant people and the earth as a whole.[3]

Fully comprehending the depth and breadth of our obligations to biblically informed global ecological ethics requires us to unpack concepts of both divine ownership and the Earth-as-gift.

BIBLICAL MOTIVATIONS FOR GLOBAL ECOLOGICAL ETHICS: GOD'S EARTH UNDER DIVINE OWNERSHIP

> Heaven and the heaven of heavens belong to the LORD your God the earth with all that is in it. (Deut 10:14)[4]

This bold claim that Yahweh the God of Israel owns the whole universe is echoed in the familiar assertion of Psalm 24:1, "To Yahweh belongs the earth and its fullness," and in the less familiar claim that God himself makes to Job in the context of the grand recital of all his works of creation: "Everything under heaven belongs to me" (Job 41:11).

The earth, then, belongs to God because God made it. At the very least this reminds us that if the earth is God's, it is not ours, even if our behavior boasts that we think it is. No, God is the earth's landlord and we are God's tenants. God has given the earth into our resident possession (Ps 115:16), but we do not hold the title deeds of ultimate ownership. So, as in any landlord-tenant relationship, God holds us accountable to himself for how we treat his property. Several dimensions of this affirmation of the divine ownership of the earth have significant ethical and missional implications.

God's creation is good. The goodness of God's creation is one of the

---

[3]Compare Paul's sermon in the Jewish synagogue in Pisidian Antioch in Acts 13:16-41 with his speech before the Areopagus in Athens in Acts 17:22-31. For the diagrammatic framework for understanding the ethical worldview of Old Testament Israel that I have developed, see C. J. H. Wright, *Old Testament Ethics for the People of God* (Downers Grove, Ill.: InterVarsity Press, 2004), pp. 182-211.

[4]All Scripture is author's translation unless otherwise noted.

most emphatic points of Genesis 1 and 2.[5] Six times in the narrative
God declares his work to be "good."[6] Several implications of this re-
soundingly simple affirmation may be noted. First, a good creation can
only be the work of a good God. This sets the Hebrew account of creation in contrast to other ancient Near Eastern accounts where powers
and gods of the natural world are portrayed in various degrees of malevolence, and where some aspects of the natural order are explained as
the outcome of that malevolence. In the Old Testament, the natural
order is fundamentally and in origin good, as the work of the single
good God, Yahweh. Part of the meaning of the goodness of creation in
the Bible is that it witnesses to the God who made it, reflecting something of his character (for example, Ps 19; 29; 50:6; 65; 104; 148; Job
12:7-9; Acts 14:17; 17:27; Rom 1:20).

Second, creation is good independently of our human presence
within it and our ability to observe it. In the creation narratives, the
affirmation that the creation was "good" was not made by Adam and
Eve but by God himself, and that three times before God created humans. So the goodness of creation (which includes its beauty) is theologically and chronologically prior to human observation, not merely a
human reflexive response to a pleasant view on a sunny day. Nor is it an
instrumental goodness in the sense that the rest of creation is good
simply because it exists for our benefit. Rather, this affirmation of the
goodness of creation is the seal of *divine* approval on the whole universe
at every phase of its creation—from the initial creation of light (Gen
1:4) to the emergence of land animals (Gen 1:25). So the created order,
including our planet Earth, has intrinsic value because it is valued by
God, the source of all value. Indeed, our own value as human beings
has its source in the fact that we are also part of the whole creation that
God already values and declares to be good.

Third, creation is good in relation to the purpose of God for it,
which has clearly included development, growth and change in "nat-

---

[5]For a discussion on the goodness of creation, see Ron Elsdon, *Green House Theology: Biblical
Perspectives on Caring for Creation* (Tunbridge Wells, U.K.: Monarch, 1992).

[6]For an intriguing culinary metaphor of creation, see Huw Spanner, "Tyrants, Stewards—or
Just Kings?" in *Animals on the Agenda: Questions About Animals for Theology and Ethics*, ed. Andrew Linzey and Dorothy Yamamoto (London: SCM Press, 1998), p. 218.

ural history," as well as human history. Of course, the meaning of being "good" includes the aesthetic sense that the creation is beautiful as a work of stupendous art and craftsmanship. But it also has a functional sense—something is good when it works according to plan, operating according to its design. Viewed from this angle, we should not envisage the goodness of creation as some kind of original, timeless or changeless perfection. Time and change are built into the very structure of created reality.

Fourth, the goodness of creation has an eschatological dimension. Creation is not yet all that God planned for it to be, even apart from the effects of the fall. God built into creation an enormous capacity for procreation—inexhaustible resources of replication, fecundity and diversity. As we experience it, the world is also suffering the effects of human sin, from which it longs to be liberated (Rom 8:19-21). So Paul locates the double hope of human redemption and cosmic liberation in the glory, the will and the Spirit of God. Nash rightly asserts that "the affirmation of the goodness of creation is also an expression of ultimate confidence in the goodness of God. . . . The creation is going on to perfection, ultimately. It is very good because it is being brought to fulfilment by a good God."[7]

These observations suggest there are surely ecologically ethical implications for regarding the created order as good in itself because of the value it has to God. It is not neutral "stuff" that we should commodify and commercialize, use and abuse for our own ends. Furthermore, as part of the whole creation, we humans exist not only to praise and glorify God ourselves, but also to facilitate the rest of creation in doing so. And if the greatest commandment is that we should love God, that surely implies that we should treat what belongs to God with honor, care and respect. Conversely, therefore, to contribute to, or collude in, the abuse, pollution and destruction of the natural order is to trample on the goodness of God reflected in creation. It is to devalue what God values, to mute God's praise and to diminish God's glory.

God's creation is sacred. Some ancient near eastern cultures consid-

---

[7]James A. Nash, *Loving Nature: Ecological Integrity and Christian Responsibility* (Nashville: Abingdon, 1991), p. 100.

ered different forces of nature divine beings (or under the control of distinct divine beings), and the function of many religious rituals was to placate or persuade these nature gods or goddesses into agriculturally beneficent action. The Bible, however, makes a clear distinction between God the creator and all things created—nothing in creation is in itself divine—ruling out nature polytheism, which was prevalent in the world around Israel.

In the true faith of Israel, the great realities of the natural world, whether forces, phenomena or objects, had no inherent *divine* existence. Such power as they had, which was undoubtedly great, was entirely the work of Yahweh and under his command. Thus, the fertility cults of Canaan were rejected, because Yahweh himself provided the abundance of nature for Israel (for example, Hos 2:8ff.). The immensely powerful and influential astral deities of Babylon were unmasked as nothing more than created objects under Yahweh's authority (Is 40:26). Concerning both fertility and astrology, Israel's distinctive beliefs about creation brought them into severe cultural and political conflict with surrounding worldviews. While the Hebrew Bible certainly teaches respect and care for the non-human creation, it resists and reverses the human tendency to divinize or personalize the natural order, or to imbue it with any power independent of its personal creator.

However, an unfortunate side effect of the Old Testament's dedivinization of nature was the popular view that the Bible "desacralized" nature. This view then rendered the natural order open to human exploration and exploitation, unfettered by religious fears or taboos. On such a view, the sole purpose of the natural order is to meet our human needs. Nature is ours to command, so whatever we do to it, we need not fear that we are insulting some inherent divine force.[8] Such a secularized view of nature is not at all what is meant here by the de-divinizing of nature.

The radical monotheism of Israel that set itself against all the so-called nature gods did not rob nature itself of its God-related sacred-

---

[8]For a helpful discussion of the roots and effects of this distortion in Old Testament theology, see Ronald A. Simkins, *Creator and Creation: Nature in the Worldview of Ancient Israel* (Peabody, Mass.: Hendrickson, 1994), pp. 82-88.

ness and significance. There is a fundamental difference between treating creation as *sacred* and treating it as *divine*. To divinize and to worship nature in any of its manifestations is to exchange the Creator for the created. But the sacredness or sanctity of creation speaks of its essential relatedness to God, not of it being divine in and of itself. The Old Testament constantly treats creation *in relation to God*. The created order obeys God, submits to God's commands, reveals God's glory, benefits from God's sustaining and providing, and serves God's purposes. This includes, but is not limited to, the purposes of providing for human beings or functioning as the vehicle of God's judgment upon them. So there is a sacredness about the non-human created order that we are called upon to honor—as the laws, worship and prophecy of Israel did.[9]

And if that is the case, are there not compelling ethical and missional implications for us who claim to worship this God as the world's creator, and for us who claim to know him also as the world's redeemer? If the earth has a sanctity derived from its relation to the creator, then our treatment of the earth will be a reflex of our own relationship with the creator.

God's creation is distinct from, but dependent on, God the creator. Affirming that "in the beginning God created the heavens and the earth" (Gen 1:1), the opening verse of the Bible implies a fundamental ontological distinction between God as creator and everything else as created. The heavens and the earth had a beginning. God was there before the beginning. The two (God and the universe) are different orders of being. This *duality* between the creator and the created is essential to all biblical thought and to a Christian worldview. It stands against both *monism* (the belief that all reality is ultimately singular—all is One, with no differentiation) and *pantheism* (the belief that God is somehow identical with the totality of the universe; altogether, everything is God). The biblical teaching on creation is thus a major point of contrast and polemic with New Age spirituality, which adopts a broadly monistic or pantheistic worldview.

---

[9]Nash, *Loving Nature*, p. 96.

Creation is distinct from God its creator, but it is also totally dependent upon God. Creation is not independent, or co-eternal. Rather, God is actively and unceasingly sustaining its existence and its functions at macro and micro levels (Ps 33:6-9; 65:9-13; 104). The world is not, in biblical teaching, an autonomous self-sustaining bio-system.[10] The Bible portrays the whole universe as *distinct from* God (its being is not part of God's being); but yet *dependent on* God for its existence and its sustenance. God is ultimate and uncreated; the universe is created and contingent. This is not to deny that God has built into the earth an incredible capacity for renewal, recovery, balance and adaptation. But the way in which all these systems work and interrelate is itself planned and sustained by God.

The whole earth is the field of God's mission, and ours. If God owns the universe, there is no place that does not belong to him. There is nowhere we can step off his property, either into the property of some other deity, or into some autonomous sphere of our own private ownership. Such claims were made in relation to Yahweh in the Old Testament (for example, Ps 139). But in the New Testament the same claims are made in relation to Jesus Christ. Standing on a mountain with his disciples after his resurrection, Jesus paraphrases the affirmations of Deuteronomy about Yahweh (Deut 4:39; 10:14, 17), and calmly applies them to himself: "All authority in heaven and on earth has been given to me" (Mt 28:18 NRSV). The risen Jesus thus claims the same ownership and sovereignty over all creation as the Old Testament affirms for Yahweh.

The whole earth belongs to Jesus by right of creation, by right of redemption, and by right of future inheritance—as Paul affirms in the

---

[10]As originally proposed, the "Gaia hypothesis" involves the interconnectedness of the whole biosphere. See James Lovelock, *Gaia: A New Look at Life on Earth* (Oxford: Oxford University Press, 1979). Lovelock suggested that the earth seems to behave like a single organism, a huge living creature. Cf. Michael S. Northcott, *The Environment and Christian Ethics* (Cambridge: Cambridge University Press, 1996), pp. 110-11. For a survey and critique of New Age ecological views and their influence on Christian thought, see Loren Wilkinson, ed., *Earthkeeping in the Nineties: Stewardship of Creation*, rev. ed. (Grand Rapids: Eerdmans, 1991), pp. 181-99; and Wilkinson, "New Age, New Consciousness, and the New Creation," in *Tending the Garden: Essays in the Gospel and the Earth*, ed. Wesley Grandberg-Michaelson (Grand Rapids: Eerdmans, 1987), pp. 6-29.

magnificent cosmic declaration of Colossians 1:15-20. So wherever we go in his name, we are walking on his property. Our mission on God's earth is not only authorized by its true owner, but it is also protected, nurtured and guaranteed by him. Since we act on his authority, there is no place for fear, for wherever we tread belongs to him already.

God's glory is the goal of creation. "What is the chief end of man?" asks the opening question of the Shorter Catechism of the Westminster Confession. It answers with glorious biblical simplicity: "The chief end of man is to glorify God and enjoy him forever." It would be equally biblical to ask the same question about the whole of creation and to give the same answer. The creation exists for the praise and glory of its creator God, and for mutual enjoyment (for example, Ps 104:27-28; 145:10, 21; 148; 150:6). That God-focused goal—to glorify and enjoy him— does not set us apart from the rest of creation. Rather it is something we share with all creation.

We may not be able to explain *how* it is that creation praises its Maker—since we know only the reality of our human personhood "from the inside," and what it means for *us* to praise him. But because we cannot articulate the *how* of creation's praise, or indeed the *how* of God's receiving of it, we should not therefore deny *that* creation praises God, since it is affirmed throughout the Bible with overwhelming conviction. Eventually, the whole of creation will join in the joy and thanksgiving that will accompany Yahweh when he comes as king to put all things right (i.e., to judge the earth, for example, Ps 96:10-13; 98:7-9).

As we consider the task of bringing glory to God, it is worth noting that several significant texts link the glory of God to the fullness of the earth, that is, the magnificently diverse abundance of the whole biosphere—land, sea and sky. The language of fullness is a feature of the creation narrative. From empty void, the story progresses through repeated fillings. For example, once the water and the sky have been separated, the fifth day sees the water teeming with fish, and the skies with birds, according to God's blessing and command (Gen 1:20-22). Not surprisingly, then, the phrase "the earth and its fullness" becomes a characteristic way of talking about the whole environment—sometimes local, sometimes universal (for example, Deut 33:16; Ps 89:12; Is 34:1; Jer 47:2; Ezek 30:12; Mic 1:2).[11] This may give added meaning to the song of the seraphim in Isaiah's temple vision, "Holy, holy, holy is Yahweh of hosts. The filling [or fullness][12] of all the earth [is] his glory" (Is 6:3).

"The fullness of the earth" is a way of talking about the whole rich abundance of the created order, especially the non-human creation (when humans are in view, they are often added as, "and those who live in it" [for example, Ps 24:1]). The earth is full of God's glory because what fills the earth constitutes (at least one dimension of) his glory (cf. Ps 104:31).

As Paul reminds us, recognizing the link between the fullness of the earth and the glory of God means that human beings are confronted daily with the reality of God simply by inhabiting the planet (Rom 1:19-20). Here again we recognize a truth of ethical and missional relevance. For all human beings inhabit a glory-filled earth which reveals and declares something of its creator and theirs. What we have done with that experience is another matter, of course. But this truth underlies not only the radical nature of Paul's exposure of universal sinfulness and idolatry, but also the universal applicability and intelligibility of the gospel. For by God's grace and the illumining power of the gospel, minds that have suppressed and exchanged this truth about the creator can be brought from darkness to light, to know their creator once more as their redeemer through the message of the cross.

BIBLICAL MOTIVATIONS FOR GLOBAL ECOLOGICAL ETHICS: EARTH AS A DIVINE GIFT AND HUMAN RESPONSIBILITY

The highest heavens belong to Yahweh,
and/but the earth he has given to the sons of Adam/humankind.
(Ps 115:16)

---

[11]For further discussion of the notion of "fullness," see Daniel I. Block's essay in chapter 5 of this volume.

[12]For this understanding of Isaiah 6:3, I am indebted to Hilary Marlowe. For further discussion in relation to the concept of the whole earth as the cosmic temple of God, see G. K. Beale, *The Temple and the Church's Mission: A Biblical Theology of the Dwelling Place of God*, ed. D. A. Carson, NSBT (Downers Grove, Ill.: InterVarsity Press, 2004), p. 49.

As we have seen, the earth belongs to God just as much as the heavens do. But unlike the heavens, the earth is the place of human habitation, for God has given it to us. Of course, the earth is the place where all God's non-human creatures also have their habitation, as Psalm 104 so evocatively celebrates. Yet the earth is never said to be "given" to the other creatures in quite the same way as it is given to humanity. So what is it about humankind that makes us the species to whom, in some unique sense, the earth has been given by God?

It is easy to say that human beings are superior, unique or special.[13] But the opening chapters of the Bible do not immediately emphasize human uniqueness. On the contrary, at point after point the Bible tells us that we have more in common with the rest of the animate creation than in distinction from it. Like the rest of the animals, we are blessed and instructed to multiply and fill the earth (Gen 1:22, 28). Indeed, they were blessed and busy filling the earth before we arrived. Humankind does not even get a separate day of creation.[14] And even to say that God has provided the resources of the earth to feed and shelter humankind is to say no more than that God does for us what God equally does for the rest of the animals, birds and fish (Ps 104).

Furthermore, it is a hoary misunderstanding of Genesis 2:7 to regard it as the origin of the human "soul," in the sense of something that the rest of the animals lack. For the conclusion of the verse, "the man became a living being," uses the same word *(nepeš)* that is repeatedly used of all the other living beings (Gen 1:20, 24, 28; 6:19).[15] So then, we are animals among animals. We are creatures, earth-creatures—*ʾādām* from the *ʾădāmâ* (or humans from the humus, or soil). And as such, of course, we are also a part of that fullness of the earth that is the very glory of God. Createdness is glory, not shame. Our shame lies elsewhere.

Human priority, the image of God, and dominion. But in the midst of all this commonality, where then does our distinctiveness lie? God

---

[13]Although the human species rightfully claims unique endowments, biological research indicates increasingly remarkable capacities within other species—capacities for tool-making, communication, play, humor, and even, according to some, for gentleness and altruism. For a discussion, see Spanner, "Tyrants, Stewards—or Just Kings?" pp. 219-21.

[14]See Daniel I. Block's essay in chapter 5 of this volume.

[15]A fact obscured by many translations (for example, NIV).

declares human life to have a particular sanctity—within the general principle that all life matters to God (Gen 9:4-6). Jesus exhorts us to trust in our heavenly Father on the grounds that we are of more value than other creatures (Mt 6:26; 10:31; 12:12; Lk 12:7, 24). Such statements do not mean that other creatures are of no value. Rather their force depends on the fact that animals *do* have intrinsic value to God.[16]

Both accounts of creation in Genesis 1 and 2 point to the priority or pre-eminence of humanity within the rest of God's good and valued creation. The ordered account of chapter 1 leads up to God's decision to create humankind in God's own image, as the penultimate climax of its sequence of days. Genesis 2 puts the human creature at the center of the whole landscape and discusses the creation of all else in relation to humanity's physical and relational nature. The message of both texts seems clearly to be that human life is supremely important (both climactic and central) to God within the context of the whole creation. Creation finds its point and its true head in this human species (a point not contradicted by the New Testament assertion that Christ is the head of the whole cosmos, for it is the *man* Jesus who occupies that role, cf. Ps 8; Heb 2).

However, only two things are said specifically about human beings that are not said about any other creature. God chose to make us in his own image, and he instructed us to rule over the rest of the creatures:

> Then God said, "Let us make humankind in our image, according to our likeness; and let them have dominion over the fish of the sea, and over the birds of the air, and over the cattle, and over all wild animals of the earth, and over every creeping thing that creeps upon the earth." (Gen 1:26 NRSV)

And having done so, God adds to the words of blessing, multiplication and filling (already spoken to other creatures), the unique mandate to "have dominion over the fish of the sea and over the birds

---

[16]Richard Bauckham, "Jesus and the Animals I: What Did He Teach?" in *Animals on the Agenda: Questions About Animals for Theology and Ethics,* ed. Andrew Linzey and Dorothy Yamamoto (London: SCM Press, 1998), p. 46.

of the air and over every living thing that moves upon the earth" (Gen 1:28 NRSV).

At one level, this is a theological expression of an obvious fact—human beings are the dominant species on the planet. We have colonized almost all of its land mass and have found ways of controlling and using almost every environment we encounter. But Genesis 1 affirms that this is much more than a simple biological fact or an accident of evolution. Rather, our position within the created order is by divine purpose and mandate. By making us in the image and likeness of God, he equipped us to rule. The two affirmations are so closely linked in the text that there can be no doubt they are meant to be related. Human beings are made to be like God; human beings are made to rule over the rest of the creation.

It is going too far to identify the two completely—that is, to argue that our dominion over nature is exclusively what constitutes the image of God in humanity. For human beings are and do very much more than all that is involved in mastering their environment. In any case, we should not so much think of the image of God as an independent "thing" that we somehow possess. God did not *give* to human beings the image of God. Rather, it is a dimension of our very creation. The expression "in our image" is adverbial (it describes the way God made us), not adjectival (as if it simply described a quality we possess). The image of God is *what we are*, rather than what we *possess*.

Nevertheless, if having dominion over the rest of creation is not what the image of God *is*, it is certainly what being the image of God *enables*. Among the many implications of being made in God's image, this one Genesis puts in the foreground: having been made by God in God's own image, human beings are instructed and equipped to exercise dominion. To put it the other way around, because God *intended* the human species to exercise dominion over the rest of his creatures, God purposefully created this species alone in his own image.[17]

So God instructs the human species not only to fill the earth (an

---

[17]This is the thrust of God's two statements expressed with two jussive clauses: "Let us make human beings in our own image and likeness, *so that* they may exercise dominion over the rest of creation."

instruction given to the other creatures, as we saw), but also to subdue it and to rule over the rest of the creatures. The words *kābaš* and *rādâ* are often noted as strong words, implying both exertion and effort and the imposing of will upon another. However, these terms do not imply violence or abuse, as contemporary ecological mythology[18] likes to caricature.[19] On one level, the first term authorizes humans to do what every other species on earth does, which is to utilize its environment for life and survival. *All* species in some way or another "subdue" the earth, to the varying degrees necessary for their own prospering. That is the very nature of life on earth. As applied to humans in this verse, it probably implies no more than the task of agriculture. That humans have developed tools and technology to pursue their own form of "subduing" the earth for human benefit is no different in principle from what other species do, though clearly vastly different in degree and impact on the total ecosphere.

The latter word, *rādâ*, is more distinctive. It certainly describes a role and function for human beings that is entrusted to no other species—ruling, or exercising dominion. It seems clear that God hereby passes on to human hands a delegated form of his own kingly authority over the whole of his creation. God installs the human species as the image, within creation, by the authority that finally belongs to God, creator and owner of the earth.

Apart from that analogy, Genesis describes God's work in regal terms, even without using the word "king." God's work of creation exudes wisdom in planning, power in execution and goodness in completion. These are the very qualities that Psalm 145 exalts in "my God and King," in relation to all his created works. Righteousness and benevolence are inherent in God's kingly power, which is exercised towards all

---

[18]The source of the widespread idea that Christianity bears major responsibility for our ecological crisis because of its instrumentalist view of nature, allegedly rooted in Gen 1:28, goes back to Lynn White, "The Historic Roots of Our Ecologic Crisis," *Science* 155 (1967): 1203-7. For decisive repudiation of White's arguments, see James Barr, "Man and Nature—The Ecological Controversy and the Old Testament," *BJRL* 55 (1972): 22, 30.

[19]For a survey of representative expressions of the notion that Christianity is therefore an intrinsically eco-hostile religion in Christian history, see Nash, "The Ecological Complaint against Christianity," in *Loving Nature*, pp. 68-92.

that he has made.[20] So the natural assumption, then, is that a creature made in the image of this God will reflect these same qualities in carrying out the mandate of delegated dominion. Whatever way this human dominion is to be exercised, it must reflect the character and values of God's own kingship. Robert Murray declares, "The 'image' is a kingly pattern, and the kind of rule which God entrusted to human kind is that proper to the ideals of kingship. *The ideals,* not the abuses or failures; not tyranny or arbitrary manipulation and exploitation of subjects, but a rule governed by justice, mercy and true concern for the welfare of all."[21] According to Spanner, "the *imago Dei* constrains us. We must be kings, not tyrants."[22] The image of God is not a license for abuse based on arrogant supremacy, but a pattern that commits us to humble reflection of the character of God.[23]

Servant-kingship. What model of kingship does the Old Testament set before us for the human exercise of dominion over creation? Possibly the most succinct statement of the ideal comes from the older and wiser advisors of the young King Rehoboam, who told him, "If you will be a servant to this people today and serve them, . . . they will be your servants forever" (1 Kings 12:7 NRSV).

Mutual servanthood was the ideal. Yes, it was the duty of the people to serve and obey the king, but his primary duty of kingship was to serve the people, to care for their needs, provide justice and protection, and avoid oppression, violence and exploitation. A king exists for the benefit of his people, not vice-versa. The metaphor that expressed this attribute of kingly rule (and which was common throughout the ancient Near East and not just in Israel) was that of the shepherd. Sheep need to follow their shepherd, but the primary responsibility of shepherds is to care for the sheep, not to exploit or abuse them. The very word shepherd speaks of responsibility, more than of rights and powers (cf. Ezek 34).

---

[20]On the Creator as King, see Robert Murray, *The Cosmic Covenant: Biblical Themes of Justice, Peace and the Integrity of Creation* (London: Sheed & Ward, 1992), p. 98.

[21]Murray, *Cosmic Covenant,* p. 98.

[22]Spanner, "Tyrants, Stewards—or Just Kings?" p. 222.

[23]For further discussion on the image of God in humanity and the verbs used to describe humanity's responsibilities in Genesis 1, see Daniel Block's essay in chapter 5 of this collection.

So, if human dominion within creation is a form of kingship, it must be modeled on this biblical pattern. Spanner writes,

> If we have dominion over God's other creatures, then we are called to live in peace with them, as good shepherds and humble servants. We cannot say that we are made in the image of God and then use that as our pretext to abuse, neglect or even belittle other species, when God does none of those things. As kings, we have the power of life and death over them, and the right to exercise it in accordance with the principles of justice and mercy; but we have the parallel duty, not only to God but to them, to love them and protect them.[24]

This concept of servant-kingship as the appropriate stance for humans towards the rest of creation is preferable to the more frequently used "stewardship" model. The teaching that we are supposed to be "stewards of creation" is widespread and popular, and of course contains some fundamental biblical truth. Above all it points to the fact that we are not owners of the earth. Rather, the One who truly owns it has entrusted it to our care. However, the concept of stewardship is vulnerable to misunderstanding and abuse. At the least harmful end is the fact that "stewardship" is commonly used in Christian circles in some cultural contexts only as a term implying appeals for money ("stewardship campaigns"). At the more harmful end, the word is used in non-Christian circles to give a moral aura to what may be unscrupulous exploitation of resources. This word speaks of the management of things, rather than of caring relationships.

A further dimension of the Old Testament concept of kingship was that it was to be exercised particularly on behalf of the weak and powerless. In Psalm 72, the psalmist prays that God will endow the king with justice so he can defend the afflicted and the needy. The essential nature of justice as conceived in the Old Testament is not blind impartiality, but intervening to set things right, so that those who have been wronged are vindicated, those who are being oppressed are delivered, the voices of the weak and vulnerable are heard, and their case attended to. Jeremiah 21:11–22:5 holds out these ideals as the criteria by which

---

[24]Spanner, "Tyrants, Stewards—or Just Kings?" p. 224.

the Jerusalem monarchy will stand or fall in God's sight (cf. 1 Kings 3:5-12). And in the climactic chapter of the book of Proverbs, King Lemuel's mother holds up the essential challenge of kingship:

Speak out for those who cannot speak,
    for the rights of all the destitute.
Speak out, judge righteously,
    defend the rights of the poor and needy. (Prov 31:8-9 NRSV)

Accordingly, to rule over the rest of creation as king, to act as the image of God the King, is to do biblical justice in relation to non-human creation. To "speak out for those who cannot speak," is a task of human kingship that could as relevantly describe our responsibility toward the rest of creation as to the human subjects of a ruler.[25]

Indeed, such compassionate justice is to be the mark, not only of kings, but of all human ethical behavior. And at least one text specifically extends the scope of such ethical duties beyond human relations to animals, "The righteous person knows the "soul" (*nepeš*) of his cattle / But the compassion of the wicked person is cruel" (Prov 12:10).

Here *nepeš* seems to mean the inner, unspoken feelings and needs of the animal (as it could do for human beings). And it is a mark of biblical righteousness to pay attention to and care for ("to know") that animal *nepeš,* just as much as for fellow humans. But the wicked (who do not care about justice, Prov 29:7), have turned compassion to cruelty. Murray writes,

The implications of this epigram are profound. Of the Hebrew virtues, the most all-embracing *(ṣedeq)* and the most deeply felt *(raḥămim),* which are used of God towards humans and of humans towards each other, are here used in speaking of right and wrong attitudes towards animals. Thus animals are brought into the sphere of human ethics.[26]

Finally, moving beyond the Old Testament, to regard our role within creation as that of kingship exercised through servanthood reflects precisely the pattern established for us by the Lord Jesus Christ. This is

---

[25]For a fuller moral and biblical case for this point, see Andrew Linzey, *Animal Theology* (London: SCM Press, 1994), pp. 28-44.
[26]Murray, *Cosmic Covenant*, p. 113.

hardly surprising. We are called to act as the image of God within creation, and Christ is the perfect image of God. So we find that his model of lordship was expressed through servanthood. And servanthood for him meant loving generosity and costly self-sacrifice for the sake of those he came to serve. There is no reason why this pattern of Christlike service to fellow human beings is not also applicable to Christlike exercise of responsibility to the natural world, which was created through Christ and for Christ. The Old Testament already gives us ample teaching about God's generous and loving care for all his creatures. (Psalms 104 and 145 are the classic expositions.) Jesus assumed this characteristic of his Father to be so axiomatic that he could build other teaching upon it (Mt 6:25-34).[27] Such servanthood is a properly biblical dimension of our kingship within creation.

We should note the balance that underlies what we have been discussing. On the one hand, created as the climax of the animal creation in Genesis 1, humankind is endowed with the necessary capacity to exercise dominion over the rest of the creatures as God's image in their midst. On the other hand, created in the context of the surrounding earth and its needs in Genesis 2, humans are put in the garden of Eden "to serve and to keep it" (author's translation).[28] *Dominion (Genesis 1) exercised through servanthood (Genesis 2) is the biblical balance for our ecological responsibility.*

Thus, the concept of human priority must be sensitively maintained by Christian ethics, in relation both to environmental issues and the emotive question of animal rights. Wherever a conflict exists between human needs and those of other animate or inanimate parts of creation—but *only when it is a conflict that cannot be satisfactorily resolved by meeting the needs of both simultaneously*—then human beings take priority. Ideally we should promote a more holistic and sustain-

---

[27]See further Bauckham, "Jesus and Animals," pp. 33-60. For discussion of the extension of Christ's model of self-giving generosity to our relationship with animals, see Linzey, *Animal Theology*, pp. 32-33.

[28]This is the literal and simplest meaning of the two verbs, ʿābad and šāmar. While the first involves work and doubtless referred primarily to the task of tilling the soil, the verb denotes primarily service. For further discussion on this model of kingship/leadership, see the discussion by Daniel Block in chapter 5 of this volume.

able regime, where environmentally friendly forms of land and water management contribute to human flourishing, and where human benefit is pursued in harmony with the good of the rest of our fellow creatures. As we shall see below, that is part of the eschatological vision of the future, but it should also guide our ecological ethics and objectives in the present.

The hope of an eschatological new creation. So the creation narratives point us back to the beginning, not just to tell us what we already know (that things are not what they should be), but also to explain *why* things are not what they were intended to be and once were. However, if Genesis tells us that sin and evil, suffering and pain, violence and destruction, frustration and loss, did not constitute

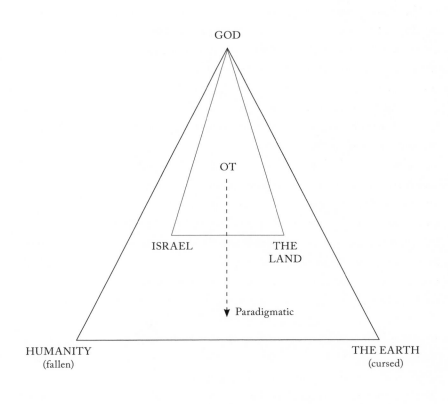

Figure 9.1.

the first word about our world, the rest of the Bible assures us that they will not be the last word either.

We began by pointing out the close analogy between the triangle of redemption (God, Israel and their land), and the triangle of creation (God, humanity and the earth). As we might expect, this interrelatedness is found not only in relation to ecological issues concerning life on earth now, but also in the Old Testament's expectations of God's redemption. Because Yahweh is both creator and redeemer, these two dimensions of Israel's faith are constantly interwoven.

We have seen already how important it is to include the Bible's strong doctrine of creation in our thinking about the earth—what we do with it, how we live on it, and for what it was created. But looking back to Genesis and affirming its great truths about our world is not enough. The Bible teaches us to value the earth, not only because of "from where it came" (or rather, because of "from whom it came"), but also because of its ultimate destiny. In other words, we need an eschatological as well as a creational foundation to our ecological ethics and mission.

The inspiring vision of Isaiah 65 and 66 portrays God's new creation as a place that will be joyful, free from grief and tears, life-fulfilling, guaranteeing work satisfaction, free from the curses of frustrated labor, and environmentally safe. This passage and others present the Old Testament foundation for the New Testament hope, which, far from rejecting or denying the earth, or envisaging us floating off to some other place, looks forward likewise to a new, redeemed creation (Rom 8:18-22), in which righteousness will dwell (2 Pet 3:10-13), because God himself will be there with his people (Rev 21:1-4). This eschatological vision for creation is overwhelmingly positive, and must affect how we understand the equally biblical portrayal of the final and fiery destruction that awaits the present world order. The purpose of the conflagration is not the *obliteration of the cosmos itself*, but rather the *purging of the sinful world order in which we live,* through the consuming destruction of all that is evil within creation, so as to establish the new creation. The world of all evil and wickedness in creation will be wiped out in God's cataclysmic judgment, but the creation itself will be renewed as the dwelling place of God with redeemed humanity[29] and restored for his glorious and eternal purpose.

This gloriously earthy biblical hope adds an important dimension to our ecological ethics. It is not just a matter of looking back to the initial creation, but of looking forward to the new creation. This means that our motivation has a double force—a kind of "push-pull" effect. It has a goal in sight. Granted it lies only in the power of God ultimately to achieve it, but, as is the case with other aspects of biblical eschatology, what we hope for from God affects how we are to live now and what our own objectives should be. This eschatological orientation protects our ecological concern from becoming centered only on human needs and anxieties, and reminds us that ultimately the earth always has and always will belong to God in Christ. Our efforts therefore have a prophetic value in pointing towards the full cosmic realization of that truth.[30]

HUMANITY'S MISSION AND RESPONSIBILITY IN THE PRESENT

Speaking personally, I share the conviction with Jannie du Preez who says, "I have, in recent years, increasingly become convinced that justice towards the earth and the entire cosmos forms an integral part of the mission of the church."[31] A biblical theology of mission that flows from the mission of God himself must include the ecological sphere within its scope, and see practical environmental action in general and aggressive responses to the climate crisis in particular as a legitimate part of Christian mission.

Creation care is an urgent issue in today's world. Only a willful blindness worse than any proverbial ostrich's head in the sand can ignore the facts of environmental destruction and its accelerating pace: large-scale

---

[29]On which, see Douglas Moo's essay in chapter 1 of this collection on the New Testament basis for environmental ethics. See also Northcott, *Environment and Christian Ethics*, p. 195.

[30]Francis Bridger, "Ecology and Eschatology: A Neglected Dimension," *Tyndale Bulletin* 41, no. 2 (1990): 301.

[31]Jannie Du Preez, "Reading Three 'Enthronement Psalms' from an Ecological Perspective," *Missionalia* 19 (1991): 122. On the link between mission and ecology see also J. A. Loader, "Life, Wonder and Responsibility: Some Thoughts on Ecology and Christian Mission," *Missionalia* 19 (1991): 44-56; and J. J. Kritzinger, "Mission and the Liberation of Creation: A Critical Dialogue with M. L. Daneel," *Missionalia* 20 (1992): 99-115.

pollution, worldwide habitat destruction and soil loss, increasing extinctions of multitudes of plant and animal species, the depletion of the ozone layer, the increase of greenhouse gases, and consequent global warming and climate change. The list is depressingly long, and to be unconcerned about it is to be either desperately ignorant or irresponsibly callous.

In the past, Christians have been concerned instinctively about great and urgent issues in every generation, and rightly included them in their overall concept of mission calling and practice. Faced now with the horrific facts of the suffering of the earth itself, we must surely ask how God himself responds to such abuse of his creation, and seek to align our mission objectives to include what matters to him. If, as Jesus tells us, God cares about his creation to the level of knowing when a sparrow falls to earth, what kind of care is required of us by our level of knowledge? It would be an utter distortion of Scripture to argue that because God cares for us *more than* for the sparrows, we need not care for sparrows *at all*, or that because we are of greater value than they are, they have no value at all.

However, our care for creation should not be merely a negative, prudential or preventive reaction to a growing problem. *Creation care must flow from love for the creator and obedience to his command.* "Love the Lord your God" is the first and greatest commandment (Mt 22:37-38). It seems quite inexplicable to me that there are some Christians who claim to love and worship God, to be disciples of Jesus, and yet have no concern for the earth that bears his stamp of ownership. They do not care about the abuse of the earth and indeed, by their wasteful and over-consumptive lifestyles, they contribute to it. "If you love me, you will keep my commandments," said Jesus, echoing as he so often did the practical ethical devotion of Deuteronomy (Jn 14:15 NRSV). And the Lord's commandments begin with the fundamental creation mandate to care for the earth. Obedience to that command is as much part of our human mission and duty as any of the other duties and responsibilities built into creation—such as the task of filling the earth, engaging in the rhythm of productive work and rest, and marriage. Being Christian does not release us from being human. Nor does a distinctively Christian mission negate our human mission, for God holds us accountable as much for our humanity as for our Christianity. As *Christian human beings*, therefore, we are doubly bound to see active care for creation as a fundamental part of what it means to love and obey God.

Creation care exercises our proper priestly and kingly role in relation to the earth. Greg Beale has rightly highlighted the theological connections between the tabernacle/temple in the Old Testament and the picture of Eden in the creation narrative, on the one hand, and the picture of the whole cosmos restored through Christ to be the dwelling place of God, and on the other hand. The temple is a microcosm, both of the primal creation reality and of the new creation reality. In both cases, we see God dwelling in the earth as his temple, with human beings serving him and it as his appointed priesthood.[32] In addition, the dual account of the mandate God gave to humanity in Genesis 1 and 2 uses the language of both kingship and priesthood. Humanity is to rule over the rest of creation; and Adam is put in the garden in Eden, "to serve and keep it." Ruling is the function of kingship; serving and keeping were major functions of the priests in relation to the tabernacle and temple.

So humankind is placed in a relationship to the earth that combines the function of king and priest: to rule and to serve. It is a quintessentially biblical combination that we find perfectly modeled in a rich range of meaning in Christ, as our perfect priest and king. But it is also the picture that we see of our restored role in the new creation (Rev 5:10). It follows then, from a creational and eschatological perspective, that ecological care in general and actions in response to climate change in particular are dimensions of our mission, inasmuch as they are dimensions of restoring the proper status and responsibility of our humanity. The earth awaits the full revealing of its appointed king and priest—redeemed humanity under the headship of Christ. Our action in the present anticipates and points prophetically towards that final goal.

Creation care tests our motivation for mission. If we start out only from the perspective of what humans do or what humans need, we will be led

---

[32]Beale, *Temple and Church's Mission.*

to an inadequate view of mission, usually including only evangelistic components and compassionate response. Although these are valid, *the ultimate starting and finishing points in our biblical theology of mission must be the mission of God himself.* The over-arching mission to which God has committed himself and the whole outworking of history is not only the salvation of human beings, but also the redemption of the whole creation. God is establishing a new creation through the transformation and renewal of creation in a manner analogous to the resurrection of his Son, and as a habitation for the resurrection bodies of his redeemed people.

Holistic mission, then, is not truly holistic if it includes only human beings (even if it includes them holistically!), and excludes the rest of the creation for whose reconciliation Christ shed his blood (Col 1:20). Those Christians who have responded to God's call to serve him through serving his non-human creatures in ecological projects are engaged in a specialized form of mission that has its rightful place within the broad framework of all that God's mission has as its goal. Their motivation flows from an awareness of God's own heart for his creation and a desire to respond to that.

Creation care is a prophetic opportunity for the church. Concern for the environment and global climate change is high on the list of anxieties in our world today. The church must respond to the realities with which the world is struggling. The Old Testament prophets addressed the contemporary realities of their own generation. Jesus did the same. What made them unpopular was their scorching relevance. If the church awakens to the urgent need to address the ecological and climate crises and does so within its biblical framework of resources and vision, then it will engage in missional conflict with at least two other ideologies (and doubtless many more). First, it must combat destructive global capitalism and the greed that fuels it. There is no doubt that a major contributor to contemporary environmental damage and climate change is global capitalism's insatiable demand for "more."[33] The bibli-

---

[33]These include greed (at any cost) for minerals and oil, land to graze cattle for meat, exotic animals and birds (to meet obscene human fashions in clothes, toys, ornaments and aphrodisiacs), commercial or tourist exploitation of fragile and irreplaceable habitats, resulting in practices that produce goods at least cost to the exploiter and maximum cost to the country and people exploited.

cal truths that covetousness is idolatry and the love of money is the root of all kinds of evil are particularly relevant here. For the church to get involved with issues of environmental protection it must be willing to tackle the forces of greed and economic power, to confront vested interests and political machination, to recognize that more is at stake than just being kind to animals and nice to people. It must do the scientific research to make its case credible. It must be prepared for the long hard road that the struggle for justice and compassion in a fallen world demands in this as in all other fields of mission.

Second, the church must stand up against *pantheistic, neo-pagan and New Age spiritualities.* Strangely, we may often find that people for whom such philosophies have great attraction are passionate about the natural order, but from a very different perspective. The church in its mission must bear witness to the great biblical claim that the earth is the Lord's. The earth is not a self-sustaining sentient being. It is not to be worshipped, feared or even loved in a way that usurps the sole deity of the one living and personal creator God. So our environmental mission is never Romantic or mystical. We are not called to "union with nature," but to care for the earth as an act of love and obedience to its creator and redeemer.

Creation care embodies a biblical balance of compassion and justice. Because to care for God's creation is essentially an unselfish form of love, compassion is exercised for the sake of creatures who cannot thank or repay us. It is a form of truly biblical and godly altruism. In this respect, it reflects the same quality in the love of God—not only in the sense that God loves human beings in spite of our unlovable enmity towards him, but also in the wider sense that "The LORD is good to all, and his compassion is over all that he has made" (Ps 145:9 NRSV; cf. Ps 145:13, 17). Again, Jesus could use God's loving care for birds and adornment of grasses and flowers as a model for his even greater love for his human children. If God cares with such minute compassion for his non-human creation, how much more should those who wish to emulate him?

In addition, *justice* is also crucial, because environmental action is a form of defending the weak against the strong, the defenseless against the powerful, the violated against the attacker, the voiceless against the greedy. And these too are features of the character of God as expressed in his exercise of justice. Psalm 145 includes God's provision for all his creatures in its definition of his *righteousness* as well as his love (Ps 145:13-17). In fact, it places God's care for creation in precise parallel with his liberating and vindicating acts of justice for his people—thus bringing the creational and redemptive traditions of the Old Testament together in beautiful harmony. Biblical mission is as holistic as biblical righteousness (Prov 12:10).

CONCLUSION

Is there, then, an ecological ethic to be derived from the Old Testament that can inform our perspective upon global environmental challenges, such as climate change? Ancient Israel may not have been anxious or fearful about the plight of the physical planet in the way that we are, for the very good reason that we have made a far greater mess of it than the ancient world ever did. So to that extent, many aspects of what we would now regard as urgent ecological ethical issues were not explicitly addressed within the Old Testament. Nevertheless, the theological principles and ethical implications that they *did* articulate regarding creation have far-reaching impact on how biblically sensitive Christians frame their ecological ethics today.[34]

Is there an ecological dimension of Christian mission? The answer has to be yes. We have seen that the two major theological pillars of Israel's faith regarding their own land were extended to include the whole earth. Thus, the whole earth is the gift of God to humanity, even as it is still held in God's ownership. These twin perspectives generate a rich variety of themes concerning human relationships with the rest of creation—both inanimate and also (especially) with the rest of the animals. The considerations articulated here are all built on the *intrinsic* value of creation to God and the mandate of God that we should care for it as he does. They do not depend on any other utility or consequence of such action, such as human benefit or evangelistic fruitful-

---

[34]For a discussion on the specific differences each person can make, see Christopher J. H. Wright, *The Mission of God* (Downers Grove, Ill.: InterVarsity Press, 2006), p. 412.

ness. We are to care for the earth because it belongs to God and he told us to. That is enough in itself.

Nevertheless, we are also part of that creation. While the short-term needs of human beings often clash with environmental good, ultimately what benefits creation benefits humanity for the long term. For this reason environmental and development issues are often intertwined. Furthermore, since the suffering of creation is bound up with human wickedness, that which is good news for the earth is part of that which is good news for people. The Gospel is indeed good news for the whole of creation.

It is not surprising, then, that Christians who take seriously our responsibility to embody God's love for creation find that their obedience in that sphere often also leads to opportunities to articulate God's love for suffering and lost people. Truly Christian environmental action is in fact also evangelistically fruitful, not because it is any kind of cover for "real mission," but simply because it declares in word and deed the Creator's limitless love for the whole of his creation (which of course includes his love for his human creatures), and makes no secret of the biblical story of the cost that the Creator paid to redeem both. Such action is a missional embodiment of the biblical truths that the Lord is loving towards all he has made, and that this same God so loved the world that he gave his only Son, not only so believers should not perish, but ultimately so *all things in heaven and earth* should be reconciled to God through the blood of the cross. God was in Christ reconciling *the world* to himself.

PART SIX

CONCLUSION

10

ENVIRONMENTAL ETHICS

Bringing Creation Care Down to Earth

David Gushee

INTRODUCING CHRISTIAN ENVIRONMENTAL ETHICS

The task of this essay is to offer elements of a constructive Christian creation care ethic grounded in scripture and relevant to evangelical and other Christians.

In recent decades, the grave challenges presented by environmental problems have evoked a sizable literature of moral analysis and response, both from within and outside the Christian tradition. This literature reflects a variety of ways of thinking about the theological and moral significance of the environment, the proper role of human beings in creation, the sources and meanings of contemporary environmental problems, and the moral principles, virtues, and rules most important for forming and directing human behavior in response to God's creation. It has been clear in the development of this literature that environmental problems have created great intellectual challenges to regnant systems of thought in most areas, including economics, political theory and international relations. Challenges of similar gravity have been felt in theology, philosophy and ethics. That environmental problems have proven so disorienting for most well-established intellectual traditions demonstrates both the novelty of the challenges ecological problems create and the difficulty we are having in responding to them.

In this chapter, a distinctively Christian theological-ethical approach will be taken to environmental problems. After surveying current theo-centric, anthropocentric and biocentric approaches to creation care, I will explore the potential of a sanctity-of-life paradigm to ground Christian moral obligation to God, our human neighbors, non-human creatures and the creation itself. This will mark a new kind of applica-tion of a familiar theme most often employed in relation to "life issues" such as abortion. I will argue that reverence for human and non-human life, and for the ecosystems that sustain such life, can be a powerful starting point for ethical response to our suffering created order. I will further claim that such reverence ultimately is based on our reverence (even worship) of God, the Creator, Sustainer and Redeemer of the earth and all that is in it. Creaturely life—beginning with human life but extending in profound ways to all of life—carries a kind of sacred-ness because of its relation to our holy God who is the source of all value. This broadening of what it means to care about the sanctity of life is important for the moral depth and credibility of evangelical moral thought and public witness.

ENGAGING THE THEOLOGICAL ETHICS OF CREATION CARE

Prior to the emergence of the modern environmental movement in the 1960s, which was a response to increasingly obvious signs of environ-mental distress, Western Christianity had lost touch with the resources for a creation care ethic that were present within the Bible and scattered in our theological tradition. We did not preach, teach or practice "cre-ation care" (the term itself is of recent origin) because we recognized neither the contemporary need to do so nor the demands of our faith that required it. Of course there were exceptions, but these were few and far between. Western Christians joined Western culture in its un-thinking drive toward modern industrial capitalism and the good life as defined by its technological advances. This is a cautionary tale in Christian cultural captivity.

Some have argued that Christianity was more than a passive by-stander in this process of ecological degradation. In a famous 1967 ar-ticle called "The Historical Roots of Our Ecological Crisis," scientist

Lynn White charged that "Christianity bears a huge burden of guilt" for the environmental problems afflicting Western society and now the whole world. White argued that the Bible desacralized nature, licensed human beings to dominate and overpopulate the earth, and created an anthropocentric view of creation.[1] The Bible has also been charged with encouraging a dualistic (spiritual vs. physical) view of reality that encouraged a contempt for this world, and with nurturing an eschatological framework in which Christ's second coming distracts Christians from an ultimate commitment to the well-being of the one Earth on which we actually live.[2] While more recent scholarship has clearly demonstrated that ecological catastrophe is not a uniquely Western or Christian problem, the sting of White's thesis lingers.[3]

Facing such criticisms over these past forty years, as well as recognizing the deepening environmental problems, more and more Christian thinkers have worked through these issues in search of a Christian theological-ethical posture adequate to address them. It is common to consider these approaches in terms of three categories: theocentric (God-centered), anthropocentric (human-centered) and biocentric (non-human life or ecosystem-centered). Let us consider each.

Theocentric approaches. "In the beginning, God created the heavens and the earth" (Gen 1:1 ESV). Theocentric approaches emphasize that "the earth is the LORD's and all that is in it, the world, and those who live in it" (Ps 24:1). Human beings must respect and care for creation precisely because it is God's creation. God is the *source* of creation; it is his amazing handiwork, and to God belongs *ownership* and *rule* over what he has created. These facts should be clear to all people, but Christians especially must be in the vanguard of those who, when they look at the world around them, do not claim it as "mine" or "ours" but instead see it as belonging fully to God its maker.

If something belongs to another rather than to me, but they have

---

[1]Lynn White, "The Historical Roots of Our Ecological Crisis," *Science* 155 (March 10, 1967): 1203-7.

[2]For a careful analysis and response, see Richard A. Young, *Healing the Earth* (Nashville: Broadman & Holman, 1994).

[3]Jared Diamond, *Collapse* (New York: Penguin, 2005), an immensely important book, tells the story of numerous societies that collapsed ecologically for a variety of reasons.

entrusted it into my care, then I must look to the example and instructions of that person for guidance as to what to do with it. Theocentric
creation care ethics devotes considerable attention to the story told in
Genesis 1–2 and to the instructions given to the first human beings as
depicted in those narratives.

Among other things, these narratives offer a primeval description of
God's creation of "the heavens and the earth" and all that is in them.
Genesis has God creating and then shaping a world in which an amaz-
ingly diverse array of ever more sophisticated creatures can flourish—
together. God creates not just humans, and not just other creatures, but
the conditions and systems and relationships that nourish and sustain
and order creaturely life. The creatures are brought forth in the contexts in which they will live—sea creatures from the sea, birds that fly
above the earth, and land creatures that move along the ground. This
offers a clue about the interconnection between creatures and their
habitats, and the dependence of the former on the health of the latter.

"Let us make humankind in our image, according to our likeness; and
let them have dominion" (Gen 1:26). Human beings are clearly treated as
the pinnacle of God's created works. But we are not alone—we are never
alone. We emerge in sequence with the other creatures. We have a particular kind of responsibility to other creatures as an aspect of our responsibility to God. But God is the center of value, not we. God has
simply chosen to relate to creation in a particular way, which involves a
special responsibility for human beings. A theocentric creation care ethic
continually draws our attention back to God. To the extent that God has
graciously entrusted creation to our care, to that very extent we must offer
creation back to God in loving gratitude and service.

In this volume, the concept of environmental stewardship has often
surfaced. Properly understood, stewardship is a theocentric form of a
creation care ethic. A steward is someone who manages something for
someone else. Christians who emphasize environmental stewardship
recognize both that "the earth is the LORD's" (Ps 24:1) and that "the
earth he has given to human beings" (Ps 115:16). The earth has been
"given" to us, but only in a provisional sense, for God remains its owner.
We are to manage it for God, and with reference to God's implicit di-

rection and explicit commands for that management. But as we manage it for God, we also are managing it on behalf of all who dwell here, with special responsibility for those creatures dependent on us for their well-being and survival. The idea that "dominion" means stewardship of God's creation is a concept featured in work by authors such as Cal DeWitt, Douglas John Hall and Loren Wilkinson, and has become a mainstream concept in contemporary Christian thought.[4] It marks a significant step forward in Christian thinking about God's creation. It works well in Christian communities in which the concept of stewardship is already familiar—usually related to stewardship of the economic resources that God entrusts to our care. A bridge can be built from caring for those financial resources as a kind of trustee of God, to caring for creation also as a trustee. Stewardship is trusteeship—responsible management of an enterprise that preceded us, will succeed us, and to which we have temporary responsibility, not on our own behalf but on behalf of its owner and beneficiaries.

Loren Wilkinson's concept of *earthkeeping* also moves in this direction: we do not own the earth, but we hold it in trust. Indeed God commands that we "serve and keep/guard it" (Gen 2:15).[5] This implies that our entire relationship to the earth is a relationship of service, which involves caring for God's creation in such a way that it is "kept" on behalf of God for the benefit of all creatures now and for future generations. One might add that we now know that if we do not "serve it" that we ultimately cannot "keep it," because the earth, its creatures and ecosystems are far more fragile than industrial-era humanity once thought. We only get to keep the earth if we serve it. And this requires a far more careful guarding of earth's creatures and ecosystems than we have been doing for many generations. *Keeping God's earth as God commands is indispensable for the well-being of all creatures, including humanity, now and in the future.*

Anthropocentric approaches. This prepares us for a consideration of *anthropocentric*, or human-centered, approaches to creation care. Where theocentric creation care is motivated by a desire to honor God as Cre-

---

[4]See "Further Reading" for references.
[5]On this translation of Gen 2:15 see Daniel I. Block in chapter 5 of this volume.

ator and obey his commands in relation to creation, anthropocentric approaches elevate human well-being to the center of concern.

If it is true, as just suggested, that honoring God's command advances human well-being, then there should not be any tension between a theocentric and anthropocentric approach. As we honor our Creator God and obey God's commands, we act in ways that advance human well-being.

This works out, however, only if human well-being is properly understood. We need an understanding of human well-being that attends to all human beings, in long-term and intergenerational perspective, with attention to every aspect of human well-being. As we think about the care of God's creation, attending to this more holistic vision of the human good creates a morally constructive kind of anthropocentric ethics. It also generates pivotal moral norms such as *environmental justice, intergenerational moral responsibility* and *ecological sustainability*. Let us say a word about each of these norms.

Justice has many definitions, and every society, ideology and worldview seems to produce its own theory of justice. Christians need to be aware that often we draw our definition of justice from non-biblical sources: Greek philosophical ethics ("to each according to his due," understood hierarchically), utilitarianism ("the greatest good for the greatest number"), elitism (justice as the rule of the meritocracy), liberalism (justice as the protection of individual autonomy in the pursuit of property and happiness), retributionism (justice as retributive punishment for wrongdoers), and so on.

On the other hand, those who attend most closely to scripture find hundreds of references to justice, few of which bear much resemblance to any of the concepts just enumerated. In the Old Testament especially, justice is rooted in the narrative of God's deliverance of his people, the Hebrew slaves, from the misery of Egyptian slavery into a covenant community in which all stood equal in value before their Redeeming God. Justice is an active concept in Scripture, emphasizing divine and human action to deliver suffering human beings from situations of oppression and denial of their basic needs. Consistently in the Old Testament, with echoes especially in Jesus' teaching in the New

Testament, justice means action to deliver the poor from their poverty, the dominated from those who bully and disempower them, the violated from those who abuse and kill them, and the excluded from those who reject them from covenant community.[6] A commitment to justice is rooted in an awareness of the neediness and vulnerability of all human beings, as well as belief in God's passionate and active concern for all, especially those who cannot protect themselves amidst unjust communities structured to disadvantage them.

Environmental justice, biblically understood, begins with the recognition of the dependence of all human beings on a healthy environment. Humans need clean air to breathe, sufficient clean water to drink, fertile and healthy soil to till, healthy neighbor-creatures for clothing, food, and medicine, reasonably stable climate systems, and temperatures within a livable range. Lack of access to these basic goods that sustain life and health can be seen as an assault on the physical well-being of persons, and perhaps also as a particularly painful example of poverty. At times, environmental injustice is part of domination and exclusion from community, when some are given access to environmental goods while others are denied them, perhaps even by force.

Environmental justice will occur if and when all human beings have access to a livable, healthy environment. Environmental injustice occurs when any groups, such as the poor, or the urban, or racial/ethnic minorities, or the powerless, are deprived of such access to a livable environment, which happens every day in our own nation and all around the world.[7] The constructive work of environmental justice involves closing the gaps between those who have access to such a living environment and those who do not.

The created order is fallen, as we know. This means that even though a good God is the Creator of this world and has provided amply for his creatures, even "normal" and "natural" circumstances involving no human wrongdoing often represent occasions for misery and suffering. Hurricanes strike. They drown people whether they live in yachts and

---

[6]Glen H. Stassen and David P. Gushee, *Kingdom Ethics: Following Jesus in Contemporary Context* (Downers Grove, Ill.: InterVarsity Press, 2003), chap. 17.
[7]See Jim Schwab, *Deeper Shades of Green* (San Francisco: Sierra Club, 1994).

estates or tenements and slums. Tornadoes blow through towns, destroying whoever and whatever happens to be in the way. In this sense, there is and can be no "environmental justice" if that is understood as a world in which no one ever suffers randomly from an environmental calamity. Where such terrors emerge as "acts of God," as the insurance companies like to say, justice simply means that everyone is treated equally in the aftermath—which, as we well know, often does not happen. But that is where human responsibility begins.

The global climate change issue has raised the interesting question of whether scientific assessment of its causes has moral significance. Certainly the matter is debated with great passion. If human beings are primarily responsible for global climate change, as now appears clearly to be the case, our responsibility to address it is to some extent heightened. We caused it, we must reverse it (if possible), and we must deal with its effects. But even if climate change were not human-induced, justice would require dealing with its effects, especially as these are distributed unevenly, with special impact on the poor and vulnerable.

Most discussions of environmental justice, of course, assume that some human beings retain access to a livable environment even while others are denied it, which is what makes the situation unjust. The grave environmental problems we now face, however, raise questions about the overall ecological health of the planet. Global climate change and even loss of biodiversity both threaten the long-term sustainability of human life. Both will be experienced as environmental justice issues first, as some groups or regions rather than others feel the effects first or most severely. If such problems continue unabated, or if they worsen, they will become environmental justice issues understood in an intergenerational sense—we may leave our grandchildren an unlivable world, enjoying our short-term lifestyle advantages at the expense of their very well-being.[8] And if even then we do not act, the language of justice hardly will seem adequate to describe a world in which fewer and fewer people and finally no human being at all can thrive (or survive). This is why ecological *sustainability* is such an important moral

---

[8]See Robert Parham, *Loving Neighbors Across Time* (Birmingham: New Hope, 1992).

norm, for it speaks to preserving the global conditions for any and all human beings to live and flourish. Sustainability is the *sine qua non* for any talk of justice. For that matter, ecological sustainability is the *sine qua non* for any talk of any other human or ethical concern. If we destroy the conditions of human life on the planet, no other concerns will be relevant at all.

Where Christians and others offer "anthropocentric" creation care efforts that are concerned for environmental justice, intergenerational responsibility and ecological sustainability, such a human-centered emphasis can be both morally and strategically constructive. The short history of the environmental movement clearly reveals that when human well-being is set against the well-being of other species, as in "save the babies, not the whales," or "save our jobs, not the snails," everyone loses. Environmentalism is seen as anti-human. But when the well-being of all humans, or the next generation of humans, or the most vulnerable humans, is stressed, environmentalism corresponds with neighbor-love in a way that most can understand and appreciate.

It should be noted that a less constructive anthropocentrism still can be found in Christian circles. What might be called a *hard anthropocentrism* is receding to some extent under the combined impact of environmental problems and environmentalism as it spreads into Christian theology. But it retains its hold in some of our most politically conservative circles, such as the work of E. Calvin Beisner in the evangelical community, and Father Robert Sirico among Catholics.[9]

These thinkers tend to emphasize the goods provided by economic growth, unfettered laissez-faire capitalism, and a "natural resources" approach to non-human creatures and the land, air and sea in which we and they dwell. Beisner, in particular, offers a reading of the Genesis materials that has moved very little from dominion understood as domination to dominion understood as stewardship. He still argues that the land, air, water and other living creatures have worth only according to their utilitarian value to humans. He is not willing to ascribe any other-than-instrumental moral value to non-human entities. He argues that

---

[9]See E. Calvin Beisner, *Where Garden Meets Wilderness* (Grand Rapids: Eerdmans, 1997).

nature was made for humans, not us for nature, that the Bible has nothing to say that might demand limits on our consumption of the resources God provides in creation, and that economic growth, rather than voluntary or state-imposed restraints on our behavior, will solve our environmental problems. It is also clear that Beisner, along with numerous conservative evangelical Christians, finds it hard to believe that God could or would permit human beings to pose any substantial long-term threat to the well-being of the creation. Here a certain understanding of God's sovereignty as well as eschatology undercuts the moral responsibility demanded in Scripture.

Biocentric approaches. Quite on the other end of the spectrum one finds a range of approaches that have attempted to find ways to ascribe intrinsic moral value to the other living creatures, the various species, and the planetary ecological order itself. These are sometimes called *biocentric* approaches because of their celebration and valuation of *life*, in all of its various forms, as well as their effort to address the significance of the biosphere as a whole.

It is clear in retrospect that the move toward biocentric ecological ethics in part was a response to an earlier stage of the environmental movement, in which the main problem was seen as the damage that human beings were doing to other species and their ecosystems. The majority culture lacked a paradigm that might generate concern for species that were being driven to extinction, or habitats and ecosystems whose destruction would affect a range of our otherwise invisible creature-neighbors. With recent developments, such as climate change, it is now clear that what happens to the other creatures, and what happens to ecosystems, eventually happens to human beings—because we are all creatures, and all interconnected, and all share a single planet.

Still, those interested in environmental issues continue to offer biocentric approaches. Some of these biocentric approaches are offered by Christians. Some Christians attempt to move toward biocentrism through revisions of classic Christian theology that stray so far from biblical categories of thought that they may constitute the abandonment of historic Christian faith. Other times the reforms stay more carefully within Christian theological boundaries.

For those who believe that biblical faith's primary sin was in desacralizing nature, robbing it of the felt sense of the divine presence, one option is to retrieve or create nature religions that redivinize nature in its individual parts or as a whole. Just as once the ancients experienced and worshiped the divine in the air, land and sea, in the various creatures, and in the mysterious processes of nature on which all life depends, such as rain, sunshine and harvest, even today some have returned to various forms of such beliefs. We are witnessing a revival of nature religions in our time, such as is found in New Age thought, Native American spiritualities, some Eastern religions, and neo-pagan religions such as the Wiccan movement. The visibility of these movements has hurt the cause of creation care among evangelicals for a long time.

Another possibility, especially appealing to some, in view of the growing appreciation of the creation as a single intricate entity, a vast ecosystem that sustains all life (the "Gaia hypothesis"), has been a retrieval of a kind of pantheism in which God is all and all is God, or a panentheism in which God is to be identified with or experienced directly in everything that exists.[10] The Earth is a single living Being, who must be revered and treated as divine.

A third move is toward a kind of feminist nature religion. Here the critique of biblical thought categories is further specified as a critique of the patriarchy or androcentrism that has distorted all of these thought categories, such as the dualism that diminishes the female in favor of the male, the natural in favor of the spiritual, the body in favor of the soul, and this life in favor of the next one.[11] In one version of this approach, the Earth is personified as our divine Mother, who/which must be loved as a whole and in her constituent elements—every tree, river and frog. Some who are attracted to this approach seek to retrieve ancient matriarchal religions which, they argue, contained elements of this kind of mysticism and spirituality and were displaced centuries ago

---

[10]The concept began as a scientific hypothesis and developed in a metaphysical/religious direction. See James Lovelock, *Gaia: A New Look at Life on Earth* (New York: Oxford University Press, 2000).

[11]Anna Peterson, *Being Human* (Berkeley: University of California Press, 2001), chap. 2.

in most of the world by the violent patriarchal religions of Judaism, Christianity and Islam.[12]

Evolutionary approaches to life on earth have been embraced by some who then weave an eco-spirituality around evolution. One approach is to find a kind of life-force spirituality at work in the multi-billion-year process by which life has unfolded on this planet and presumably elsewhere. All life is related to all other life, all life seeks to extend itself, and in the development and infinite elaboration of life forms on this planet one has much material for religious awe and wonder, as well as the basis of an ethic of reverence and respect for life in all its forms.[13]

One influential philosophical rather than theological move has been the embrace of a kind of eco-utilitarianism by the philosopher Peter Singer. Singer offers a new kind of moral universalism in which at least some non-human creatures are valued equally to human beings and thus become the bearers of moral claims that must be respected by human beings. Unfortunately, the way Singer grounds his elevation of the moral status of the higher mammals is by establishing a consciousness-based or capacity-based evaluation of that status. This simultaneously elevates the moral status of the higher mammals that have been shown to be near or equal to human beings in their capacities and consciousness while demoting human beings who lack such capacities and consciousness. This move lies at the root of Singer's horrifying proposal that infanticide and euthanasia should be permitted. For Singer, the capacities of an infant or an Alzheimer's patient fall below those of a fully functioning gorilla, and their respective rights should be treated correspondingly.[14]

Another move suggested in recent literature has been more explicitly political. It involves a rethinking of political community to include all creatures. If one thinks of modern history as involving a gradual recognition of the moral and thus political status of all hu-

---

[12]See, for example, Riane Eisler, *The Chalice and the Blade* (Gloucester, Mass.: Peter Smith, 1994).

[13]Thomas Berry, *The Dream of the Earth* (San Francisco: Sierra Club, 1988), esp. chap. 10.

[14]Peter Singer, *Practical Ethics*, 2nd ed. (Cambridge: Cambridge University Press, 1993).

man beings, and not just some categories of human beings (men, landowners, white people), then the extension of this status to non-human creatures can be seen as the next logical step. Animals join humans in the kingdom of ends, to reframe Immanuel Kant. In an extension of the categorical imperative, they must count as among those who are viewed as ends also and not merely as means to someone else's ends. This ultimately leads to a reframing of the concept of citizenship, with animals included in a kind of global earth community with rights that must be respected even if they cannot speak for themselves.[15]

I have already suggested that a number of Christian theologians have attempted to reframe Christian theology in radical ways that, in my view, essentially introduce elements of nature religions into Christian faith. While this is not the place to offer an introduction to all of these approaches, what they have in common is generally the explicit abandonment of core doctrinal elements of Christian faith and often the introduction of theological concepts and images that have little precedent in biblical or historical theology. Two examples of this are the mystical panentheism of Matthew Fox's creation spirituality, and the feminist embrace of a kind of Mother Earth theology such as Sallie McFague's suggestion that the earth should be viewed as God's body.[16]

Perhaps it is easy for evangelicals to dismiss all of the foregoing moves as dangerous overreactions. They should instead be viewed as relevant evidence of the Earth's distress and of culture's responses to that distress—and some of our Christian brothers' and sisters' responses. Some represent the retrieval of centuries of wisdom about sustainable human living on this planet. Even those that go too far should speak to us about our own need as perhaps more carefully orthodox Christians to respond far better than we have done.

---

[15]This can be framed philosophically, as an expansion of Kant (as in Paul Taylor, *Respect for Nature* [Princeton: Princeton University Press, 1986]) or Mill (as in Peter Singer, *Animal Liberation*, [New York: Harper Perennial, 2001]), or theologically (as in Larry Rasmussen, *Earth Community, Earth Ethics* [Maryknoll, N.Y.: Orbis Books, 1996]).

[16]Matthew Fox, *Original Blessing* (Santa Fe: Bear, 1983); Sallie McFague, *Models of God* (Minneapolis: Augsburg Fortress, 1987).

THE EMERGENCE OF A SANCTITY-OF-HUMAN LIFE ETHIC

In late twentieth-century Christian ethics, a central moral norm emerged: the "sanctity of human life." The impetus for the articulation of this moral norm in much of the Western world in the 1970s was the full legalization of abortion and, secondarily, the reality or possibility of the legalization of assisted suicide. Even today the term is often used, either by its advocates or its foes, as applying primarily to those two issues. Those who were in favor of abortion sometimes sought explicitly to undercut the validity of a sanctity-of-human-life ethic, no one more stridently than Australian philosopher Peter Singer.[17] After a while, many Christians wearied of the association of "sanctity of life" with the Christian Right and the "pro-life movement" and dropped or rejected this particular moral vocabulary for other terminology. Even today most politically progressive Christians shy away from the term.

We need to reclaim the concept of the sanctity of human life while at the same time freeing it of this crippling hyper-association with the abortion fight and the culture wars. The idea that every human life has immeasurable, God-given value worthy of the highest respect is actually the culmination of the best of the Jewish, Christian and Western moral traditions—and a sifting out of elements of those same traditions that fall short of that ideal.

In this sense, it is incorrect to describe the sanctity of human life as a new moral norm. It is as old as the Genesis concept of the *imago Dei*, and as new as the liberation ethics of the twentieth century. It is as old as the demand to love our neighbors as ourselves, and as new as twentieth century theological personalism, the post-Holocaust writings of Elie Wiesel and Irving Greenberg on resanctifying human life after Auschwitz, Catholic social teaching from Vatican II to John Paul II, anti- and post-colonial writing, feminist thought and the thinking of the leaders of America's civil rights movement. What all of these disparate sources have in common is a profound sense of the grandeur and dignity of the human person (each and every person) and a profound resistance to his or her dehumanization and degradation.

---

[17]For example, Peter Singer, *Unsanctifying Human Life* (Oxford: Blackwell, 2002).

The working definition I have developed for the sanctity of human life has come to be articulated as follows:

> The sanctity of life is the conviction that all human beings, at any and every stage of life, in any and every state of consciousness or self-awareness, of any and every race, color, ethnicity, level of intelligence, religion, language, nationality, gender, character, behavior, physical ability/disability, sexual orientation, potential, class, social status, etc., of any and every particular quality of relationship to the viewing subject, are to be perceived as sacred, as persons of equal and immeasurable worth and of inviolable dignity. Therefore they must be treated with the reverence and respect commensurate with this elevated moral status, beginning with a commitment to the preservation, protection, and flourishing of their lives.
>
> The belief that human life is sacred flows from biblical faith. In particular, life is sacred because, according to Scripture, God created humans in his image, declared them precious, ascribed to them a unique status in creation, blessed them with unique, god-like capacities, made them for eternal life, governs them under his sovereign lordship, commands in his moral law that they be treated with reverence and respect—and forever elevates their dignity by his decision to take human form in Jesus Christ and to give up that human life at the Cross.[18]

There are many reasons to embrace this ethic as a/the central Christian moral norm. As articulated carefully here, this statement of what the sanctity of life means emphasizes as starkly as possible the *universality* of human moral obligations to other human beings. I have sought to craft language here that emphasizes the length, breadth, height and depth of human moral obligation to other humans. No one can be excluded, for any reason. All must be viewed as sacred and treated with reverence and respect. To each and to all I owe particular moral *obligations*, focusing first on the protection and preservation of their lives and finally, in an open-ended way, to their flourishing in every aspect of what it means for them to flourish as human creatures made in the image of God.

---

[18]David P. Gushee, *Sanctifying Human Life* (Grand Rapids: Eerdmans, forthcoming). This definition is a composite of numerous other definitions along with my own contributions.

And yet, it is not at all clear that this kind of Christian ethic is sufficient for addressing the particular challenges created by the ecological degradation of the planet that we face today and into the rest of the twenty-first century. In fact, it can be argued that a sanctity-of-human-life ethic is part of the problem and cannot be part of the solution. It would be quite a paradox if the highest expression of a Christian ethic that values human life turns out to be at the same time a source of the ongoing devaluation of the rest of God's creation.

PROBLEMS OF A SANCTITY-OF-HUMAN-LIFE ETHIC
FOR THE CARE OF CREATION

Here are a few of the possible problems with this ethic.

First, it sharpens our sense of the immense value of the human person, but offers no account even of the existence, let alone the value, of other beings. We are trained to see human beings as the pinnacle of creation, the height of God's creative work, and the center of God's concern when it comes to the affairs of this planet—and indeed, of the entire universe. Even the broad sanctity ethic proposed here still focuses the entirety of its attention on human beings. The drama of salvation history remains the question of the response of the human being to God our Maker and Redeemer; the drama of ethics remains the question of the response of the human being to other human beings.[19]

As for the existence of other sentient beings, and the creation itself, this account of life's sanctity remains silent. At least in Western Christianity we have lacked even the language to discuss that which goes beyond and yet includes both the vertical and the horizontal, the divine-human and human-human dramas. An earlier generation might have spoken of God's relationship with the angels or the heavenly court. They disappear here. And no mention is made of fish, squirrels or dolphins, or of trees, rivers, air and crabgrass. A sanctity approach does at least push Christians to pay attention to ethics and not just theology, to how people are treated and not just whether they believe in Jesus, but it

---

[19]Young, *Healing the Earth*, p. 48.

does nothing to raise the visibility of the millions of other creatures with whom we share the created order, or the created order itself.

Even when Christians do move in the direction of a theology of creation and the other creatures, a common theological move is quickly to sharpen the ontological distinctions between human and non-human creatures. The first step in this direction is to define the content of the *imago Dei* through some delineation of the ways in which only human beings are made in God's image. Often this is done through the specification of certain capacities of the human that are set against the lack of capacity of other creatures. We say only humans can reason, or plan, or create, or love, or invent and speak languages. Only humans have a "soul" that can relate to and love God. This is sometimes called "human exceptionalism," or criticized as human egocentrism, or speciesism, and it goes deep in Christian thought.[20] Imagine how different our view of the world would be if our teachings about creation emphasized all that we shared in common with other creatures instead of all that makes humans different. Instead, our tradition tends to emphasize human uniqueness and superiority in fateful ways.

This move toward a capacity-based construal of the divine image is also susceptible to empirical attacks from those who propose or show that the distinctions between the reasoning, creative, emotive, linguistic, relational or even spiritual capacities of humans over against the higher mammals, for example, have been overdrawn. We end up risking a core element of our theology with every new discovery about the surprisingly advanced capacities of other creatures.

This is one very good reason, by the way, for us to follow the suggestions of a number of biblical scholars that the image of God should be understood in terms of our unique *responsibilities*, not our unique *capacities*, which connects to the language of environmental stewardship.[21] We image God as we bear God's delegated authority to care for the earth and its creatures. This emphasizes our unique power and re-

---

[20]On the problem of "exceptionalism," see the excellent discussion in Anna L. Peterson, *Being Human* (Berkeley: University of California Press, 2001), chap. 2.

[21]For example, Claus Westermann, *Creation*, trans. John J. Scullion (London: SPCK, 1974). See also Daniel Block's essay in chapter 5 of this volume.

sponsibility in the earth, rather than our increasingly tenuous claim to have unique capacities.

One consequence of defining the *imago Dei* in this better-than, over-against paradigm is the implicit or explicit degradation of the status and value of non-human creatures relative to human beings. Other creatures are less-than us because they cannot reason, emote, relate, love, create or speak. It becomes very important in this approach to delineate the many specific ways in which other creatures are indeed inferior to us in their capacities. Not made in the image of God, not destined for eternal life with God, they occupy an ambiguous and certainly less important role in the divine economy. They are not part of the ultimate drama of salvation, nor are they part of the penultimate drama of ethics. They are barely more than "scenery" on the stage of the divine-human drama.[22] Human uniqueness and status are bought at a high price here—the denigration of the status of each and every one of the other creatures on the planet.

Incidentally, this way of defining what it really means to be human, what it really means to be made in the image of God, has dramatic unintended consequences—especially a weakening of the moral status of those human beings who lose or never have those distinctive capacities that we have identified as constituting the image of God. A child in the womb does not qualify as *imago Dei* material as defined by capacities. The best we can really say is that one day, if all goes well, this developing child will have those capacities. A person in a persistent vegetative state lacks some or all of the capacities we have named. So does a person with grave mental illness or in the last stages of Alzheimer's. These weaknesses of a capacity-based defining of the image have been exploited ruthlessly by those who have had reason to do so, from the Nazis in their euthanasia campaign until today. How tragic, that the effort to buttress the elevation of what it means to be human has sometimes contributed to the degradation of lives that do not quite qualify by the definitions we have created.

A review of our exalted definition of the sanctity of human life re-

---

[22]This was actually claimed by Emil Brunner, *Revelation and Reason* (Philadelphia: Westminster Press, 1946), p. 34.

veals huge implications for how human beings are to be treated by other human beings, but it sets no ethical framework for human responsibility to other creatures and the creation itself. We can see that each and every human being is to be viewed with reverence and respect, and to be treated in a manner that contributes to the preservation, protection and flourishing of their lives. This is concise, challenging and clear. But how are we to view and to treat the monkeys, rats and dogs, or the roses, oceans and air?

TOWARD A BROADENED CHRISTIAN SANCTITY-OF-LIFE ETHIC

If properly modified, the sanctity of life still can be the organizing framework or paradigm that we need for an era of ecological crisis. If this effort is successful, concern for God's creation can be, at least in part, anchored in a moral commitment that is already widely shared in the churches, which is a considerable advantage for those trying to affect the beliefs and behaviors of the average Christian today.

In biblical thought, the majesty and holiness of God, together with the free decision of God, entirely grounds any ascription of anything like "sanctity" to humanity. Therefore it is wrong to say even that human beings and their lives are somehow *intrinsically* sacred, if we are not at the same time saying that what makes human lives sacred is God's action and declaration toward them. Perhaps a more precise way to say it is that in theocentric perspective all creational value is *derived value*, in that God the Creator is the one who authoritatively declares and demonstrates the value of all things that he has made. Only after we are clear about this can we then venture to say that an entity has *intrinsic value*, which means that God has already and permanently made his valuation of that entity clear.

In the critical Psalm 8, for example, it is God's name that is "majestic . . . in all the earth" (v. 1). It is God's decision to choose to be "mindful" of humanity amidst all of God's other majestic creations (v. 4). It is God who made us "a little lower than God [Heb., the *ʾĕlōhîm*]" (v. 5), and "crowned [us] with glory and honor" (v. 5). It is God who chose to make us ruler "over the works of [his] hands" (v. 6). If human life can be described as sacred, it is so only insofar as the majesty, holiness, presence, love and care of God touch it, are related to it, and are directed toward it. To honor human life and treat it with reverence is an appropriate theological, spiritual and ethical response to God.

Insofar as ecological degradation and catastrophe hurt human beings (those creatures toward whom God's actions and declarations reveal such exalted value), Christians are duty bound to respond with steps to ease the suffering of their human neighbors. Therefore one of the best responses that concerned Christian environmentalists can make to advance their commitments is to (1) remind their fellow Christians of their sacred obligations toward their human neighbors, whom God loves so dearly, and (2) show concretely how ecological degradation is already sickening and killing those neighbors. This is not hard to do. Here theocentrism and anthropocentrism come together.

But then we must also find ways to demonstrate biblically that the other creatures, and the ecosystems that sustain them, and the creation as a whole, are also in some sense sacred, as in, valued highly by God. Biblically, I believe it is important to say that they are not sacred to the same degree (cf. Lk 12:6-7) or in the same way that human beings are, especially if we tie sacredness in any strong way to the *imago Dei*, and if we preserve some species uniqueness as part of that divine image. But they are indeed sacred—if we understand sacred, again, to mean "sacred as a result of God's action and declaration toward them and relationship with them." If even human beings are viewed as having a God-derived and God-declared rather than intrinsic sacredness—as being touched by the sacred because touched by the divine who makes sacred—then perhaps we can open ourselves to the possibility that other creatures might also have their own kind of God-derived sacredness. *What makes creaturely life sacred is God's relation to it, not any particular characteristic we might claim for ourselves or any other creature.* Radical theocentrism therefore overrides chauvinistic human speciesism. All creatures bow before the majestic Creator who alone gives them value. In this way, a reframed sanctity of life ethic pulls together all of the themes we have been considering. It is simultaneously biocentric and anthropocentric because it is so deeply theocentric.

When we then re-open the text of the Bible and look especially for

God's relationship to other creatures and the creation, we find a God who creates other creatures and the creation (Gen 1–2), who declares them good (Gen 1:31), who feeds and sustains them (Ps 104; Mt 6:26), who makes covenant with them (Gen 9), who protects them in his laws (Lev 25; Deut 6:14), who hears their groaning (Rom 8:28), and who promises their ultimate liberation from bondage to decay (Rom 8:29) in the renewal of all things (Mt 19:28). We have ample biblical grounds for looking upon them and treating them with reverence and respect.

It is not too much to say that to the extent Christians have failed to acknowledge God's sacred relationship to other creatures and the creation, we have failed God, we have sinned against him and against other creatures and the creation we share with them. Our sins demand repentance, which includes both grief over sin and new commitment to a different way of relating. We must learn to perceive our moral obligations as God's people to those other creatures loved and valued by God, and to the ecosystems that God prepared and still employs to sustain all of our lives.

CONCLUSION

In the face of the charge that Christians and Christianity bear grave responsibility for our environmental crisis, we dare not simply move into a sulk of defensiveness. We must instead claim the profound resources for creation care that have been there from the very beginning in Scripture. We must tell our own story more adequately, understand our own holy texts more profoundly. Only then will we be prepared to address specific contemporary issues such as urbanization, water, biodiversity and climate change.

Even as we do our own intellectual homework, eventually we must live out the implications of our findings. There is an important place for a book like this one, which seeks to move care of God's creation right into the center of American evangelical life. But eventually, we must all live out the implications of what we are discovering about Scripture and about our environmentally distressed world. John says that "everyone who does what is right is righteous," just as Jesus is righteous (1 Jn 3:7). Eventually—actually, now—we need to do more than get our theology right. We need to get our lives right.

WHEN THE GARDENER RETURNS

An Ecological Perspective
on Adam's Dominion

Douglas J. Green

THE DIVINE GARDENER OF GENESIS 1–2

The story of creation in Genesis 1 begins with a problem that needs to be solved. That problem is stated simply at the beginning of verse 2: "Now the earth was *tōhû wābōhû*." The KJV translated this Hebrew phrase "without form and void" and established a tradition—at least among the English versions—that has seen only minor variation in the following four centuries. Unfortunately, this translation is neither accurate nor clear (What would a "formless and void" earth actually look like?). Recently, however, David Tsumura has eliminated some of the chaos of this verse by arguing that *tōhu wābōhû.* does not refer to a shapeless mass but had a much more concrete and comprehensible meaning, and that the opening clause of verse 2 should be translated "the earth was desolate and empty."[1] This, then, is the twofold problem that God must "solve" during the creation week. Land exists, but it is desolate, a desert devoid of vegetation (most likely because it is covered by a vast cosmic sea—the Deep of Gen 1:2). Furthermore, because the land is uninhabitable it is also unin-

---

[1]David T. Tsumura, *Creation and Destruction: A Reappraisal of the* Chaoskampf *Theory in the Old Testament* (Winona Lake, Ind.: Eisenbrauns, 2005), p. 34. See also Kenneth A. Mathews, *Genesis 1–11:26,* NAC 1A (Nashville: Broadman & Holman, 1996), pp. 130-31.

habited, or empty. So the story of creation does not begin with chaos, formlessness or nothingness, but with desolation and emptiness, in a desert without vegetation and without creatures. "Now the earth was desolate and uninhabited."

Against this backdrop, the two movements within the six of days of God's creative activity now make more sense. The initial phase of God's workweek reaches its climax on day three, with a double act of creation. First, God draws back the waters of the Deep that cover the earth so that the land is exposed (Gen 1:9-10), and then on this newly revealed dry ground he brings forth vegetation, specifically the kind that grows without the aid of human agriculture: "plants bearing [lit., sowing] seed" (i.e., cereal crops like wheat, barley and oats[2]) and "fruit trees" (Gen 1:11-12). In this way, on day three, the problem of *tōhû*, desolation, is solved. On this day the Lord reveals himself as the divine gardener who turns earth's original barrenness into verdant, fruitful land.

The other problem of Genesis 1:2, the *bōhû*—earth's primeval uninhabitedness or emptiness—will be answered at the end of the second three-day phase, on day six, with another double act of creation: first, the "living creatures" (Gen 1:24-25) and then humanity, whose calling is to "fill the earth" and in so doing reverse its original emptiness (Gen 1:26-28). So by the end of day six, the Lord has overcome all the "anti-creational" elements that existed at the beginning of his workweek: the darkness replaced by light (day 1), the Deep pulled back from the land (day 2), desolation turned to fruitfulness (day 3) and empty land now filled with creatures (day 6). God creates, but as he does so he gains dominion over the cosmos. This presentation of God as the creator-king is reinforced by the fact that on day seven he rests by ceasing from his work. Read in a wider ancient Near Eastern and Israelite literary context, God's *inactivity* on this final day of the creation week actually shows that he exercises complete sovereignty

---

[2]Bryan Paradise, "Food for Thought: The Septuagint Translation of Genesis 1.11-12," in *A Word in Season: Essays in Honour of William McKane*, ed. James D. Martin and Philip R. Davies, JSOTSup 43 (Sheffield, U.K.: JSOT Press, 1986), p. 182.

over all that he has created.[3] As Jon Levenson puts it,

> The creation narratives . . . are best seen as dramatic visualizations of the uncompromised mastery of YHWH. He alone is "the Lord of all the earth," and when the cosmogonic events are complete, his lordship stands beyond all doubt. He reigns in regal repose, "majestic on high," all else subordinate to him.[4]

Thus Genesis portrays God not merely as a creator but as a creator-king, and one dimension of this kingship is his role as a gardener who greens the wasteland of Genesis 1:2, making unproductive land productive (Gen 1:11-12). Moreover, even when the wide-angle lens of Genesis 1 gives way to the more narrowly focused narrative of Genesis 2, we still see the divine gardener at work: "Now the LORD God planted a garden in Eden" (Gen 2:8).

HUMANITY—GOD'S "VICE GARDENER"

If the opening chapters of Genesis present the Lord as the king over his creation, they also show that he intends to exercise his royal dominion *indirectly*, through the rule of one of his creatures. More specifically, God's plan is to rule creation through a vice regal representative, a creature who stands in God's place and rules over the rest of creation on his behalf. The creature who occupies this position of mediatorial kingship is, of course, humanity, with Adam, *the* human of chapter 2, taking the role of the individual king, or vice regent over creation.

Humanity's role as kings over creation is clear from Genesis 1:26-28. God creates humanity and then grants them the authority to "subdue" the earth and "rule over" its creatures. Their dominion over the land and the creatures that inhabit it cannot be separated from God's kingship over the world he has created. While we must not forget that animals and humans are both creatures of the sixth day, and our shared creatureliness has important theological and ethical implications that

---

[3]Bernard F. Batto, "The Sleeping God: An Ancient Near Eastern Motif of Divine Sovereignty," *Bib* 68 (1987): 153-77.

[4]Jon D. Levenson, *Creation and the Persistence of Evil: The Jewish Drama of Divine Omnipotence* (San Francisco: HarperCollins, 1988), p. 3.

are often neglected,[5] we cannot escape the fact that humans are the only creatures made in God's image. As Richard Middleton has argued, their status as bearers of the divine image means that humans are not only "*like God* in exercising royal power on earth"—their rule mirrors or is analogous to God's rule—but also they are God's *representatives*, entrusted with the office and task of exercising God's rule and power in the world *on his behalf*.[6] In other words, humanity is "the earthly embodiment of the divine sovereign."[7]

If humanity's rule over creation mirrors God's dominion, then the mandate given to them to "subdue" the earth and "rule over" its creatures must, at least to some degree, derive its definition from the way God exercises his kingship over creation, especially on days three and six. When God "subdues" the land, he makes it verdant and fruitful and when he "rules over" the creatures, their numbers increase and they fill the earth. So if God's vice regents are to exercise dominion on his behalf, then *their* subduing and ruling *must* have the same creation-enhancing character.

ADAM—THE GARDENER-KING

In Genesis 2 the wide-angle view of the whole earth narrows to the "ground" or "soil," that is, agricultural or arable land.[8] Similarly, the focus narrows from "Man" understood collectively as "humanity" to "the human," Adam. He is the one in whom all that is true for the collective humanity is individualized, concentrated and epitomized. He is the quintessential human.

Not surprisingly, given the portrayal of humanity in chapter 1 as the Godlike kings who rule on behalf of the heavenly king, the presentation of Adam in Genesis 2 is rich with royal connotations, even though these connections may not be immediately obvious to modern

---

[5]For a corrective to the view that overstates the difference between humanity and animals, see Michael Williams, "Man and Beast," *Presb* 34 (2008): 12-26.

[6]J. Richard Middleton, *The Liberating Image: The* Imago Dei *in Genesis 1* (Grand Rapids: Brazos, 2005), p. 88.

[7]John T. Willis, "The Divine Sovereign: The Image of God in the Priestly Creation Account," in *David and Zion: Biblical Studies in Honor of J. J. M. Roberts,* ed. Bernard F. Batto and Kathryn L. Roberts (Winona Lake, Ind.: Eisenbrauns, 2004), p. 179.

[8]Gordon J. Wenham, *Genesis 1–15,* WBC 1 (Waco, Tex.: Word, 1987), p. 58.

readers. In Genesis 2:7 we learn that Adam is created "from the *dust of the ground*." The inclusion of the word "dust" hardly seems necessary—after all, the animals are formed "from the ground" (Gen 2:10)—but when connected to the enthronement formula spoken to Baasha in 1 Kings 16:2 ("I lifted you up *from the dust* and made you leader of my people Israel"), the creation of Adam should also be understood as the moment when the Lord grants him the authority of kingship.[9] The literal making of the man is the metaphorical raising up of a king.[10]

In Genesis 2 Adam exercises the same dual authority over land and creatures described in Genesis 1. First, he rules over the animals by naming them (Gen 2:19-20).[11] Second, he subdues the earth by imaging "God's gardening" on day three of the creation week: "The Lord God took the human and he settled him in the Garden of Eden to work [i.e., cultivate] it and to care for it" (Gen 2:15).[12] In other words, like God, Adam is a gardener. Genesis 2:5 even suggests that the Lord *needs* the human to make the land fertile and productive. Creation is incomplete without the human gardener. Only with Adam can creation become what it was meant to be: productive, fruitful, verdant. Therefore, the most appropriate place for the primal gardener to inhabit is that section of the arable land known as the Garden of Eden. This is not like a vegetable or flower garden but more like a botanical garden or park with a rich diversity of exotic plants and trees. In fact, in light of archaeological discoveries during the last century, the Hebrew word ʿ*ēden* can best be translated as "luxuriance" or "abundance, fertility."[13] The name describes the place: a well-watered garden of lush vegetation.

---

[9]See Walter A. Brueggemann, "From Dust to Kingship," *ZAW* 84 (1972): 1-18.

[10]Nicolas Wyatt, "'Supposing Him to Be the Gardener' (John 20,15): A Study of the Paradise Motif in John," *ZNW* 81 (1990): 35.

[11]Gerhard von Rad, *Genesis. A Commentary*, OTL, rev. ed. (Philadelphia: Westminster Press, 1972), p. 83: "namegiving in the ancient Orient was primarily an exercise of sovereignty, of command." See also Mathews, *Genesis 1–11:26*, p. 221.

[12]As Daniel Block has argued in his contribution to this volume, this can also be translated as "to *serve it* and to protect/care for it," which would make the point even more strongly that Adam was placed in Eden at least as much for the garden's benefit as for his own.

[13]A. R. Millard, "The Etymology of Eden," *VT* 34 (1984): 103-7; Tsumura, *Creation and Destruction*, pp. 123-25.

To be sure, there is a clear anthropocentric dimension to Adam's role as gardener. Gardeners cultivate the soil for their own benefit, but they use the earth in a way that preserves and protects it for future use. The gardener image captures a delicate balance. It recognizes a legitimate utilitarian use of the environment by humans, but the need to preserve that environment for future productivity ensures that human "taming" of the land (Gen 1:28) does not devolve into a rapacious and destructive model for dealing with the earth. The relationship between the human (Hebrew, 'ādām) and the soil from which he was formed (the 'ădāma) is thoroughly symbiotic.

The royal dimension of Adam's role as a gardener becomes clearer when we learn that throughout the ancient Near East, the mark of successful kings was their ability to make their land productive and fruitful. More specifically, the kings' greatest achievements included the large "pleasure gardens"—like the Garden of Eden—that they planted and cultivated in their capital cities. In Assyria, where the title "Gardener" was used as a royal epithet,[14] the royal inscriptions often contained the boast that the king "had laid out a pleasure garden . . . in which he planted all the spice-trees of the Hittite land (and) the fruit-trees of every mountain."[15] Closer to Israel, the seventh-century Ammonite king Amminadab defined the accomplishments of his reign as "the vineyard and the garden and the irrigation-channel and the reservoir."[16] What appears to us as fairly unexciting activities—irrigation projects and the cultivation of a garden and a vineyard—were for the ancients clear evidence of royal greatness. Finally, the Israelites themselves made the same connection between kingship and horticultural activities. In Ecclesiastes 2:4-6, the "son of David, king in Jerusalem" (1:1) surveys all the "great projects" that marked him off as a successful monarch: "I built houses [i.e., palaces] for myself and I planted vineyards, I made gardens and parks and planted all kinds of fruit trees

---

[14]Terje Stordalen, *Echoes of Eden: Genesis 2-3 and the Symbolism of the Eden Garden in Biblical Hebrew Literature*, CBET 25 (Leuven: Peeters, 2000), p. 98. See also Manfred Hutter, "Adam als Gärtner und König (Gen 2,8.15)," *BZ* 30 (1986): 258-62.

[15]"Bull Inscription" of Sargon II, lines 41-42 (A. Fuchs, *Die Inschriften Sargons II. aus Khorsabad* [Göttingen: Cuvillier, 1994], pp. 66-67).

[16]"The Tell Sīrān Inscription," translated by Walter E. Aufrecht (*COS* 2.25:139-40).

in them. I made reservoirs to water groves of flourishing trees . . ." Like the Assyrian emperors and king Amminadab of Ammon, Israelite kings saw themselves as paradise-makers. The creation of well-watered, fertile and fruitful garden-space was one of the abiding marks of true kingship. The botanical garden, filled with exotic trees and flowing streams, was the parade example of the king's life-giving role as gardener, and visible proof that his wise rule brought fertility and fruitfulness to his whole land.[17]

Genesis 1 and Genesis 2 portray humanity—and the representative human—in highly exalted terms. Adam is the creature most like God, charged with representing him and mediating his life-giving rule over the world. He is the viceroy of creation, ruling under and on behalf of the great King of heaven. Adam is, as Psalm 8 puts it, "a little lower than the heavenly beings [and] crowned with [God's] glory and honor." In fact, all creation is "under his feet." But the good news for creation is that while Adam's feet tread with royal authority on earth's soil, they are also the feet of a gardener, walking carefully across his garden, ensuring its continued fertility and protecting it from reverting back to pre-creation desolation. As long as God's royal gardener reigns, the garden will flourish. So Adam shows us what a high and noble vocation—a Godlike and yet truly human calling!—creation-care was meant to be.

WAITING FOR THE GARDENER-KING OF THE NEW CREATION

Adam's sin has been analyzed in terms of a loss of righteousness and corruption of human nature, but less has been said about its ecological impact. When the first humans sinned, the king was dethroned[18] and cast from his garden-kingdom to work the arable land from which he was first formed (Gen 3:23). But now that land is cursed; thorns and

---

[17]David Stronach, "The Garden as a Political Statement: Some Case Studies from the Near East in the First Millennium B.C.," *Bulletin of the Asia Institute* 4 (1990): 171-72. See also Stordalen, *Echoes of Eden*, p. 97.

[18]If Adam's creation from the dust (Gen 2:7) is also his enthronement as king, then the pronouncement "to the dust you will return" (Gen 3:19) describes not only his mortality but also his dethronement from his position as vice regent over creation. See Brueggemann, "From Dust to Kingship," pp. 2-3.

thistles mingle together with edible plants (Gen 3:17-18).

To use Paul's language, this curse subjects creation to "futility" and places it in "bondage to decay" (Rom 8:20-21). Creation now falls short of and away from what God originally intended it to be. Adam must still work the soil (Gen 3:23), but he does so in constant fear that the land will be infertile and unproductive.[19] And so creation "groans" as it longs for the day of transformation and renewal. But if the role played by Adam in the first creation is any guide, the Lord will only achieve that *re*-creation by working through a human representative, a new Adam, who must be his gardener-king. After the Fall, the old Adam continues to work the ground, but now as a struggling farmer and no longer as the gardener of Eden's fertile soil. As a king dethroned and banished from his garden-kingdom, he is apparently powerless to bring the fertility of the Garden to a wider world.

Therefore, as creation groans for renewal, it also longs for the return of the Lord's Gardener-King, the re-enthronement of the divine image-bearer who will rule the world on God's behalf. In short, without a new Adam to care for the earth there can be no new creation. This expectation fueled the royal ideology of the ancient Near East which viewed each new king as a reborn Primal Man and his coronation as the day of new creation. Little wonder that kings planted "pleasure gardens" as symbols of their (limited) power to restore nature to its pristine, fertile and fruitful condition. Of course, all such kings—even Israel's kings—were mere shadows of a reality that was yet to come: the eschatological Gardener-King who would one day renovate creation by cultivating a new garden, this time not limited to the walled enclosure of Eden but breaking beyond those boundaries to bring fertility and fruitfulness to the whole earth.

THE RETURN OF THE GARDENER-KING

John's Gospel tells the story of Jesus, using the creation week as a frame. "In the beginning" (Jn 1:1) is an obvious echo of Genesis 1:1, and Jesus'

---

[19]Daniel E. Fleming, "By the Sweat of Your Brow: Adam, Anat, Athirat and Ashurbanipal," *Ugarit and the Bible: Proceedings of the International Symposium on Ugarit and the Bible, Manchester, September, 1992*, ed. G. J. Brooke, A. H. W. Curtis and J. F. Healey, UBL 11 (Münster: Ugarit-Verlag, 1994), pp. 93-100, proposes that the image of the sweating brow suggests anxiety rather than toil.

dying cry, "It is finished! (Jn 19:30) is almost certainly a reference back to Genesis 2:2: "by the seventh day God finished his work." Christ's death brings the old creation to an end, and his resurrection, on the first day of the new week (Jn 20:1, 19), marks the first day of a new creation.[20] The opening scene on this new day is set outside a tomb in a garden (Jn 19:41)—the place where the old creation (symbolized by the tomb) gives way to the new (symbolized by the garden). A man approaches Mary Magdalene and asks, "Why are you crying?" John, ever the master of irony, no doubt smiles as he introduces Mary's response: "*Thinking he was the gardener . . .*" (Jn 20:15). In fact, Mary's misunderstanding is a deep comprehension of what has happened. The man standing before her *is* the Gardener. Not a worker in the garden of Joseph of Arimathea, but *the* Gardener, the King of the New Creation![21] This is the man destined to bring all of creation into order, harmony and abundance.

While the day of the final curse-lifting renewal still lies out in our future (Rom 8:19-22), in Christ's resurrection the age to come has broken into this present age, and the Gardener has already taken up his royal vocation of subduing the earth on God's behalf. Accordingly, the reborn Gardener of Genesis 2 calls his subjects—the renewed humanity of Genesis 1—to live as true humans, by living *from* the first definition, found in Genesis 1–2, of what it means to be human, but especially by living *toward* the gospel's vision of what humanity will be in the age to come. With our "ethical eyes" looking back to our origin and forward to our destiny, we are called to live as ambassadors of the New Creation, who give the watching world a foretaste of what life in that kingdom will be like. Surely this should be good news for creation as Christians seek to live the royal, second-Adam life as God's gardeners. Yes, Christians may work the earth for human benefit, but we must do so in a protective and caring way that previews and anticipates the great day of renewal when Jesus, the Gardener-King, will finally deliver the natural realm from its bondage to decay and at last transform the whole world into a new and better Eden.

---

[20]See N. T. Wright, *The Challenge of Jesus: Rediscovering Who Jesus Was and Is* (Downers Grove, Ill.: InterVarsity Press, 1999), pp. 175-77.

[21]Wyatt, "Supposing Him to Be the Gardener," pp. 36-37; Wright, *Challenge*, p. 176.

RECOMMENDED FURTHER READING

FURTHER READING ON ESCHATOLOGY AND ENVIRONMENTAL ETHICS

DeWitt, Calvin, ed. *The Environment and the Christian: What Does the New Testament Say About the Environment?* Grand Rapids: Baker Academic, 1991.

McGrath, Alister E. *The Reenchantment of Nature: The Denial of Religion and the Ecological Crisis.* New York: Doubleday, 2002.

Polkinghorne, John. *The God of Hope and the End of the World.* New Haven, Conn.: Yale University Press, 2002.

Reumann, John. *Creation and New Creation: The Past, Present, and Future of God's Creative Activity.* Minneapolis: Augsburg, 1973.

Schaeffer, Francis A. *Pollution and the Death of Man: The Christian View of Ecology.* Wheaton, Ill.: Tyndale House, 1970.

FURTHER READING ON CITIES AND THE GLOBAL ENVIRONMENT

Benton-Short, Lisa, and John Rennie Short. *Cities and Nature.* New York: Routledge, 2008.

Berquist, Jon L., and Claudia V. Camp, eds. *Constructions of Space II: The Biblical City and Other Imagined Spaces.* LHB/OTS 490. New York: T & T Clark, 2008.

Brand, Peter, and Michael J. Thomas. *Urban Environmentalism: Global Change and the Mediation of Local Conflict.* New York: Routledge, 2005.

Brown, William P. *The Ethos of the Cosmos: The Genesis of the Moral Imagination in the Bible.* Grand Rapids: Eerdmans, 1999.

Brueggemann, Walter. *The Land: Place as Gift, Promise, and Challenge in Biblical Faith.* 2nd ed. Minneapolis: Fortress, 2002.

————. *Using God's Resources Wisely: Isaiah and Urban Possibility.* Louisville, Ky.: Westminster John Knox, 1993.

Bullard, Robert D., ed. *Growing Smarter: Achieving Livable Communities, Environmental Justice, and Regional Equity.* Cambridge, Mass.: MIT Press, 2007.

Burdett, Richard, and Deyan Sudjic, eds. *The Endless City: The Urban Age Project by the London School of Economics and Deutsche Bank's Alfred Herrhausen Society.* New York: Phaidon, 2007.

Cronon, William. *Nature's Metropolis: Chicago and the Great West.* New York: W. W. Norton, 1991.

Davis, Ellen F. *Scripture, Culture, and Agriculture: An Agrarian Reading of the Bible.* New York: Cambridge University Press, 2009.

Ellul, Jacques. *The Meaning of the City.* Biblical and Theological Classics Library. Carlisle, U.K.: Paternoster, 1997.

Forman, Richard T. *Urban Regions: Ecology and Planning Beyond the City.* Cambridge: Cambridge University Press, 2008.

Fritz, V. *The City in Ancient Israel.* Sheffield, U.K.: Sheffield Academic Press. 1995.

Geus, C. H. J. de *Towns in Ancient Israel and in the Southern Levant.* Palaestina Antiqua 10. Leuven: Peeters, 2003.

Gonzalez, George. *Urban Sprawl, Global Warming, and the Empire of Capital.* New York: SUNY Press, 2009.

Gottlieb, Roger. *Reinventing Los Angeles: Nature and Community in the Global City.* Cambridge, Mass.: MIT Press, 2008.

Grabbe, Lester L., and Robert D. Haak, eds. *"Every City Shall Be Forsaken": Urbanism and Prophecy in Ancient Israel and the Near East.* JSOTSup 330. Sheffield, U.K.: Sheffield Academic Press, 2001.

Habel, Norman C. *The Land Is Mine: Six Biblical Land Ideologies.* Overtures to Biblical Theology. Minneapolis: Fortress, 1995.

Heynen, Nik, Maria Kaika and Erik Swyngedouw, eds. *In the Nature of Cities: Urban Political Ecology and the Politics of Urban Metabolism.* New York: Routledge, 2006.

Kaika, Maria. *City of Flows: Modernity, Nature, and the City.* New York: Routledge, 2005.

King, Philip J., and Lawrence E. Stager. *Life in Biblical Israel.* Library of Ancient Israel. Louisville, Ky.: Westminster John Knox, 2001.

Klineberg, Eric. *Heat Wave: A Social Autopsy of Disaster in Chicago.* Chicago: University of Chicago Press, 2002.

Marlow, Hillary. *Biblical Prophets and Contemporary Environmental Ethics.* Oxford: Oxford University Press, 2009.

Massey, Doreen. *World City.* Cambridge: Polity, 2007.

Meeks, Wayne. *The First Urban Christians: The Social World of the Apostle Paul.* 2nd ed. New Haven, Conn.: Yale University Press, 2003.

Newman, Peter, Timothy Beatley and Heather Boyer. *Resilient Cities: Responding to Peak Oil and Climate Change.* Washington, D.C.: Island Press, 2008.

Pelling, Mark. *The Vulnerability of Cities: Natural Disasters and Social Resilience.* London: Earthscan, 2003.

Pellow, David Naguib. *Garbage Wars: The Struggle for Environmental Justice in Chicago.* Cambridge, Mass.: MIT Press, 2002.

Pierce, Neil R., and Curtis W. Johnson. *Century of the City: No Time to Lose.* New York: The Rockefeller Foundation, 2008.

Platt, Harold L. *Shock Cities: The Environmental Transformation and Reform of Manchester and Chicago.* Chicago: University of Chicago Press, 2005.

Portney, Kent E. *Taking Sustainable Cities Seriously: Economic Development, the Environment, and Quality of Life in American Cities.* Cambridge, Mass.: MIT Press, 2003.

Prasad, Neeraj, Rederica Rangheri, Fatima Shah, Zoe Trohanis, Earl Kessler and Ravi Sinha. *Climate Resilient Cities: A Primer on Reducing Vulnerabilities to Disasters.* New York: World Bank, 2008.

Rogerson, John W., and J. J. Vincent. *The City in Biblical Perspective.* Biblical Challenges to the Modern World. London: Equinox, 2009.

Sze, Julie. *Noxious New York: The Racial Politics of Urban Health and Environmental Justice.* Cambridge, Mass.: MIT Press, 2007.

FURTHER READING ON BIOLOGICAL DIVERSITY

Adams, Jonathan, Lynn Kutner and Bruce Smith, eds. *Precious Heritage: The Status of Biodiversity in the United States*. Oxford: Oxford University Press, 2000.

Berry, R. J., ed. *Environmental Stewardship: Critical Perspectives—Past and Present*. New York: T & T Clark, 2006.

Block, Daniel I. "All Creatures Great and Small: Recovering a Deuteronomic Theology of Animals." Forthcoming in the Elmer Martens Festschrift.

Borowski, Oded. *Every Living Thing: Daily Use of Animals in Ancient Israel*. Walnut Creek, Calif.: AltaMira Press, 1998.

Bouma-Prediger, Steven. *For the Beauty of the Earth: A Christian Vision for Creation Care*. Grand Rapids: Baker, 2001.

Brown, William P. *The Ethos of the Cosmos: The Genesis of Moral Imagination in the Bible*. Grand Rapids: Eerdmans, 1999.

A Christian Approach to the Environment. N.p.: The John Ray Initiative, 2005 (www.jri.org.uk).

Fretheim, Terence E. *God and World in the Old Testament: A Relational Theology of Creation*. Nashville: Abingdon, 2005.

Gaston, Kevin, and Kevin Spicer. *Biodiversity: An Introduction*, 2nd ed. Malden, Mass.: Blackwell Science, 2004.

Gottlieb, Roger S. *A Greener Faith: Religious Environmentalism and Our Planet's Future*. Oxford: Oxford University Press, 2006.

Hannah, L., and T. E. Lovejoy, eds. *Climate Change and Biodiversity*. New Haven, Conn.: Yale University Press, 2006.

Houston, Walter. *Purity and Monotheism: Clean and Unclean Animals in Biblical Law*. JSOTSup 140. Sheffield, U.K.: JSOT Press, 1993.

Linzey, Andrew. *Animal Theology*. Urbana: University of Illinois Press, 1995.

———. *Christianity and the Rights of Animals*. New York: Crossroad, 1987.

Linzey, Andrew, and Dorothy Yamamoto, eds. *Animals on the Agenda: Questions About Animals for Theology and Ethics*. Chicago: University of Chicago Press, 1998.

Mang, Johanna, Pamela Stedman-Edwards and Alexander Wood, eds.

The Root Causes of Biodiversity Loss. London: Earthscan, 2000.

Phillips, Anthony. "Animals and the Torah," pp. 127-38. In *Essays on Biblical Law.* JSOTSup 344. Sheffield, U.K.: Sheffield Academic Press, 2002.

Reed, Esther D. "Animal Rights and the Responsibilities of 'Dominion,'" pp. 133-46. In *The Ethics of Human Rights: Contested Doctrinal and Moral Issues.* Waco, Tex.: Baylor University Press, 2007.

Riede, Peter. *Im Spiegel der Tiere: Studien zum Verhältnis von Mensch und Tier im Alten Testament* OBO 187. Göttingen: Vandenhoeck & Ruprecht, 2002.

Rodd, Cyril. S. "Animals" and "Nature," pp. 207-49. In *Glimpses of a Strange Land: Studies in Old Testament Ethics.* OTS. Edinburgh: T & T Clark, 2001.

Rolston, Holmes. *Environmental Ethics: Duties to and Values in the Natural World.* Philadelphia: Temple University Press, 1988.

Van Dyke, Fred. *Conservation Biology: Foundations, Concepts, Applications.* New York: Springer, 2008.

Wennberg, Robert N. *God, Humans, and Animals: An Invitation to Enlarge Our Moral Universe.* Grand Rapids: Eerdmans, 2003.

Wilkinson, Loren, ed. *Earthkeeping in the Nineties: Stewardship of Creation.* Rev. ed. Eugene, Ore.: Wipf & Stock, 2003.

Wright, Christopher J. H. "Ecology and the Earth," pp. 103-45. In *Old Testament Ethics for the People of God.* Downers Grove, Ill.: InterVarsity Press, 2004.

FURTHER READING ON WATER RESOURCES

Barlow, Maude, and Tony Clarke. *Blue Gold: The Fight to Stop the Corporate Theft of the World's Water.* New York: New York Press, 2002.

Bisson, Robert, and Jay H. Lehr. *Modern Groundwater Exploration: Discovering New Water Resources in Consolidated Rocks Using Innovative Hydrogeologic Concepts, Exploration, Drilling, Aquifer Testing, and Management Methods.* Hoboken, N.J.: John Wiley & Sons, 2004.

Buras, Nathan, ed. *Reflections on Hydrology: Science and Practice.* Washington, D.C.: American Geophysical Union, 1997.

Chapelle, Francis H. *The Hidden Sea: Groundwater, Springs, and Wells.*

Tucson, Az.: Geoscience Press, 1997.

Daily, Gretchen C. *Nature's Services: Societal Dependence on Natural Ecosystems.* Washington, D.C.: Island Press, 1997.

Dalley, S. *Myths from Mesopotamia: Creation, the Flood, Gilgamesh and Others: A New Translation.* World's Classic. Oxford: Oxford University Press, 1991.

Glennon, Robert. *Water Follies: Groundwater Pumping and the Fate of America's Fresh Waters.* Washington, D.C.: Island Press, 2002.

Gunton, C. E. *The Triune Creator: A Historical and Systematic Study.* Edinburgh Studies in Constructive Theology. Edinburgh: Edinburgh University Press, 1998.

Harland, P. J. *The Value of Human Life: A Study of the Story of the Flood (Genesis 6-9).* Supplement for Vetus Testamentum 64. Leiden: Brill, 1996.

Kandel, Robert. *Water from Heaven: The Story of Water from the Big Band to the Rise of Civilization, and Beyond.* New York: Columbia University Press, 1998.

Pearce, Fred. *Keepers of the Spring: Reclaiming Our Water in an Age of Globalization.* Washington, D.C.: Island Press, 2004.

Postel, Sandra, and Brian Richter. *Rivers for Life: Managing Water for People and Nature.* Washington, D.C.: Island Press, 2003.

Reisner, Marc. *Cadillac Desert: The American West and Its Disappearing Water.* New York: Penguin, 1986.

Rothfeder, Jeffrey. *Every Drop for Sale: Our Desperate Battle over Water in a World About to Run Out.* New York: Penguin Putnam, 2001.

Royte, Elizabeth. *Bottlemania: How Water Went on Sale and Why We Bought It.* New York: Bloomsbury, 2008.

Tsumura, D. T. "The *'Chaoskampf'* Motif in Ugaritic and Hebrew Literatures," pp. 473-99. In *Le Royaume d'Ougarit de la Crète à l'Euphrate. Nouveaux axes de Recherche,* ed. J.-M. Michaud. Proche-Orient et Littérature Ougaritique II. Sherbrooke: GGC, 2007.

———. *Creation and Destruction: A Reappraisal of the* Chaoskampf *Theory in the Old Testament.* Winona Lake, Ind.: Eisenbrauns, 2005.

———. "The Doctrine of *creatio ex nihilo* and the Translation of *tōhû wābōhû*" in a volume for The International Workshop on the Study of the Pentateuch with Special Emphasis on Its Textual Transmission History in the Hellenistic and Roman Periods (8/28-31/07) [to be published by E.J. Brill].

————. *The Earth and the Waters in Genesis 1 and 2: A Linguistic Analysis.* Journal for the Study of the Old Testament Supplement Series 83. Sheffield, U.K.: Sheffield Academic Press, 1989.

Villiers, Marq de. *Water: The Fate of Our Most Precious Resource.* Boston: Houghton Mifflin, 2001.

Ward, Diane Raines. *Water Wars: Drought, Flood, Folly, and the Politics of Thirst.* New York: Riverhead Books, 2002.

Watson, R. A. *Chaos Uncreated: A Reassessment of the Theme of "Chaos" in the Hebrew Bible.* Beihefte zur Zeitschrift für die alttestamentliche Wissenschaft 341. New York: Walter de Gruyter, 2005.

FURTHER READING ON GLOBAL WARMING

Berry, R. J., ed. *When Enough Is Enough: A Christian Framework for Environmental Sustainability.* Nottingham, U.K.: Apollos, 2007.

DiMento, Joseph F. C., and Pamela Doughman, eds. *Climate Change: What It Means for Us, Our Children, and Our Grandchildren.* Cambridge, Mass.: MIT Press, 2007.

Elsdon, Ron. *Green House Theology: Biblical Perspectives on Caring for Creation.* Tunbridge Wells, U.K.: Monarch, 1992.

Emanuel, Kerry. *What We Know About Climate Change.* Cambridge, Mass.: MIT Press, 2007.

Houghton, John. *Global Warming: The Complete Briefing*, 4th ed. Cambridge: Cambridge University Press, 2009.

Kent, J., and N. Myers. *Environmental Exodus: An Emergent Crisis in the Global Arena.* Washington, D.C.: Climate Institute, 1995.

Linzey, Andrew, and Dorothy Yamamoto, eds. *Animals on the Agenda: Questions About Animals for Theology and Ethics.* London: SCM Press, 1998.

Lynas, Mark. *Six Degrees.* New York: HarperCollins, 2008.

Monbiot, George. *Heat: How to Stop the Planet Burning.* London: Penguin Books, 2007.

Murray, Robert. *The Cosmic Covenant: Biblical Themes of Justice, Peace and the Integrity of Creation.* London: Sheed & Ward, 1992.

Nash, James. *Loving Nature: Ecological Integrity and Christian Responsibility.* Nashville: Abingdon, 1991.

Northcott, Michael. *A Moral Climate.* Maryknoll, N.Y.: Orbis, 2007.

Spencer, Nick, and Robert White. *Christianity, Climate Change, and Sustainable Living.* London: SPCK, 2007.

Volk, Tyler. *CO$_2$ Rising: The World's Greatest Environmental Challenge.* Cambridge, Mass.: MIT Press, 2008.

FURTHER READING ON ENVIRONMENTAL ETHICS

Beisner, E. Calvin. *Where Garden Meets Wilderness.* Grand Rapids: Eerdmans, 1997.

Berry, Thomas. *The Dream of the Earth.* San Francisco: Sierra Club Books, 1988.

Bouma-Prediger, Steve. *For the Beauty of the Earth: A Christian Vision for Creation Care.* Grand Rapids: Baker, 2001.

Cobb, John B. *Is It Too Late? A Theology of Ecology.* Denton, Tex.: Environmental Ethics Books, 1995.

DeWitt, Calvin B. *Caring for Creation: Responsible Stewardship of God's Handiwork.* Grand Rapids: Baker Books, 1998.

Diamond, Jared. *Collapse: How Societies Choose to Fail or Succeed.* New York: Penguin, 2005.

Granberg-Michaelson, Wesley. *Ecology and Life: Accepting Our Environmental Responsibility.* Dallas: Word, 1988.

Hall, Douglas John. *The Steward: A Biblical Symbol Come of Age.* New York: Friendship, 1982.

Hessel, Dieter. *After Nature's Revolt: Eco-Justice and Theology.* Minneapolis: Fortress, 1992.

Martin-Schramm, James B., and Robert L. Stivers. *Christian Environmental Ethics: A Case Method Approach.* Maryknoll, N.Y.: Orbis, 2003.

McFague, Sallie. *The Body of God: An Ecological Theology.* Minneapolis: Fortress, 1993.

Moltmann, Jürgen. *God in Creation: A New Theology of Creation and the*

Spirit of God. New York: Harper & Row, 1985.

Murphy, Charles M. *The Cosmic Covenant: Biblical Themes on Justice, Peace, and the Integrity of Creation*. London: Sheed & Ward, 1992.

Nash, James A. *Loving Nature: Ecological Integrity and Christian Responsibility*. Nashville: Abingdon, 1991.

Parham, Robert A. *Loving Neighbors Across Time: A Christian Guide to Protecting the Earth*. Birmingham, Ala.: New Hope, 1992.

Peterson, Anna. *Being Human: Ethics, Environment, and Our Place in the World*. Berkeley: University of California Press, 2001.

Rasmussen, Larry L. *Earth Community, Earth Ethics*. Maryknoll, N.Y.: Orbis, 1996.

Ruether, Rosemary Radford. *Gaia and God: An Ecofeminist Theology of Earth Healing*. New York: HarperCollins, 1992.

Schwab, Jim. *Deeper Shades of Green: The Rise of Blue-Collar and Minority Environmentalism in America*. San Francisco: Sierra Club Books, 1994.

Singer, Peter. *Unsanctifying Human Life*. Oxford: Blackwell, 2002.

Sleeth, Matthew J. *Serve God, Save the Planet*. Grand Rapids: Zondervan, 2006.

Taylor, Paul W. *Respect for Nature: A Theory of Environmental Ethics*. Princeton, N.J.: Princeton University Press, 1986.

Wilkinson, Loren. *Earthkeeping in the Nineties: Stewardship of Creation*. Grand Rapids: Eerdmans, 1991.

Wilson, E.O. *The Creation: An Appeal to Save Life on Earth*. New York: Norton, 2007.

Woyjtla, Karol (Pope John Paul II). *The Gospel of Life*. New York: Random House, 1995.

Young, Richard A. *Healing the Earth: A Theocentric Perspective on Environmental Problems and Their Solutions*. Nashville: Broadman & Holman, 1994.

CONTRIBUTORS

Daniel I. Block is the Gunther H. Knoedler Professor of Old Testament at Wheaton College. He is a regular essayist at scholarly conventions and contributor to scholarly journals, and he lectures frequently in international contexts. Among his numerous publications are major commentaries on Ezekiel and on Judges and Ruth, the monograph *The Gods of the Nations: Studies in Ancient Near Eastern National Theology;* "All Creatures Great and Small: Recovering a Deuteronomic Theology of Animals" in *Essays on the Old Testament and Issues in the Life of God's People;* Festschrift for Elmer Martens; and a commentary on Deuteronomy (NIVAC; Grand Rapids: Zondervan, 2010). Dr. Block's passion is to recover the Old Testament as authoritative and living Scripture for the church. He and his wife, Ellen, are gardeners. When they are not traveling to see their children and grandchildren, they are happiest at home creating and enjoying their own little Eden in the backyard.

M. Daniel Carroll R. (Rodas) is Distinguished Professor of Old Testament at Denver Seminary. Prior to his appointment to Denver Seminary, he was professor of Old Testament and ethics and director of graduate studies at El Seminario Teológico Centroamericano in Guatemala City, Guatemala, and remains an adjunct professor there. He was instrumental in the establishment of the Spanish-language training program at Denver Seminary. Dr. Carroll is the author of several books, including *Amos—the Prophet and His Oracles: Research on the Book of Amos.* He has edited *Rethinking Context, Rereading Texts: Contributions from the Social Sciences to Biblical Interpretation* and *Theory and*

Practice in Old Testament Ethics, and has coedited five books, most recently *Character Ethics and the Old Testament: Moral Dimensions of Scripture*. His latest work is *Christians at the Border: Immigration, the Church and the Bible*. Dr. Carroll and his wife, Joan, have two adult sons, Matthew and Adam.

Fred Van Dyke is Chair of the Department of Biology and Director of the Environmental Studies Program at Wheaton College (Illinois), where he teaches courses in environmental science, environmental ethics and conservation biology. A former wildlife biologist with the Montana Department of Fish, Wildlife and Parks and consultant to the Forest Service and National Park Service, Fred is the author of numerous articles on wildlife ecology and environmental ethics, a contributor to the books *The Greater Yellowstone Ecosystem: Redefining America's Wilderness Heritage*; *The Smithsonian Book of North American Mammals*; and *Vertebrate Conservation and Biodiversity*, and the author of *Conservation Biology: Foundations, Concepts, Applications* and *Redeeming Creation: The Biblical Basis of Environmental Stewardship*. Fred's students have received the Morris K. Udall Scholarship and the Au Sable Leadership Fellowship in environmental conservation. Fred enjoys cycling and running 5ks, and managed to win his age group in his first triathlon in February 2008.

Douglas J. Green is Professor of Old Testament and Biblical Theology at Westminster Theological Seminary (Philadelphia, Pennsylvania). He was formerly an environmental lawyer in Sydney, Australia. He has contributed to a number of publications, including *A Complete Literary Guide to the Bible* and the *Dictionary of Biblical Imagery*. His research interests range from ancient Near Eastern royal ideology to Christian interpretation of the Psalter. Dr. Green and his wife, Rosemarie, have two children, Mitchell and Adelaide.

Michael D. Guebert is Professor of Geology and Environmental Science at Taylor University in Upland, Indiana. Prior to his appointment at Taylor University in 1999, he held faculty positions at Middle Tennessee State University and Wheaton College, Illinois. Dr. Guebert's scholarly interests include water source delineation and protection, soil and water conservation in agricultural settings, and water resources in developing countries. He regularly teaches an international service-learning course in Central America focused on appropriate technologies in water resources, sanitation and hygiene. His initiatives in experiential education and community engagement have earned widespread acclaim, including the 2007 Teaching Excellence and Campus Leadership Award at Taylor. Dr. Guebert and his wife, Carolyn, have four children, Alyssa, Emily, Davis and James. They enjoy water activities such as kayaking the Outer Banks of North Carolina, sailing Sand Lake in Minnesota, and canoeing the Mississinewa River in Indiana.

David P. Gushee is the Distinguished University Professor of Christian Ethics at Mercer University. Prior to joining the faculty at Mercer, Dr. Gushee served as Graves Professor of Moral Philosophy at Union University. Beyond his work at Mercer, he is a columnist for Associated Baptist Press, and a contributing editor for *Christianity Today*. Dr. Gushee also currently serves as co-chair of the Scriptural/Contextual Ethics Group of the American Academy of Religion and on the Christian Ethics Commission of the Baptist World Alliance. He has published twelve books, including *Kingdom Ethics*, *Righteous Gentiles of the Holocaust*, *Only Human*, *The Future of Faith in American Politics*, and *The Scholarly Vocation and the Baptist Academy*. He has authored more than eighty scholarly essays, book chapters, articles, and reviews, and hundreds of magazine articles and opinion pieces. He was the principal drafter of both the Evangelical Climate Initiative and the Evangelical Declaration against Torture. Dr. Gushee's current research interests focus the intersection between Christian faith, ethics and public policy. His current book project explores the theological and ethical roots and implications of belief in the sanctity of human life.

Sir John Houghton is Professor Emeritus of Atmospheric Physics at University of Oxford. One of the world's foremost climatologists, Sir John served as co-chair of Working Group I of the Intergovernmental Panel on Climate Change (IPCC) and was lead author of three IPCC Assessment Reports. Over the past twenty-five years, Houghton has held a number of scientific and administrative posts, having served as Director General of the Britain's Meteorological Office, as Chair of the Royal Commission on Environmental Pollution, and President of the John Ray Initiative. During his distinguished career, Houghton has received the Rank Prize for Optoelectronics, the Royal Astronomical Society Gold Medal, and the International Meteorological Organization Prize, among others. He is an honorary scientist at the Hadley Centre for Climate Prediction and Research and in 2006 was awarded the prestigious Japan Prize for his lifetime work on climatology. Sir John is the author of numerous publications, including *The Physics of Atmospheres*, *Global Warming: The Complete Briefing*, *Does God Play Dice?: A Look at the Story of the Universe* and *The Search for God: Can Science Help?*

Douglas Moo is Blanchard Professor of New Testament at Wheaton College. He has written nine books, including commentaries on Romans, Second Peter and Jude, James, and Colossians and Philemon, as well as an introduction to the New Testament (with D. A. Carson). His research focuses on the letters and theology of Paul. Dr. Moo is married with five grown children and four grandchildren. He and his wife, Jenny, love to photograph the natural world.

David Toshio Tsumura is Professor of Old Testament at Japan Bible Seminary in Tokyo, Japan, and a foremost authority on the early chapters of Genesis, especially the creation and flood accounts. He serves as head of the translation committee for the revision of the New Japanese Bible (Shinkaiyaku), chairman of the Tokyo Museum of Biblical Archaeology and editor of *Exegetica: Studies in Biblical Exegesis*. Dr. Tsumura is the author of *Creation and Destruction: A Reappraisal of the Chaoskampf Theory in the Old Testament*. He is coeditor of *I Studied Inscriptions from Before the Flood: Ancient Near Eastern, Literary, and Linguistic Approaches to Genesis 1–11*. His most recent publication is a major commentary on *The First Book of Samuel* (NICOT). Dr. Tsumura and his wife, Susan, have two sons and one grandson. He enjoys gardening, walking with his wife and listening to classical music.

Noah J. Toly is Director of Urban Studies and Assistant Professor of Politics and International Relations at Wheaton College in Wheaton, Illinois. He teaches courses on environmental politics, global cities and urban theory. His research interests are in urban environmental politics and policy, the intersection of urban environmental politics and global environmental politics, and global cities. Dr. Toly is the author of or contributor to numerous publications on energy and environmental policy. He is coeditor of *Transforming Power: Energy, Environment, and Society in Conflict*. He enjoys spending time with his wife, Becky, and their three children.

Rev. Dr. Christopher J. H. Wright is the International Director of the Langham Partnership International, a group of ministries founded by John Stott, providing literature, scholarships, and preaching for pastors in Majority World churches and seminaries. He has taught Old Testament at Union Biblical Seminary in India, and served on the faculty of All Nations Christian College, a crosscultural training college in England, where he was Principal from 1993-2001. He serves as the Chair of the Lausanne Theology Working Group and has written several books, including commentaries on Deuteronomy and Ezekiel, *Old Testament Ethics for the People of God, The Mission of God*, as well as *Knowing Jesus, Knowing the Holy Spirit*, and *Knowing God the Father through the Old Testament*. An ordained Anglican on the staff of All Souls Church, Langham Place, London, England, Dr. Wright and his wife, Liz, have four adult children and several grandchildren, and live in London.

Subject Index

Scripture Index